PITTSBURGH THEOLOGICAL MONOGRAPH SERIES

General Editor

DIKRAN Y. HADIDIAN

6

WHEN MAN BECOMES GOD

Humanism and Hybris in the Old Testament

PITTSBURGH THEOLOGICAL MONOGRAPH SERIES

Already Published

1. *Rhetorical Criticism; essays in honor of James Muilenburg*. Edited by Jared J. Jackson and Martin Kessler. 1974

2. Francois C. Gérard: *The Future of the Church; the theology of renewal of Willem Adolf Visser't Hooft*. 1974

3. *Structural Analysis and Biblical Exegesis; interpretational essays by R. Barthes, F. Bovon, F. J. Leenhardt, R. Martin-Achard and J. Starobinski*. Translated by Alfred M. Johnson, Jr. 1974

4. John Bowman: *The Samaritan Problem; Studies in the Relationships of Samaritanism, Judaism and Early Christianity*. With a new introduction. Translated by Alfred M. Johnson. 1975

5. *The Tale of the Tell; archaeological studies by Paul W. Lapp*. Edited by Nancy L. Lapp. 1975

6. Donald E. Gowan: *When Man becomes God; Humanism and Hybris in the Old Testament*. 1975

Forthcoming

7. John Bowman: *The Fourth Gospel and the Jews; a study of R. Akibah, Esther, and the Gospel of John*. 1975

8. *The Informal Groups in the Church*. Papers of the Second Cerdic Colloquium. Strasbourg, May 13-15, 1971. Edited by René Metz and Jean Schlick. Translated by Matthew J. O'Connell. 1975

9. Jack M. Maxwell: *Worship and Reformed Theology; the liturgical lessons of Mercersburg*. 1975

10. Robert G. Heath: *Crux Imperatorum Philosophia: Imperial Horizons of the Cluniac Liturgical Community, 964-1109*. 1975

11. *The New Testament and Structuralism,* a collection of essays edited by Alfred M. Johnson, Jr. 1975

12. *Liberation Ideaology and the Message of Salvation*. Papers of the Fourth Cerdic Colloquium. Strasbourg, May 10-12. Edited by René Metz and Jean Schlick. Translated by David Gelzer. 1976

13. Louis Marin: *The Semiotic of the Passion Narratives*. Translated by Alfred M. Johnson, Jr. 1976

14. Richard Reitzenstein: *The Hellenistic Mystery Religions*. Translated by John Steely. 1976

WHEN MAN BECOMES GOD

Humanism and Hybris in the Old Testament

by

DONALD E. GOWAN

THE PICKWICK PRESS

PITTSBURGH, PENNSYLVANIA

1975

1504784
Jin 9-11-96

Library of Congress Cataloging in Publication Data

Gowan, Donald E
    When man becomes God.

    (Pittsburgh theological monograph series ; no. 6)
    Includes bibliographical references and index.
    1. Man (Theology)--Biblical teaching.
2. Pride and vanity--Biblical teaching. 3. Myth
in the Old Testament. I. Title. II. Series.
BS661.G68   218   75-17582
ISBN 0-915138-06-9

To my wife

CONTENTS

ABBREVIATIONS

AJA	American Journal of Archaeology
AJSL	American Journal of Semitic Languages and Literatures
AJT	American Journal of Theology
ALUOS	Annual of the Leeds University Oriental Society
AngThR	Anglican Theological Review
ANES	The Ancient Near East: Supplementary Texts and Pictures, ed. J. B. Pritchard (Princeton: Princeton University Press, 1969).
ANET	Ancient Near Eastern Texts, ed. J. B. Pritchard (2nd ed., Princeton: Princeton University Press, 1955).
ASTI	Annual of the Swedish Theological Institute, Jerusalem
ATANT	Abhandlungen zur Theologie des Alten und Neuen Testaments
ATD	Das Alte Testament Deutsch
BA	The Biblical Archaeologist
BASOR	Bulletin of the American Schools of Oriental Research
BH^3	Biblica Hebraica, 3rd edition
BJRL	Bulletin of the John Rylands Library
BKAT	Biblischer Kommentar, Altes Testament
BS	Biblische Studien
BSOS	Bulletin of the School of Oriental Studies, London
BZAW	Beihefte, Zeitschrift für die Alttestamentliche Wissenschaft

CBQ	Catholic Biblical Quarterly
ChQR	Church Quarterly Review
EvTh	Evangelische Theologie
HAT	Handbuch zum Alten Testament
HKAT	Handkommentar zum Alten Testament
HThR	Harvard Theological Review
IB	The Interpreter's Bible
ICC	The International Critical Commentary
IDB	The Interpreter's Dictionary of the Bible
IEJ	Israel Exploration Journal
JAAR	Journal of the American Academy of Religion
JAOS	Journal of the American Oriental Society
JBL	Journal of Biblical Literature
JBR	Journal of Bible and Religion
JEA	Journal of Egyptian Archaeology
JNES	Journal of Near Eastern Studies
JQR	Jewish Quarterly Review
JR	Journal of Religion
JRAS	Journal of the Royal Asiatic Society
JSS	Journal of Semitic Studies
JTS	Journal of Theological Studies
LXX	The Septuagint Version of the Old Testament
PEQ	Palestine Exploration Quarterly

RA	Revue d'Assyriologie et d'Archéologie Orientale
RBibIt	Revista Biblica (Italiana)
RGG³	Die Religion in Geschichte und Gegenwart, 3rd ed.
RHR	Revue de l'Histoire des Religions
SBT	Studies in Biblical Theology
StTh	Studia Theologica, Lund
TDNT	Theological Dictionary of the New Testament
ThLZ	Theologische Literaturzeitung
TWNT	Theologische Wörterbuch zum Neuen Testament
TZ	Theologische Zeitschrift
VT	Vetus Testamentum
VTS	Supplements to Vetus Testamentum
WMANT	Wissenschaftliche Monographien zum Alten und Neuen Testament
WO	Die Welt des Orients
ZAW	Zeitschrift für die Alttestamentliche Wissenschaft
ZDMG	Zeitschrift der Deutschen Morgenländischen Gesellschaft

PREFACE

For a long time we have been complaining about the kind of
exegesis which stops short once a detailed and careful historical-
critical analysis of a text has been made, as if that were all that
an interpreter of Scripture was supposed to provide for those who
are concerned about what the Bible has to say to them. At the same
time, Biblical scholars and others as well have protested the kind of
theology and homiletics which does not take exegesis seriously. The
study which follows is an effort to respond to those complaints and
to offer something more complete. It attempts to put together in one
book a study of a Biblical theme which moves from the technical work
of exegesis to theological affirmations, and in places to the borderline of homiletics. To many it may thus appear to be a mixed genre;
parts of it seem properly to belong in technical journals and monographs while other parts seem to belong to a more popular realm of
religious literature, directed toward pastors and laymen. That may
be what it is, but my effort has been to produce a new genre in
which the work of the interpreter of Scripture appears as a totality.
Since I have not consciously been following a previous model this
attempt may not prove to be satisfactory but I believe the effort,
at least, needs to be made. An inspiration for the work, if not a
model, has been found in the expository writings of George Adam
Smith, which were remarkably successful in their day in combining
technical exegetical work with the affirmation of what these texts
mean to a person of faith.

After completing a doctoral dissertation on the oracles against
the nations in Ezekiel several years ago I found that further thought
about the "mythological" materials in those passages suggested that
they had something important to contribute to the Old Testament doctrine of Man--Man outside the covenant, if you will--and that what
they were saying leads us inevitably to use the Greek word <u>hybris</u>,
and to apply it above all to government. Those ideas seemed worth
pursuing, both because they promised to open new insights into one
aspect of Old Testament theology and because of the suggestion that
the ancient texts may be saying something very important to modern
societies. Further impetus for my work on the Old Testament doctrine
of Man was provided by Eric Fromm's book, <u>You Shall Be As Gods</u> (New
York: Holt, Rinehart & Winston, 1966), which dealt with some of the
same texts and themes but from a non-theistic point of view. To
some extent this book is an answer to Fromm, although I have not
carried on an overt dialogue with his work in what I have written.

        Since the book has grown out of some of the work I did for
my doctorate I should express my thanks here to Professors J.
Coert Rylaarsdam and Gosta Ahlström of the Divinity School of
the University of Chicago for their helpful criticisms of the
dissertation. I must also thank my wife Darlene for her patience
and for help with typing and indexing, and the general editor,
Dikran Y. Hadidian, for accepting the book as a part of the
Pittsburgh Theological Monograph Series.

PROLOGUE

WHEN MAN BECOMES GOD

"Every man would like to be God, if it were
possible; some few find it difficult to admit
the impossibility."   Bertrand Russell[1]

"You shall be as gods."   The Serpent[2]

"To be a man means to reach toward being God."
                              Jean-Paul Sartre[3]

"God in man is nothing other than the essence
of man."   Ludwig Feuerbach[4]

"Man has, as it were, become a kind of pros-
thetic god."   Sigmund Freud[5]

"But God, if a God there be, is the substance
of men which is man."   A. C. Swinburne[6]

It is not part of the language of Christian piety to speak of
men becoming gods. The possibility of attaining that goal has been
denied from the beginning and the desire to reach it, although
recognized, has often been identified as the root of all sin. Yet
there is a current of thought in our time which takes seriously
the possibility that man might in some meaningful sense be called
a god, and it may be that there is a strong element of truth in
those affirmations. Two factors make possible such a tendency;
the rise of secularism with the general waning of consciousness
of the presence and reality of a transcendent God, and the tremendous increase in human ability, through science and technology,
to exercise the kind of control over the world which has previously
been ascribed to God.

If God is Creator--man's creative powers have not as yet
reached their limits and may soon include the creation of life.
If God is Lord of the earth--it is man who exercises evident lord-
ship and does as he wishes with its resources. If God is Judge of
humankind--it is man who rules his fellows and manipulates their
lives as he pleases, for good or ill. And he does so with apparent

1

impunity; no thunderbolts or loathesome diseases strike down the impious in the sight of their victims. And much that he has done has been for the betterment of his fellow men.

No wonder that humanism, which emphasizes the importance of man[7] and his well-being, and which displays confidence in his capacity to deal successfully with the problems of life has often found God to be a totally unnecessary concept.[8]

> Modern nonreligious man assumes a new existential situation; he regards himself solely as the subject and agent of history, and he refuses all appeal to transcendence. In other words he accepts no model for humanity outside the human condition as it can be seen in the various historical situations. Man makes himself, and he only makes himself completely in proportion as he desacralizes himself and the world. The sacred is the prime obstacle to his freedom. He will become himself only when he is totally demysticized. He will not be truly free until he has killed the last god.[9]

Humanism may find it necessary to fight against the very idea of God, as in the works of P.-J. Proudhon, who believed that if God exists he must be essentially hostile to human nature, so that man must become victor over the idea of God and put his faith in human progress if he is to become true master of his destiny.[10] Or it may be more blandly asserted, as in the Humanist Manifesto of 1933, "that the nature of the universe depicted by modern sciences makes unacceptable any supernatural or cosmic guarantees of human values".[11]

Yet others have found that the idea of deity cannot be done away with entirely, and if they can recognize no transcendent God, then man becomes the logical candidate. We have quoted examples of such thoughts at the beginning of this chapter. They do not represent some new kind of mythology but are serious evaluations of the possibilities for man in a world which has no transcendent God.[12] They believe that man has, or can seek to gain the power to do all that has traditionally been ascribed to the power of God (or all of that which is meaningful to them) and have recognized that those who possess such power must also assume the moral responsibilities which have been part of the nature of God in the higher religions. Thus everything significant that has been said about God in the past must now be said about man, at least proleptically, in the faith that it can one day be achieved.

Now it is not the intention of this book to argue against this tendency to think of man as a god, but rather to study a series of Old Testament passages which suggest that such affirmations may be partly right. One exponent of such a view, Eric Fromm, has said the serpent's offer, "You shall be as gods," is a real promise to be taken seriously and worked toward.[13] Our study will often be in tacit dialogue with Fromm's book, for he believes that he has found in the Old Testament and Rabbinical teachings evidence for an evolution of the God-concept from that of an absolute monarch to non-existence, leaving man with the possibility of achieving complete freedom.[14] His recognition of what may perhaps legitimately be called the "radical humanism" of the Old Testament (although I would not use the term in precisely his sense) will be partly re-affirmed in this book, but alongside his assertion that man can achieve his full humanity only by obtaining complete freedom from the concept of God must be placed the Old Testament's insistence that if there is no God then there is no such thing as humanity. Our studies must emphasize another side of the question, one which has concerned many others who have thought about whether man might aspire to become a god.

> "I said, 'You are gods, and all of you are the sons of the Most High,' but you shall die like man."
> Psalm 82:6f

> "The only original rule of life today: to learn to live and to die, and, in order to be a man, to refuse to be a god." Albert Camus[15]

> "Man is neither angel nor beast, and the mischief is that he who would play the angel plays the beast." Blaise Pascal[16]

> "Strive not to be a Zeus . . . Mortal aims befit mortal men." Pindar[17]

> "We do not trust ourselves as gods. We know what we are." Archibald MacLeish[18]

A full and honest recognition of man's true potential brings with it a profound uneasiness. We can do so many wonderful things we may even dare to stretch the language and think of ourselves as almost gods, and yet . . . We are not always sure that it is a good thing for men to become gods.

> There is, in truth, a terror in the world,
> and the arts have heard it as they always do.
> Under the hum of the miraculous machines and the
> ceaseless publications of the brilliant physi-
> cists a silence waits and listens and is heard.
>
> It is the silence of apprehension. We do
> not trust our time, and the reason we do not
> trust our time is because it is we who have made
> the time, and we do not trust ourselves. We
> have played the hero's part, mastered the mon-
> sters, accomplished the labors, become gods--
> and we do not trust ourselves as gods. We know
> what we are.
>
> In the old days when the gods were someone
> else, the knowledge of what we are did not
> frighten us. There were Furies to pursue the
> Hitlers, and Athenas to restore the truth. But
> now that we are gods ourselves we bear the
> knowledge for ourselves. Like that old Greek
> hero who learned when all the labors had been
> accomplished that it was he himself who had
> killed his sons.[19]

Long ago the Greeks experienced a related kind of uneasiness.
They became convinced that the gods jealously guarded their prerogatives from human encroachment, and called the efforts at encroachment which inevitably occurred, hybris. This word remains the most
convenient term available to us to denote the tragic perversion of
true humanism which concerns observers of modern society, which has
also been a traditional part of the Christian doctrine of sin and
which, as we shall show, plays a special role in the Old Testament
doctrine of man. We shall use it, in the absence of a comparable
Hebrew word, as we deal with an Old Testament concept which, though
not identical to the Greek idea, is close enough that its definition
can legitimately be modified to fit the different context. And we
must prefer it to any available English term since our language,
like Hebrew, has no single word which is quite its equivalent.

The idea is clearly present among us--though we must borrow
a Greek word to denote it--that there is a danger to us in our
very greatness; that to be godlike is at the same time almost
irresistibly attractive and terribly frightening. So the equations
of humanity and deity continue to appear, but with warnings attached.
Malcom Muggeridge has preached on the folly of hybris in his sermon,
"Men Like Gods".[20] Edmund Leach has warned, "Unless we teach those
of the next generation that they can afford to be atheists only if
they assume the moral responsibilities of God, the prospects for

the human race are decidedly bleak."[21] Leroy Augenstein has
pleaded for a careful and thoughtful approach to the ethical
decisions which medical technology thrusts before us in his
Come, Let Us Play God.[22] As technology enables us to do ever
more and government becomes ever stronger the concern over what
man can do to man becomes more and more frequently expressed.

The aim of this book is to contribute something further to
modern man's willingness to recognize his near divinity and to
accept it as both a great blessing and an awesome danger by
means of an interpretation of a series of Old Testament passages
which are startlingly "humanistic" in their outlook.[23] Most of
them come from rather obscure parts of the Hebrew Scriptures,
but it is my hope to be able to show that they are coherent with
the mainstream of Israelite thought, that they add something
significant to what has previously been said about man in biblical theologies, and that they can be heard speaking to the modern
state with peculiar directness. The reader will soon see that
the Old Testament materials which deal with hybris have two notable
pecularities. They are concerned not so much with Israelites as
with the great nations of the earth, and they are more significantly related to the myths of the ancient Near East than almost any
other part of the Bible. The latter peculiarity makes Chapter I
and the Excursus necessary. Since there are many points of contact between the Old Testament hybris passages and other texts from
antiquity it will be helpful to devote the first chapter to a
survey of the various understandings of man which can be identified
among Israel's neighbors. And since myths are involved in our
comparative study, the complex and controverted subject of what is
meant by "myth" and how myths are to be interpreted cannot be
ignored. In order not to break the continuity of the argument the
rather lengthy treatment of the problem of myth which I found it
necessary to produce has been appended as an excursus.

Chapter II lays the Old Testament background for our study by
showing how a concern for hybris is related to more general teachings about pride. It includes studies of the vocabulary and brief
interpretations of passages such as Gen. 11:1-9, Isa. 2:6-22, 10:
5-19, and 37:23-29. All of this leads up to Chapters III-V, which
deal with those relatively obscure yet highly remarkable passages,
Isa. 14:1-21, Ezek. 28:1-19, 31:1-18 and Dan. 4:1-37, which I believe
to be addressed not merely to certain bygone kings of Babylon, Tyre
and Egypt, but to be more broadly applicable to every powerful
state.[24] The conclusions which I have drawn about these passages
as hybris texts depend almost entirely on the detailed analysis of
each of them using an approach which finds form criticism and
comparative mythology to be the most helpful tools. Further,
rather personal comments on their relevance will appear in the

Epilogue, centering on the Old Testament's preoccupation with the
nations and with the prominence of death in every passage which
speaks of hybris.

Most discussions of hybris have seen it as a failing of
individuals.[25] It was that for the Greeks and it has been that
in most of Christian theology. If that were the extent of the
danger of hybris, the beautiful summation of biblical humanism
by Rabbi Bunam might be an adequate guide:

> A man should carry two stones in his pocket.
> On one should be inscribed, "I am but dust and
> ashes." On the other, "For my sake was the
> world created." And he should use each stone
> as he needs it.[26]

But we shall see that the Old Testament does not really believe
that an individual is capable of true hybris, rivaling God himself,
but that the state does have that potential. And for that special
reason it is important to hear such overlooked words as those which
the Old Testament has addressed to the great nations of the earth.
We are living in the same kind of situation which those passages
describe.

> America is striving to win power over the sum
> total of things, complete and absolute mastery
> of nature in all its aspects. This bid for
> power is not directed against any nation, class
> or race . . . The stake is higher than dictators'
> seats and presidential chairs. The stake is the
> throne of God. To occupy God's place, to repeat
> his deeds, to recreate and organize a man-made
> cosmos according to man-made laws of reason,
> foresight and efficiency: that is America's
> ultimate objective.[27]

Whether this indictment of America be true or not, we can recognize
in it enough that we know or fear to be true about the centers of
power in our world that it makes us shiver. And for that reason
this book was written; to use the technical tools of biblical exegesis to attempt to add a paragraph to a neglected part of Old
Testament theology, in the hope that those whose theology and
ethics depend on the biblical witness may be offered a glimpse of
new insight into the nature of the state in the eyes of God, and
encouragement in the difficult and usually frustrating struggle
against the forces of de-humanization.

CHAPTER I

MAN VERSUS GOD IN ANTIQUITY

Humanism appears to us now to be the product of a technological society in which man can for the first time hope to be his own master. Is this true? Did archaic man ever feel, as we do, that he could get along without God, or did he deify humanity in the place of God? Did he talk of being self-sufficient, or of freeing himself from the domination of the gods? Were any of these ideas suggested as attainable possibilities, or, if not, were they conceived, then rejected as dangerous and impossible? If we are to understand our own time, we need to know the answers to such questions lest we remain at the mercy of what seem to be utterly new ideas without the ability to see them in historical perspective. Although our chief concern in this book is the Old Testament understanding of man, we ought also to make ourselves aware of other views of man in antiquity--first, in order to justify our feeling of having a special relationship to the Old Testament and, second, to make the Old Testament concept more clear by comparing it with the views held by contemporaries and predecessors of the Israelites. Hence, this chapter will be devoted to a brief survey of materials from Egypt, Mesopotamia, Ugarit, and Greece which will attempt to show what men of the past had concluded about the relationship between humanity and divinity. The choice of materials has been limited by geographical and chronological propinquity to ancient Israel, and by the accident of discovery, which enables us to know more about this aspect of some cultures than of others.[1] In addition, a comparative statement concerning the "humanism" of the Old Testament will be provided without documentation at this point as an introduction to one of the emphases of this book; that a special Israelite contribution to our own understanding of man is the appreciation of man's remarkable likeness to God himself and the awareness of the terrible danger in which that puts him.[2]

Ancient Egypt

If we ask of the contemporaries of the ancient Israelites whether they felt a strong sense of deprivation because of their humanity (i.e., because they lacked something the gods possessed) we shall receive several widely varying answers, and if we then

ask of those who felt deprived whether they were willing to resign
themselves to their deprivation or rebelled against it we shall
find representatives of both reactions. That is true not only as
we go from one culture to another but within a given culture as it
changes in time. What we know of man in ancient Egypt makes that
apparent. John A. Wilson has given us an attractive description
of Old Kingdom man (2700-2200 B.C.; long before Israelite times)
which speaks directly to the questions just posed. The Old Kingdom
was a time of tremendous intellectual and physical advances and it
produced (or was the product of) a spirit of self-reliance and
optimism. As Wilson says,

> Man was enough in himself. The gods? Yes, they
> were off there somewhere, and they had made this
> good world, to be sure; but the world was good
> because man was himself master, without need for
> the constant support of the gods.[3]

I suppose Wilson's picture is so attractive to us because much about
it sounds so modern, but of course the Old Kingdom Egyptian was no
secularist. He never thought of denying the existence of the sacred,
and magic was important to him. But he felt no sense of deprivation
at being human, no envy of the gods; rather life in this world was
fully man's to enjoy and the next world was expected to be the same.[4]
No rebellion here then--certainly there might be hybris of a super-
ficial kind; one might think more highly of himself than he ought to,
but that was a social error which would result in loss of status, not
a sin against one's creator.[5] The gods punished sin, but did it not
directly but through their upholding of ma'at.[6] So when we learn
that pictures of the gods are totally absent from monuments set up
by ordinary men during the Old and Middle Kingdoms,[7] we may think it
was because such men experienced little feeling of nearness to, need
for, or direct responsibility to the gods.[8]

Change did come in the ancient Egyptian's estimate of himself,
beginning with the First Intermediate Period (2200-2050 B.C.), and
it culminated in a quite different outlook on his relationship to
the gods by the period of the New Kingdom (1465-1165 B.C.).[9] The
disturbing events of the First and Second Intermediate Periods
brought into the Egyptian's view of life that element of uncertainty
which had been missing earlier. So, during the New Kingdom caution
was the rule; he was advised to live as a conformist in this life,
submissive to the will of the gods, so that he might look forward
to a better life in the next world.[10] He no longer thought himself
to be master of his life, but began to seek oracles so as to have
divine guidance for his behavior.[11] He had become more or less
painfully aware of what he lacked that the gods possessed, as he

expressed it in the often quoted proverb: "The god is (always) in his success, (whereas) man is (always) in his failure. One thing are the words which men say, (but) another thing is what the god does."[12] So he felt himself to be dependent upon the gods for success and good fortune, sought to live in submission to them ("silence"), and developed a much stronger sense of his personal relationship to god.[13] But he still does not seem to have been deeply disturbed by what he lacked, nor is there any evidence at all of rebellion against the gods. For a way had been provided to a certain and blessed afterlife, and in that he could center his attention and could take comfort.[14]

From what we know of Egypt in the early periods, then, we would judge that the temptation of _hybris_ was not a danger the Egyptian would have recognized (save in the form of pride as a social fault), for it does not appear that he coveted anything that the gods possessed nor that he was aware of the danger of attempting to usurp their private privileges. Despite the changed attitude which we find in the New Kingdom, and despite the complaints against the injustice of the present world disorder which appeared during the Intermediate Periods,[15] the new spirit which developed was one of submission rather than rebellion, and we nowhere find expressed the desire to grasp for man what is reserved for the gods.[16]

Ancient Mesopotamia

In sharp contrast to the Egyptian understanding of humanity stand the views of the inhabitants of ancient Mesopotamia, with their strong sense of deprivation. They believed that from creation on man's position on earth was one of servitude and insecurity. Unlike the Egyptians, whose creation stories seem to draw no conclusions about man's obligations to the gods from their accounts of how and when he was made,[17] the Sumerians and their successors in the Tigris-Euphrates valleys are explicit in telling why man was made. He is always created to be the servant of the gods, the builder of their sanctuaries and their breadwinner.[18] So the basic relationship with which Mesopotamian religion worked was that between master and slave.[19] The prime virtue was thus obedience, and man could expect that if he obeyed the gods they would reward him with health and prosperity as a master does his faithful slave.[20]

In reality life was very uncertain, however, and the conviction that man's fate lay not in his own hands but in the unpredictable whims of the gods[21] surely was the result of generations of experience with the hardships of life in a land whose climate was severe and which had neither a natural unity nor natural defenses.

Kramer has described the dominating characteristic of the Sumerians as an aggressive drive for pre-eminence,[22] and perhaps such a character was necessary in order to create and maintain a civilized culture in Mesopotamia. The continuing conflicts among the city-states and the periodic struggles with invaders from inside or outside the Fertile Crescent had their counterparts in stories of intrigues and battles among the gods.[23] Hybris plays a prominent role in the myths, as we shall see later, and we should also expect to find it in the human sphere, under these circumstances, if man could be believed capable of it.

The keen sense of deprivation which the Mesopotamian man felt certainly led him to long for a way of gaining what only the gods possess; mastery of his destiny and freedom from death. But an ordinary man could not dream of challenging the gods; he could complain of the injustice of the world order,[24] and he could disobey and be punished for it, but nothing more. Erica Reiner has commented on this in her publication of a text concerning the apkallu's, legendary sages of the antediluvian period, in which foggy reminiscences of a series of human acts of rebellion led by the sages seem to be preserved.[25] She believes that such acts of hybris were so contrary to the dominant spirit of Mesopotamian religion during the periods which are well documented that they were almost completely suppressed. Man's longing for something better was expressed only in stories of semi-divine heroes, such as Gilgamesh or Adapa (to be discussed in more detail later). They, and not the ordinary man, might be bold enough to insult one of the gods, as Gilgamesh did in killing the Bull of Heaven[26] and in resisting Ishtar's advances,[27] and as Adapa did in breaking the wing of the south wind.[28] Their superior qualities are demonstrated by the fact that they not only dare to do such things but can get by without punishment (though poor Enkidu dies for his part in the Bull of Heaven affair). Another semi-human figure who was able to thwart the will of the gods is the hero of the flood story, Atrahasis or Utnapishtim (Ziusudra in the Sumerian version).[29] He outwitted the gods' determination to destroy mankind and (with the help of a personal god) survived the flood. But the contrast between Gilgamesh and Utnapishtim is more significant than either of their successes; the latter and his wife are the only beings who have been granted immortality by the gods, something which eludes Gilgamesh, and so we see that it is not the success of Gilgamesh and Adapa in insulting gods with impunity but their failure to obtain immortality which contains a statement of belief about human destiny. Their failures represent the conviction of the ancient Mesopotamian that to gain what man most deeply desires is impossible. Not even the semi-divine heroes of the distant past could overcome the curse of human destiny, which is to be afflicted by the gods and eventually to die.

Although hybris is one of the clearly identifiable themes of
Mesopotamian literature, it appears only in stories of the gods
such as Zu's attempt to usurp the kingship of the gods for himself, and in stories about such more than human heroes as Gilgamesh
and Adapa. That an ordinary man might seriously challenge the gods
is apparently not considered. Man was created in a brutish state,
given civilization only as a gift from the gods,[30] has only a precarious hold on even this place in the cosmos,[31] and is best
counseled to resign himself to his lot.[32] What he longs for the
gods hold jealously, and he dares to express his desire to usurp
the divine prerogatives only in the form of tales about men who
were already partly divine.

Ugarit

We know very little about the concepts of man which were held
by the peoples of Canaan, Phoenicia, and Syria in the pre-Israelite
period. The only literature available is from Ugarit, and its
nature is such that we learn little from it about man beyond some
information about social structures, etc.[33] At least one student
of the Ugaritic literature has suggested that the theme of hybris
appears in it, however; in the AQHT text.[34] Here we find no
aggression against the gods, no coveting something which is reserved for the gods alone, but there is a certain presumptuousness
in Aqhat which reminds us of Gilgamesh. He was a prince, the son
of Danel, who had been given by his father a magnificent bow which
had been made by the divine artisan, Kathir wa-Hasis. The goddess
Anat coveted the bow and offered him first riches, then immortality
in exchange for it, but he scorned her. She lied, he said, in
telling him he could become immortal, for that is not man's lot;
and furthermore of what use could such a bow be to a mere woman?
(II, vi, 15-39). Anat took her revenge for this insult and had
Aqhat killed (III, i, 29-40). The novelty of this story is that
it is a deity who feels deprived of something which man possesses,
but that this detail reveals no strikingly different concept of man
from the others we have surveyed is shown by the fact that the gods
have their way in the end, even royalty is at their mercy, and to
defy them only leads to disaster.

The sketchy evidence from Ugarit suggests that the concept
of man held in ancient Syria had much in common with the understanding we have found in Mesopotamia and that there is no trace of the
peculiar views which we shall find in the Old Testament.

Ancient Greece

Such a wide variety of speculations about the nature of man
has been preserved in ancient Greek literature that generalizations
are bound to be risky. Statements about the relationship between
man and the gods obviously do not apply to the thought of atheistic
philosophers at all, for example. We shall not attempt to cover
the whole spectrum of Greek thinking about man, but shall only try
to describe certain ideas which appear to have been widespread and
to have influenced both the philosophical schools and those who were
not philosophically oriented.

A text from Pindar gives an answer to our questions with which
many Greeks apparently would have agreed:

> Of one kindred, one only, are men and gods, and
> of one mother do we both draw our breath; but
> by difference of power we are utterly divided:
> man is a thing of nought, but for the gods the
> bronze floor of heaven stands as a seat unshaken
> for ever. Nevertheless we bear some likeness to
> the Immortals, either in greatness of spirit or
> in bodily form; although we know not where, from
> day to day or in the night watches, it is written
> by fate that we should end our course.[35]

The tendency among the Greeks to narrow the distance between the
gods and man in one way or another is in striking contrast to the
concepts of god held in the Middle East. But, outside of atheism,
they never succeeded in fully overcoming the distance, and indeed
the difference of power and privilege was of critical importance to
them.[36]

The narrowing of the distance was brought about from both
directions; men were glorified while the estimate of the gods was
a rather low one. That the Olympian gods were thought of in completely anthropomorphic terms is well known.[37] In appearance and
behavior, inwardly and outwardly, they were but gross human beings
whose behavior was often shocking if it could be taken seriously.[38]
At the same time the Greeks raised their heroic ancestors to a
divine or semi-divine status and the cult of heroes was extensive,[39]
so that in the case of individuals the gulf between humanity and
divinity could be bridged again and again--or had been in the past.
For as Pausanias describes it:

> The men of those days, because of their right-
> eousness and piety, were guests of the gods,
> eating at the same board; the good were openly

honoured by the gods, and sinners were openly
visited with their wrath. Nay, in those days
men were changed to gods, who down to the present
day have honours paid to them . . . But at the
present time, when sin has grown to such a height
and has been spreading over every land and every
city, no longer do men turn into gods, except in
the flattering words addressed to despots, and
the wrath of the gods is reserved until the sinners
have departed to the next world.[40]

Pausanias has introduced the idea that modern man has fallen upon
bad times, a notion as familiar to the ancient Greeks as it is to
us. It was one of two common theories about the early state of man;
one which was derived largely from Hesiod and which held that man
had once lived in a Golden Age, from which he had retrogressed to
his present, unsatisfactory condition.[41] The Golden Age was a time
when food was plentiful, when men were free from toil and grief,
and when death was like sleep.[42] But successive generations, of
silver, bronze, and iron, brought mankind to a life filled with
labor, trouble and sorrow.[43] Such a view was quite obviously
motivated by a strong feeling of deprivation and it produced
expressions of fear and resentment of the gods which we shall
examine shortly.

The other theory about man's early state said that he was a
brutish creature who has, with help and by his own efforts, improved
his lot immensely. By the classical period this was the most
commonly held view, although it could be combined in various ways
with some concept of a Golden Age.[44] There were two competing ideas
about what started man on his way to civilization; the gift of fire
(due to Prometheus) and that of agriculture (as taught in the
religion of Demeter).[45] In either case the idea of gradual progress
from a wretched existence, worse than that of the animals,[46] to the
glories of the Greek city states tended to emphasize the powers of
man. For this had been accomplished largely against the will of
the gods, as the Prometheus myths make clear. As Xenophanes said,
"The gods did not reveal to men all things in the beginning, but
in course of time, by searching, they find out better."[47] The prevailing belief appears to have been that man was able to rise above
his original brutish state only through trickery and that Zeus had
ever since made the life of man precarious in his anger.[48]

This conviction about the hostility of the gods is frequently
expressed in Greek literature. Its characteristic form is to be
found in the teaching about phthonos theōn, the jealousy of the
gods; an appropriate concept, it would seem, for a people whose
deities were so man-like and who kept their distance from mortals

only through power. The gods, it was believed, could not abide
too much human success, so that the ambitious, boastful, or
merely lucky man was in serious danger.[49] Such a teaching reflects a deep insecurity and anxiety on the part of the Greeks,
especially when it took a completely amoral form, as it sometimes did.[50] In Homer, for example, are to be found the stories
of how Apollo and Artemis slew the sons and daughters of the
mortal Niobe because she had dared to compare herself with their
divine mother Leto, who had borne only two (_Iliad_ xxiv. 605-612);
and of the death of Eurytus at Apollo's hand because he challenged
him to a contest with the bow (_Odyssey_ viii. 223-228). When
moralized, it becomes an aspect of Zeus' concern for justice and
an affirmation of his wrath against insolent men.

This brings us finally to _hybris_. In early times this word
meant any violation of the law,[51] but in its developed sense of
human aggrandizement against the gods it became one of the characteristic doctrines of Greek religion.[52] It has been translated
in many ways; as pride, haughtiness, presumption, insolence,
arrogance, wantonness; and its place in Greek thought has been
examined by several authors on Greek religion.[53] According to
Nilsson, the concept was developed and defined by the introduction
of a new word, _koros_ (surfeit, satiety, complacency), which enabled
it to be given a moral interpretation in terms of just retribution.[54]
So surfeit led to _hybris_ which was met by _nemesis_ (the ill will or
indignation of the gods). But it was observed that _nemesis_ or
reversals of fortune beset men who were not haughty or arrogant,
so in order to preserve its relationship with _nemesis_ the concept
of _hybris_ was broadened to include good fortune as well.[55] This
would clearly depreciate the moral factor for now _hybris_ might
simply denote the feeling that one had good luck on his side.[56]
A further depreciation occurred whenever it was said that the gods,
because of _phthonos_, beguiled men into _hybris_ in order to bring
misfortune upon them.[57] The result of all this was to impress
upon men the precariousness of their lives and especially the
dangers attending success or even happiness.[58] The concept with
those attending it could provide a rather accurate description of
human behavior: _olbos_ (comfort) leads to _koros_ (complacency),
which produces _hybris_ (insolence), the result of which is _atē_
(moral blindness and the ruin which results).[59] _Atē_ is the minister
of the gods whose anger (_nemesis_) has been provoked by _hybris_, and
she has as her own instrument _peitho_ (temptation).[60] But when the
jealousy of the gods was emphasized and they were thought to in-
flict _hybris_ upon men so that any human success might be brought
low, the effects of such a belief could surely have been nothing
but negative.[61] Such ideas do appear often in the literature; one

striking quotation should adequately illustrate them:

> You see that it is always the largest animals
> that Heaven smites with his thunderbolt, and
> will not suffer them to make a show of bravery;
> but the small ones do not chafe his anger. You
> see also how his bolts fall always upon the
> highest houses and trees; for Heaven loves to
> dock the things that stand out above the rest.
> So also a great host is utterly destroyed by a
> few men, when Heaven in his jealousy sends
> upon them panic, fear or thunder, whereby they
> perish unworthily. For Heaven will suffer
> none but himself to have high thoughts.[62]

Man clearly felt himself to be a rival of the gods, then, for
he was so much like them. But he could do little or nothing that
was effective to overcome his secondary status, for he lacked their
power. His challenges of their power never really threatened them
seriously, and to him they were always fatal.

* * * * * * *

We have been speaking of an unbridgeable distance between the
gods and man in several cultures in spite of the clearly evident
fact that it was thought to be possible for certain individuals
to lose their humanity (especially their mortality) and to become
divine. The Pharaoh was obviously a special case, god incarnate;
more important to us is the Egyptian belief, from the Middle Kingdom on, that anyone who made the proper preparations could become
a god at death.[63] We know that in Mesopotamia such figures as
Gilgamesh and Tammuz were believed to have been kings of an early
period who became gods after death. The same belief was held for
every king among the Hittites. And in Greek mythology half-divine
figures, children of mixed divine-human parentage, occur very
frequently. The gap between god and man was frequently bridged
in antiquity, then, but when we survey these cases it becomes
evident that the bridges in no way narrow the distance between
the gods and the ordinary man in this life. All involve the rite
de passage of birth or death. If one is born human his only
option in this life is to live in submission to the gods. And
although in some cultures some men might be promised divinity
after death, that made no change in man's relationship to the
gods in this life.[64]

We have now reached the point where a contrast between the concepts of man just described and that of the Old Testament can be sketched in a preliminary fashion. As yet we have not found outside the Old Testament any serious attempt to depict man as a rebel against heaven who attempts to become his own god. (We shall look more carefully for it in a later chapter.) The idea had occurred to the Greeks but they created no myths about it. Prometheus, it must be recalled, was a god not a man, and his rebellion against Zeus was only to gain the benefits of fire for mankind, not to usurp the kingship of the gods. That a man might actually aspire to grasp the position of the high god for himself thus appears to be an idea which is a distinctive development in the Old Testament. The preceding discussion suggests two reasons why others came so near to speaking about man's _hybris_ in the same terms as the Old Testament but without developing it explicitly.

1) The distance between man and the gods was so wide that never could a mortal be considered a serious competitor of the gods. He could only disobey; the thought that somehow he could be free from the gods and be his own master seems never to have been seriously entertained. That is to say, even the Egyptians with their self-sufficiency and the Greeks with their heroes may be said to have had a lower conception of man than the Old Testament.

2) We have seen that the deification of _certain individuals_ could be easily accepted by these cultures alongside their conviction that humanity has its immutable place far below the gods. This was possible without scandal simply because they were polytheists. The creation of another deity or two created no problem for their doctrine of god, and since these were special cases involving the loss of humanity for those who were deified, they did not affect their doctrine of man as it applied to the average individual.

The problem in the Old Testament is produced by its monotheistic conception of God (contrary to 2) alongside an exceptionally high doctrine of man (contrary to 1). Man was created from the dust (Gen. 2:7), as in several Mesopotamian texts,[65] but he is made in the image of God (Gen. 1:26f.), only a little less than God (Ps. 8:5), and he has been given dominion over all the earth (Gen. 1:28; Ps. 8:6). This does not mean that Old Testament man was above those admonitions to humility, circumspectness, and submission which other cultures produced. The Old Testament warns against pride in much the same ways used by Egyptians and Greeks. Rather it means that the Old Testament also believes man to be subject to a more insidious danger than the others recognized. If he can rule the world for God, if he can act as a creator much as God does,[66] if he can make himself so wise and clever as to be able to control his own destiny, why be content with "a little less than God"? Certain of the writers of the Old Testament were conscious of that temptation and they believed the occasional deification of an individual by their contemporaries to be the result of giving in to it. But no one may truly become a god, for the Old Testament writers. There is but one God and it is he who has given to men this glory which is theirs. To fail to acknowledge that, to claim to be one's own master and to take full credit for one's glory is for these writers to claim a divinity which God will not permit to any man.

How could they describe this sin? In Hebrew they had no word like hybris nor weak compounds such as "self-deification". They used roots meaning "to be high", as we shall see in the following chapter, but the terminology is far less important than the type of literature they employ. In the ancient Near East there did exist myths about rebellion against the high god and attempts to usurp his throne, but the rebel is always a lesser deity, never a man. These are the only myths which are brought over into the Old Testament almost intact. All other points of contact between the Old Testament and myths of other peoples are fragmentary and distorted, and the only other mythological theme which appears with comparable frequency is that of the slaying of the dragon, which is alluded to but never cited at any length. Certain facts now converge to point to the line of research which this book will follow: they are the monotheistic conception of God, the high doctrine of man, the consequent heightening of the dangers of hybris and the apparent necessity of using mythological language to talk about the danger.

Now perhaps it becomes more clear why it was necessary to begin with this brief and admittedly inadequate survey of certain aspects of the conception of man in neighboring cultures. It was not simply to try to show the superiority of the Old Testament, in traditional fashion, but to reveal how the uniqueness of the Old Testament's concept of man can be thoroughly appreciated only when we have explored the ways in which Hebrew thought is dependent upon and in tension with the thought of other peoples. In a certain sense such passages as Isa. 14:4-21 can only remain bizarre literary fragments and cannot become revelation for us until we take seriously the ancient near eastern materials out of which it was fashioned.[67] This is what the central portion of this book will attempt to do. But before we begin that study, two more preliminary efforts must be undertaken. They are: 1) a survey of the broad semantic field of words in Hebrew which are related to our subject, which will help to show how the passages to be studied in detail are related to the Old Testament as a whole, and 2) a consideration of what may

CHAPTER II

PRIDE GOETH BEFORE DESTRUCTION

The idea that man can go it on his own without a god to help
him or call him to account is a rare one in the cultures of the
ancient Near East, but it has been suggested that it does appear
in the Old Testament. Now we ought to survey the Old Testament
evidence in order to find out just how common the idea is, in what
contexts it appears and how it fits into the broad spectrum of
Israelite thought about man and his relationship to God. It is a
curious thing that while the Biblical understanding of _hybris_ is
frequently discussed in dogmatics, and indeed is often called the
essence of sin, modern theologies of the Old Testament usually do
not mention it at all. A check of the indices of twenty-nine Old
Testament theologies and histories of the religion of Israel published in this century revealed only four that discuss _hybris_, or
even the broader word, pride.[1] By contrast, not only has pride
been one of the traditional seven deadly sins in Christendom,[2]
but in so influential a modern work as Reinhold Niebuhr's _The
Nature and Destiny of Man_, to take only one example, pride is described as "basic sin".[3] In Niebuhr's work and in Christendom as
a whole the epitome of pride is man's "effort to usurp the place
of God",[4] which is precisely our subject. Hence, it might appear
that the subject is a natural one for a systematic theologian but
that as an Old Testament scholar I should have to justify paying so
much attention to it.[5]

There is one predecessor who has begun some work on this subject in the Old Testament field. He is the French scholar Paul
Humbert, whose article on the vocabulary of pride in Hebrew shows
a special interest in getting at what the Old Testament says of
démesure or l'hybris anti-divine.[6] His work can provide the start-
ing point for our thinking in this chapter, in that he has identified
the relevant vocabulary and has provided brief analyses of the
passages in which it occurs.

The Vocabulary of Pride

We shall deal with the terminology rather briefly, although in
another context a more extensive study of the semantic field of pride
would be worthwhile. We have seen already that there is no single

Hebrew word which corresponds exactly to the Greek _hybris_, but that we must work with a series of terms, any of which may be translated in some contexts by the English "pride". "Pride" is a much broader term than _hybris_, but includes it, as we have noted above in mentioning Christian theology.[7] What we shall find as we survey the Biblical vocabulary is that the Hebrew words do not possess the broad range of meanings denoted by "pride" and that they emphasize the external more than the internal; behavior more than attitude. Furthermore, when attitude is described it frequently borders on what might be called _hybris_.

In Christian hamartiology as Niebuhr analyzes it there are three types of pride: pride of power, pride of knowledge, and pride of virtue.[8] The Old Testament is barely aware of the last two of these but is acutely conscious of the first. So we shall find ourselves dealing with discussions of the misuse of power and with the attitudes engendered in those who let power go to their heads, for the most part. In addition, we shall find that even attitudes tend to be described in terms of their outward effect, so that the introspective character of many Christian discussions of pride will be largely lacking. But it should be emphasized that it is the nature of the Hebrew language to describe one's emotions and attitudes in terms of what is visible.[9] Also the terms which are used to denote pride have not become abstractions like the English word, for they are still used in a purely physical sense as well as to denote a moral quality.

The most common roots which are used to indicate pride are _gbh_, _g'h_, and _rwm_, and each of them means "to be high". The sense of haughtiness or exalting oneself is thus the basic meaning of all the words derived from these roots when they are used in a moral sense. The root _gdl_ "to be great", and others denoting turbulence and violence have derivatives which are used in the same semantic field, but the idea of height tends to dominate discussions of pride. That the physical sense is never completely lost is shown by the use of the tall tree as a symbol of overweening pride in Ezek. 31 and by the leveling of everything high as God's judgment against pride in Isa. 2.[10]

The root which comes nearest to providing a description of the inner attitude of pride is _gbh_, which appears in this sense twenty-three times in five forms.[11] As Hebrew psychology makes use of parts of the body to indicate emotions, so _gbh_ is used of lifting up the eyes (Isa. 2:11, 5:15; Ps. 101:5), heart (Ezek. 28:2, 5, 17; Ps. 131:1; Prov. 16:5, 18:12; 2 Chron. 17:6, 26:16, 32:25,26) and face (Ps. 10:4), as well as the spirit (Prov. 16:18; Eccl. 7:8). The "haughty" attitude is what the various forms of this root most often describe. It results in "arrogant" speech (_'tq_, 1 Sam. 2:3) and in a refusal to listen to God (Jer. 13:15). Its opposites are the patient spirit ('erek-rū^aḥ, Eccl. 7:8) and humility or lowness (špl, Isa. 5:15, 2:11,17; šwḥ, Isa. 2:11,17; '^anāwā, Prov. 18:12; knʿ, 2 Chron. 32:26). Little is said about the effect of such an attitude on others, for normally only the eventual humbling of the haughty is described in these texts (Prov. 16:5,18, 18:12; Isa. 2:11,17; Zeph. 3:11, Ps. 101:5). The feeling of self-sufficiency which this term denotes is expressed most clearly in a verse which reminds us of our main theme:

> The wicked, when his face is haughty, does not seek (God);
> All his thoughts are, "There is no God." (Ps. 10:4)

Closely related to gbh in meaning and use is the root rwm, which also means "to be high". Indeed the notion of physical height seems almost never to be lost, even when the root is used in a moral sense (Mic. 2:3 is the only exception).[12] Here, too, certain parts of the body are connected with the word in order to describe an attitude. The heart (Deut. 8:14; 17:20; Hos. 13:6; Jer. 48:29; Ezek. 31:10; Dan. 11:12) and the eyes (Isa. 10:12; Ps. 18:28; Prov. 6:17, 21:4) are used in idioms which are familiar to us, but a distinctive use is with the hand (Exod. 14:8; Num. 15:30, 33:3), apparently to describe a defiant action, not unlike our expression "high-handed", as Num. 15:30 reveals. Again humility and lowness are the obvious opposites, while the outward effect of this attitude is well described by Ps. 75:5-6:

> I say to those who boast, "Do not boast,"
> And to the wicked, "Do not raise up (rwm) a horn,
> Do not raise up your horn on high,
> Or speak with insolent ('tq) neck."

The boastfulness which is an expected result of pride appears else-where in association with this root (e.g., Jer. 48:29f.), and the occurrence here of the strong word 'tq "insolent" points us toward the equation of pride with arrogance which will soon appear. The inner effect of the attitude described by this term is similar to that in Ps. 10:4, although not put so strongly; viz. when one's heart is lifted up he forgets God (Deut. 8:14; Hos. 13:6).

The other terms tell us less about one's inner attitude toward God but more about how pride affects one's attitude and behavior toward other men. The root g'h also denotes height and is used in a moral sense thirty-seven times in four forms.[13] The form which Bertram says is the main one underlying the Septuagint's use of hybris is gā'ōn, but that seems to be a less significant term in the Old Testament than several of the others in that it is almost entirely confined to the sense of power, wealth and prestige.[14]

In Amos 6:8 the "pride" of Jacob is parallel to "strongholds", and frequently the idea expressed involves physical humbling of wealth and power (Lev. 26:19; Isa. 14:11, 25:11; Jer. 13:9; Ezek. 16:56, 32:12; Zech. 9:6, 10:11). So the special sense of this word denotes external possessions, rather than either attitude or behavior. The other forms of g'h tend to describe behavior of an unjust, arrogant sort. They are used of the wicked (Job 40:11-12; Ps. 10:2), of those who follow the way of evil with perverted speech (Prov. 8:13), of liars (Ps. 31:19), of the arrogant and ruthless (zēd, 'ārīṣ, Isa. 13:11), of the violent (Ps. 73:6), of those who oppress the widow and the poor (Prov. 15:25, 16:19), who close their hearts to pity (Ps. 17:10). Now the full effects of pride on behavior become clear, and what the various forms of g'h tell us is reinforced by the other strong words which are used in association with the roots we have already discussed. What we would call the proud man is what the Hebrews called the man whose heart, or eyes, or face, or spirit is exalted; i.e., he considers himself to be above others (said explicitly in Deut. 17:20), to need no one (cf. Jer. 13:15 and the context of Isa. 10:12), and to be responsible to no one. As we have seen, that includes even God, and it is apparent that such an attitude leads one to become insufferably arrogant toward those he considers to be beneath him; to live in disregard of others' feelings and rights.

Another root, zwd, is probably correctly associated with the words for pride by Humbert and Bertram, although it occurs only once in the same context with those we have been discussing (Isa. 13:11). The root means "to boil" and the forms which concern us tend to be stronger in meaning than those forms of g'h which convey arrogance. "Willfulness" is a broad term covering many of its uses (e.g., the prophet who speaks although God has not sent him, Deut. 18:20,22, etc.), and under that category specific disobedience of the law is often denoted (Deut. 1:43, 17:12,13; Ps. 19:14, 119:21, 85; Prov. 13:10). This willful, lawless behavior can be of a violent sort, as other occurrences show (Exod. 18:11, 21:14; Prov. 13:10; Jer. 43:2; Mal. 3:15,19; Ps. 86:14, 119:51,69,78,122). So it is appropriately translated by "arrogant", "insolent", "willful", and especially by "presumptuous"; but "proud" seems less appropriate (as in the RSV: Jer. 49:16, 50:31,32; Ezek. 7:10; Prov. 11:2, etc.). "Godless" (in five of the six occurrences in Ps. 119, RSV) is somewhat bold but probably acceptable, since that idea is present within this semantic field.

The most important elements of the field have now been introduced. In one passage which heaps up words for pride, Jer. 48:29, many of these terms appear together:

> We have heard of the prestige (g^e'ōn) of Moab,
>   He is very proud (gē'ē);
> His haughtiness (gābᵉhō) and his prestige (g^e'ōnō)
>   and his insolence (ga'^{a}wātō)
>   And the arrogance (rūm) of his heart.

Here are the roots gbh, rwm, and g'h, with three forms of the latter being used. (The parallel passage, Isa. 16:6, uses only the three forms of g'h.) Two of these roots appear together six other times (Isa. 2:11,12,17; Zeph. 3:11; Ps. 131:1; Prov. 16:18), showing how closely related they are. While gbh and rwm tend to describe an attitude, the forms of g'h most frequently denote the effects of that attitude on behavior. On the fringes of the field are other words which may be noted briefly. Of interest is gdl in seven occurrences, six of which describe men's magnification of themselves over against God (Isa. 10:12; Jer. 48:26,42; Dan. 8:11, 11:36,37; also Isa. 9:8). In one passage gbr is used in the same way (Job 15:25). Other words, of less importance for us, are yāhīr (Hab. 2:5; Prov. 21:24), 'allīz (Zeph. 3:11, etc.), 'abārā (Isa. 16:6, etc.), 'rṣ (Isa. 13:11), 'tq (1 Sam 2:3; Ps. 31:19), rhb (Ps. 101:5; Prov. 21:4, 28:25), tip'eret (Isa. 10:12) and hnp (Isa. 9:16, 10:6, 33:14; Job 8:13, 13:16, 17:8, 20:5, 27:8, etc.).[15]

The results of this word study show us that the Old Testament says little about how pride affects a man within, but that in the prophetic books, Psalms and Proverbs it rather frequently declares that the proud man is to be numbered with the wicked, the arrogant, the presumptuous and the insolent. Hence, the Old Testament conception of pride is rather similar to the Greek hybris, and like hybris it may produce presumption and insolence toward God himself.

Humbert has noted the remarkable fact that some of the most prominent "hybris passages" in the Old Testament use none of the words we have been discussing; proof to him that there is in Hebrew no word with the force of the Greek term.[16] I have already suggested that there is a special kind of language which the Old Testament prefers to use for this subject, that borrowed from myth, but in order to complete our survey of this aspect of Old Testament thought we ought to look first at the few significant hybris passages which do not use myth.

The Israelite and Pride

The preceding study of the Hebrew vocabulary of pride has revealed the borderline where pride becomes hybris. It is clear that the Old Testament authors believed that the willfulness, arrogance, and insolence which they described could lead some men

to a denial that there was any God who could hold them responsible
for their actions (cf. Zeph. 1:12). Extended descriptions of this
kind of individual may be found especially in Ps. 10 and Job 15.
Such a man says: "There is no God (Ps. 10:4b); . . . God has forgotten, he has hidden his face, he will never see it (vs. 11); . . .
You will not call to account (v. 13)." He seems to "limit wisdom
to himself" (Job 15:8b), he has turned his spirit against God (vs.
13a), and he has "stretched forth his hand against God and bids
defiance (hitgabber) to the Almighty" (vs. 25). These are among
the strongest condemnations of "the wicked" to be found in the
Israelite world. These extremes of behavior and attitude are
perhaps already partly the result of sin, for seldom is the
Israelite warned against this sort of thing although he is warned
of many other sins time and again. The eighth chapter of Deuteronomy
is significant here because it is one of the few passages where a
warning against putting oneself in the place of God is issued to
Israel. The rhetoric and the theology make an extended passage worth
quoting:

> Be careful lest you forget Yahweh your God, so that
> you do not keep his commandments, his ordinances
> and his statutes which I am commanding you today;
> lest you eat and are satisfied, build good houses
> and live in them, your herds and flocks are great,
> your silver and gold are multiplied and everything
> which you have is multiplied, and then you are
> proud of yourself and you forget Yahweh your God
> who brought you out from the land of Egypt, from
> the house of bondage, who led you in the great and
> terrible wilderness of fiery serpents and scorpions
> and arid places where there was no water, who brought
> you water from the flinty rock, who gave you manna
> to eat in the wilderness (which your fathers did not
> know), in order to afflict you and to test you and
> afterwards do good to you; and then you say to your-
> self, "My strength and the might of my hand has made
> this wealth for me." But remember Yahweh your God,
> that he is the one who gives you strength to get
> wealth, in order to confirm his covenant which he
> swore to our fathers, as at this day. For if you
> ever forget Yahweh your God and follow other gods
> to serve them and bow down to them, I testify to you
> this day that you shall certainly perish. Like the
> nations which Yahweh made to perish before you, so
> shall you perish, because you did not obey the voice
> of Yahweh your God. (Deut. 8:11-20)

The possibility that wealth may lead one to take such pride in his own skill, wisdom, and power that he pushes God out of mind is in itself dangerous enough to destroy Israel.

But frankly Israel was not often that wealthy or powerful, and perhaps that is why this kind of admonition does not appear frequently. Usually when the Old Testament describes the kind of sin which approaches hybris it speaks of mankind in general or of foreign kings, and when it reaches the extreme of using mythological language the subjects are always pagan rulers.[17]

The Primordial History

We can see already, then, that hybris in the fullest Biblical sense of the word is something extraordinary and outside the normal range of Israelite experience.[18] It is to be found in stories of the beginnings of human history. The irresistable temptation in the Garden of Eden is "You shall be as gods" (Gen. 3:5).[19] One of the major themes of the story of the Tower of Babel is hybris (Gen. 11:1-9). Humbert considers the strange fragment in Gen. 6: 1-4 to be another example of the démesure-fall pattern.[20] This account of the origins of the Nephilim tells of an attempt to blur the absolute distinction between God and men, spirit and flesh, as Humbert interprets it, by producing half-divine creatures through cohabitation. Such a move is thwarted by the Almighty as he re-affirms man's mortality, limiting his life-span to 120 years. In the misty past, then, the Israelites could believe there existed ancestors of the present races of man who had the ability and the temerity to overstep the bounds set upon humanity by the Creator of all. In these beliefs they differed little from their prede-cessors in Mesopotamia and later neighbors in Greece; indeed similar ideas are to be found in the folklore of many peoples.[21] The story of the Tower of Babel is distinctive enough and of great enough interest that it ought to be discussed at some length, how-ever.

> Once the whole earth had only one language, with
> few words. And as men journeyed in the East they
> found a plain in Shinar and settled there. And
> each one said to his neighbor, "Come on, let us
> make bricks and burn them with fire." (For they
> used bricks for stone and bitumen for mortar.)
> And they said, "Come on, let us build ourselves
> a city and a tower with its top in the heavens,
> and let us make a name for ourselves lest we be
> scattered over the face of the earth." But Yahweh

came down to see the city and the tower which the
sons of Man had built. And Yahweh said, "See,
they are one people and all of them have one
language. They have begun to do this and now
nothing they devise to do will be impossible for
them. Come on, let us go down and confuse their
language so that one will not understand the
language of his neighbor." So Yahweh scattered
them from there across the face of all the earth
and they left off building the city. Because of
that its name was called Babel, for there Yahweh
made a babble of the languages of all the earth,
and from there Yahweh scattered them across the
face of all the earth.

This is a puzzling story. It must be a fragment of one which
was once more complete, or perhaps of two which have been conflated.[22]
We are not told why the people are afraid of being scattered, what
their precise sin was or what became of the tower. But early interpreters had no question about its meaning. This was clearly a hybris
passage to them. They believed the building of the tower to be an
effort to storm the heights of heaven by insolent men, and the story
was elaborated accordingly with great detail.[23] To the story as
elaborated by Jewish interpreters there are many parallels in world
folklore, and most of these are concerned with hybris, too.[24] But
some modern scholars have questioned whether a heaven-scaling tower
and hybris are really parts of the story.[25] With this in mind we
shall look with some care at the text of the passage, putting everything to one side except the question of whether the present form of
the story has to do with hybris. (This means ignoring possible
earlier recensions, Babylonian local color, etc., all of which are
discussed in the commentaries.)

Two questions which the story is intended to answer are evident:
How did the family of Adam become so greatly disunified, scattered
all over the earth and divided from one another in many ways? And,
more specifically, Why do Adam's descendents speak many different
languages? Interpreters of the passage have added a third question
which they think the story answered: What is the origin of the
ruined temple tower which travellers have seen in Babylon (or
Borsippa)?[26] One of our questions will be whether the evidence
really points to that third concern as a motive for the Biblical
story.

Questions such as the first two in the preceding paragraph
belong to an aspect of human thought which is expressed in myth and
folklore all over the world; the conviction that something has gone
wrong--with the world itself, with man, with his systems.[27] It seems

fair to assume, then, that although this passage does not speak very explicitly of sin and punishment it does assert that the divisions among men are a perversion of things as they ought to be. Now, the "loss of paradise" is explained in myth and folklore in various ways; as the result of sin, as the result of divine jealousy or pique, or simply as an unfortunate accident. What is the motivating factor in the Tower of Babel story? It is clearly not an accident, for men are afflicted because of God's reaction to something they have done. One has to consider divine jealousy as a possible motive, for one of the few hints at what moves God to act is, "and now nothing they devise to do will be impossible for them" (vs. 6b).[28] But since this story appears in a document in which the nature and consequences of human sin are mapped out with care, we must also inquire whether the confusion of tongues was thought to be a just punishment for sin.[29]

We have already observed that from earliest interpreters on the sin of the building of the tower has been taken to be an effort to storm heaven itself. This would be _hybris_ in its grossest form and might then in some contexts be taken as a real threat to God (especially with vs. 6b to support it) but in the present setting it is depicted as a vain threat from the beginning. Every commentator observes the ironic way in which the storyteller has God go down from Heaven in order to get close enough to see that tower which was so enormous in man's sight. If the magnitude of the effort was due to sin, it is an effort, and a sin, which is ridiculed by the story in its present form. But other interpretations of the building project have been suggested by modern scholars. Perhaps building a tower to heaven is not the sinful deed at all; then vs. 4b may be taken as the clue to what men did that was wrong. Men had been commanded to "fill the earth" (Gen. 1:28) and this they refused to do, so God forced them to scatter by means of the confusion of tongues.[30] This reading of the passage would make the scattering a fulfillment of God's will rather than solely a punishment.[31]

Another interpretation sees this text as part of the Yahwistic writer's judgment of human culture.[32] Nothing specifically sinful is cited here; only two natural attributes of man: energy and the desire for fame (plus perhaps anxiety). These are necessary forces for the creation of culture, but they _also_ are the preconditions for _hybris_, and this story seems to suggest that such a sin is the inevitable result of the development of culture.[33] Or, perhaps the story is even more explicit. Men are concerned about being scattered, so they attempt by their own efforts to insure their future.[34] They build a city with a tower. The tower is what has impressed everyone who has read the story, because it was to have "its head in the heavens" (vs. 4a), and yet that expression may not

refer to an effort to scale the heavens at all. It was, for one
thing, the kind of expression used of the Mesopotamian temple
towers to indicate their sacred purpose as points of contact
between heaven and earth, with no thought of men ascending to
heaven by means of them.[35] And it is a rather ordinary Hebrew
expression used in the Bible to mean "sky-high". "Great cities
with fortifications in the heavens" are mentioned in Deut. 1:28,
and it has been argued that nothing more than this is meant by
the reference to the tower in Gen. 11.[36] This view has not been
favorably received by other scholars,[37] but perhaps it deserves
more weight than it has been given. For it is not the tower but
the city which is emphasized. "City and tower" are mentioned together twice (vss. 4,5), but at the end the tower is forgotten;
only the abandonment of city-building is cited. It may be, then,
that the initial emphasis on a city with a sky-high tower is simply
intended to depict men making a grasp for power, to secure themselves against all dangers through a unified effort. But it is an
effort which leaves out God.

Perhaps the emphases and major concerns of the story are becoming clearer, now that we have considered a series of interpretations of it. If there once existed a story about building a
tower to ascend to the heavens, and if such a story was connected
by the Hebrews with the Mesopotamian temple towers, we must admit
that we have lost almost all trace of it now. What we now have
is a judgment of human culture in its urban form, where power tends
to be concentrated most alarmingly. The two points of emphasis are
the city and "scattering"; i.e., concentration of power in human
hands and dispersion of it. The motives which lead men so to grasp
power are touched upon very lightly ("to make a name for ourselves")
and the divine explanation for thwarting men's efforts is tantaliz-
ingly open. "And now nothing that they devise to do will be impossible for them." Divine jealousy? The text does not rule it
out. But let us be a bit bold and suggest another meaning; divine
concern for human welfare. Now that man can do anything, who is
really threatened; God, or man himself? Man can do everything, and
so he does it, whether it is good or evil. He is neither wise
enough nor good enough to use well the power which he is capable of
grasping for himself, and since that is so it may be permissible to
interpret God's intervention, limiting what man can do, as at least
partly an act of grace. Whether the Yahwist thought this way it is
difficult to prove; his language is not that precise, but it is
language which leaves itself open to the kind of interpretation
which impresses itself upon the mind of a dweller in an urban
culture: perhaps to be divided and scattered could be interpreted
as preferable (for the future of humanity) to the possession by
sinful men of uncontrolled power.

Is this a hybris passage? We conclude that intimations of concern about usurpation of God's place and power are present, but in a subdued form. Although it is open to several interpretations, it is essentially the kind of negative judgment of urban culture which has appeared in many forms from the nomads to the free-land advocates of late twentieth-century America. Its relationship to hybris itself is in its awareness of the possibility that society, more than any individual, has within it the power to become a god over mankind, without limitations of its power, unless there is a God who intervenes.

The Nations: Pride of Power

It is the possession of great power and the desire for more which provides the most likely occasion for hybris to arise, the story of the Tower of Babel has suggested. We now may turn to a group of passages which develop this suggestion further and which put it in quite specific terms. The greatest accumulation of power in human hands has traditionally been found in government. Ecclesiastical and industrial power centers have been important at times, but have only been occasional rivals of government. Since this is true it ought not to be surprising to find the greatest concentration of concern about the dangers of hybris in the Old Testament in passages which are concerned with the great nations of the earth. The theme occurs with considerable prominence in these contexts in the book of Isaiah and we must now center our attention on certain passages in that book which bring us a step nearer to the climax of Israelite thought concerning self-aggrandizement. They are Isa. 37:22-29 (parallel in 2 Kings 19:21-28) and Isa. 10:5-19.

An issue which is extremely important for the citizen of any modern state is considered, perhaps for the first time in any depth, in the book of Isaiah. That is, how does/can/should one react to overwhelming power: a) when he possesses it, or b) when it is wielded against him? The issue arose in Isaiah's time because Assyria, in the late eighth and early seventh centuries, was the first really impressive example to appear in history of a world power. Certainly there had existed great civilizations long before, extensive trade networks, ambitious empire-builders, but none before Assyria made so explicit and effective a claim to possess the brute power to dominate the world. That is how they saw themselves, as the royal inscriptions reveal, and that is how subject or threatened peoples saw them, as we can learn from works such as Isaiah and Nahum.

The power of the great Assyrian empire builders went to their heads. The extravagant boasting of their inscriptions is well known, but let us cite a few instructive examples:

> Sargon, prefect of Enlil, exalted priest of Assur, elect of Anu and Dagan, the great king, the mighty king, king of the universe, king of Assyria, king of the four quarters (of the world), favorite of the great gods, rightful ruler, to whom Assur, Nabû and Marduk have intrusted an unrivaled kingdom, and whose name they have caused to attain unto the highest renown; . . .
> Mighty hero, clothed with terror, who sent forth his weapon to bring low the foe; the king, since the day of whose (accession) to rulership, there has been no prince equal to him, and who has not seen a conqueror in war or battle, who has smashed all lands like pots and who has cast bonds upon the four regions (of the earth); . . .[38]
> In my all-embracing wisdom and the fertile planning of my brain, which thinking Ea and Bêlit-ilâni had made to surpass that of the kings, my fathers, (and) following the prompting of my heart, I built a city . . .[39]
> Sennacherib, the great king, the mighty king, king of the universe, king of Assyria, king of the four quarters (of the earth); the wise ruler (lit., shepherd, "pastor"), favorite of the great gods, guardian of the right, lover of justice; who lends support, who comes to the aid of the needy, who turns (his thoughts) to pious deeds; perfect hero, mighty man; first among all princes, the flame that consumes the insubmissive, who strikes the wicked with the thunderbolt; the god Assur, great mountain, has intrusted to me an unrivaled kingship, and, above all those who dwell in palaces, has made powerful my weapons; from the upper sea of the setting sun to the lower sea of the rising sun, all humankind (lit., the black-headed race) he has brought in submission at my feet and mighty kings feared my warfare . . .[40]

Of course these kings were religious men and their religion taught them that they were servants of the gods, who held their kingship by divine appointment, so that due humility before the gods was expected. They believed that they went to war because it was the will of the gods that they do so, and that they ought to give the gods credit for victory.[41] This was done as called for, but where do they put the emphasis? On what I have done, on my greatness, ferocity, invincibility and wisdom. As individuals these men knew moments of panic and weakness, as the prayers of Esarhaddon and Ashurbanipal reveal;[42] but in the wielding of power they admitted no restraints. In practice there were certain controls over what the king could and could not do at a given time, as the omen texts reveal[43] (not to mention the limitations of practical politics); but there is no evidence of any moral restraint whatever on the power of the king in international affairs. It was experienced by Assyria's neighbors as uncontrolled power, used only for the glory of the great king.

That is to say, when a nation, or a ruler, achieves power enough to determine the destiny of the rest of the world, as Assyria did (to say nothing of the United States and Russia in the present), then it becomes very probable that a virtual deification of the power to govern will occur. God is on the side with the strongest battalions. Power is deified when those who have it refuse to accept any moral controls on how they use it. It is deified when those against whom it is wielded panic in the face of it and agree that there is no other kind of power that matters. This is what George Adam Smith described as the Atheism of Force and the Atheism of Fear.[44] He did so in his exposition of Isa. 10:5ff., and it has been meditation upon the implications of that passage and Isa. 37:22ff. which has produced the preceding paragraphs.

The date and authorship of these passages in the book of Isaiah is not an essential issue for our interpretation of their significance, but a brief discussion of these questions, plus a more detailed study of the form and tradition-history of the oracles may be helpful before we consider their theology. There is general agreement among scholars that part, but not all of Isa. 10:5-19 is the work of the prophet Isaiah. The judgment oracle in vss. 16-19 is usually ascribed to another author,[45] but there is little agreement about which parts of vss. 5-15 are Isaianic.[46] There has been much less discussion of Isa. 37:22-29, probably because of its location in the midst of the interesting and problematic accounts of Sennacherib's threat to Jerusalem in 701 B.C. A great deal of work has been done on reconstructing the history of the period and on comparing Isa. 36-39 with the parallels in 2 Kings 18-20. Beyond this, the concern for Isaiah's work has centered on theories about the role he actually played in the crisis of 701, with a consequent tendency to devote little attention to the value of the oracle in itself. But since it appears to be better preserved than the material in chapter 10, it is actually the better place with which to begin our study.

She scorns you, she mocks you,   22b
    The virgin daughter of Zion.
She wags her head at you,
    The daughter of Jerusalem.
Whom have you reproached and reviled,   23
    And against whom have you raised your voice
And lifted your eyes to the heights?
    Against the Holy One of Israel!
By means of your servants you have reproached the Lord,   24
    (And you said) "With my many chariots
I have ascended the high mountains,
    To the recesses of Lebanon;
And I cut stands of cedar,
    From the choicest junipers,
And I entered its extremest height,
    The forest of its Carmel.
I dug, and I drank water,   25
And I dried up with the sole of my foot
    All the mountain streams . . ."
Have you not heard long ago   26
    That I did it?
In days gone by I formed it,
    And now I bring it forth;
And fortified cities
    Become desolate heaps of ruins,
And their inhabitants are weak,   27
    Terrified and ashamed;
They are like plants of the field
    And green grass,
The tender grass of rooftop and terrace,
    Before it rises.
Your going out and your coming in I know,   28
    And your raging against me.
Because you have raged against me   29
    And your roaring has come up to my ears,
Therefore I will put my hook in your nose
    And my bit in your lips,
And I will send you back by the way you came.

The only question about the unity of the passage which needs to
be raised has to do with vs. 22b, which appears to introduce the poem
as a taunt sung by the daughter of Zion, while vss. 23-29 are best
understood as a prophetic word in which God himself addresses the
Assyrian king. Since there appears to have been a collection of
oracles inserted into the narrative at this point,[47] it may be that
vs. 22b is a fragment of a popular taunt (which might be compared

with Nahum 2-3) which could have originated in the sense of relief
felt by Jerusalem when Sennacherib's siege was raised in 701 or
much later when Nineveh fell (612). The remainder of the section,
vss. 23-29, however, is a masterfully organized unit. It begins
with an accusing question, "Whom have you reviled?" (vs. 23)
answering, "The Holy One of Israel." Then the king's boasting
is quoted, in the first person, in words almost identical to some
of the Assyrian inscriptions we now possess (vss. 24-25). It is
difficult to believe that the author of this passage was not
acquainted with the language of the royal annals.[48] The boasting
is now interrupted by another question which asserts that Sennacherib
ought to have known that all this is the doing of the Holy One of
Israel, and the continuation of the listing of the king's exploits
is now put in its proper context as a description of what Yahweh had
planned for him (vss. 26-27). This makes it clear why Sennacherib
is accused of scorning Yahweh; because he had been claiming as signs
of his own greatness what was actually the work of the God of Israel.
This is summed up briefly in vs. 28, then a typical prophetic judgment oracle concludes the passage (vs. 29).

The concluding verse is the key to most of what the poem intends to say, as a study of its form and the history of its tradition
will make clear. The form of this sentence is one which is characteristic of prophetic speech. It has two parts, called by some "invec-
tive" or "reproach" (vs. 29a) and "threat" (vs. 29b), and by others
"reason" (Begründung) and "judgement speech".[49] This is the typical
way by which the prophets of Israel announced the judgment of God;
by declaring what God was about to do to punish his people and at
the same time justifying it, explaining what they had done to deserve
judgment.[50] The same form is used in oracles against foreign nations
and the contents of some of those oracles provide the necessary background for understanding Isa. 37:29.

It has been shown that the ancient institution of holy war provided the original setting for oracles directed against foreign
nations.[51] Holy war as a sacral institution was apparently only
practiced for a short time during the period of the Judges,[52] but
its ideology had a lasting effect on Israelite traditions. This
is not surprising since most of the Israelite beliefs about war can
be shown to have been commonplace in the war ideologies of their
neighbors throughout ancient near eastern history. The characteristics of holy war as they have been delineated by Gerhard von Rad
are:

1. Israel was called to the holy war by a blast of the trumpet
(Judg. 3:27, 6:34; I Sam. 13:3). Messengers would be sent to the
neighboring tribes (Judg. 6:35, etc.). Sometimes they might carry a
piece of flesh as a sign of the call to battle (Judg. 19:29; 1 Sam.
11:7).

2. The volunteer army which was thus gathered together was called the "people of Yahweh" (Judg. 5:11,13, 20:2).

3. The soldiers, their weapons, and the camp were holy (Josh. 3:5; 1 Sam. 21:6; 2 Sam. 1:21), and they were to take careful precautions to preserve their sanctity during the war.

4. Before the battle a sacrifice was offered (1 Sam. 7:9, 13:9,12).

5. Especially important was the request for a divine oracle (Judg. 20:23,27; 1 Sam. 7:9, 14:8ff.,37, 23:2,4,9-12, 28:6, 30:7f.; 2 Sam. 5:19,23).

6. On the basis of the divine decree, the leader declared to the soldiers, "Yahweh has given . . . into your hand" (Josh. 2:24, 6:2,16, 8:1,18, etc.).

7. When the army marched to battle, Yahweh went out before them (Judg. 4:14; 2 Sam. 5:24).

8. The war was Yahweh's war and the enemies were his enemies. He fought against and defeated the enemy on behalf of Israel (Exod. 14:14; Josh. 10:14,42, 11:6, 23:10; Judg. 20:35).

9. Because of this Israel was reassured that there was no cause for fear. "Fear not," is a common component of the divine call to war (Exod. 14:13; Josh. 8:11, 10:8,25, 11:6).

10. The effect of Yahweh's presence on the battlefield was to create panic among the enemy forces and because of this the army of Israel could triumph (Exod. 23:27f.; Josh. 5:1, 10:2, 11:20, 24:12; 1 Sam. 4:7f., 14:15,20).

11. The battle was begun with a war cry ($t^e r\bar{u}'\bar{a}$), the result of which was the above-mentioned panic, although when Yahweh was displeased with Israel and deserted them on the battlefield, the panic might befall Israel instead of the enemy (Josh. 7:5; 1 Sam 17:11).

12. The consequence of victory in the holy war was that all booty was to be put under the Ban (herem), to be devoted to Yahweh (Josh. 6:18f.; 1 Sam. 15).[53]

According to von Rad it was the prophets who were largely responsible for preserving the holy war traditions long after it ceased to be a living institution. There is evidence for the regular participation of prophets in preparations for battle,[54] and the forms and themes which originally belonged to the holy war appear frequently in the prophetic books.[55] A key passage which links the traditional ideology of warfare with the oracles against foreign nations as we have them in the prophetic books is 1 Kings 20:1-34. It is no holy war which is being described here but the situation would have called for one in earlier times. Israel had been invaded by Ben-Hadad of Syria with an army of overwhelming strength. But twice, as Ahab prepared to defend himself in this desperate situation, a prophet came to him with an oracle from

Yahweh: "I will give them into your hand" (vss. 13, 28). Many
of the characteristics of the holy war are missing in Ahab's time;
the charismatic leader and volunteer troops are a thing of the
past, but it is clear that prophets are keeping alive the tradition
of Yahweh as the God who goes forth to battle with Israel's armies
to give them victory when they are in danger from their enemies.

The most striking of the oracles quoted in this chapter is in
vs. 28:

> Because the Syrians have said, "Yahweh is a god of
> the hills but he is not a god of the valleys,"
> therefore I will give all this great multitude into
> your hand, and you shall know that I am Yahweh.[56]

The form is identical to Isa. 37:29: a reason-judgment oracle with
the reason introduced by the same particle (ya'an "because"). The
judgment promises the downfall of a foreign oppressor of Israel,
and in both cases the reason given is the foreigner's belittling
of Yahweh. The use of a quotation of the foreigner's own words in
20:28a also reminds us of the quotations in the poem preceding
37:29.

This is no coincidence. The influence of the holy war ideology
on Isaiah's message has been observed by several scholars,[57] and
such influence is not confined to Isaiah, among the prophets. It
can be shown that Amos consciously uses the ideology in a novel way,
to declare that Yahweh is about to go to war as of old, but this
time to include Israel and Judah among his enemies.[58] The series
of reason-judgment oracles in Amos 1:2-2:8 makes use of the kind of
oracle which prophets had been used to deliver to a king about to
go out to battle, promising him victory, but uses it for a new
purpose; to promise Yahweh's world-wide judgment of the nations.
We shall find such a reversal of the holy war ideology elsewhere in
the prophets (Isa. 2, e.g.) but in the Isaiah passages which concern
us now we are closer to the original sense of the traditions.

The poem in Isa. 37:23-29 thus appears as one which is typical
of the thought of the prophet Isaiah in two respects; its use of
the holy war tradition and its emphasis on pride.[59] The two
features go together naturally, for it is customary for the war
ideologies of the ancient Near East to cite the sins of the enemy
as the reason for attacking him and to include as a prominent sin
his despite for and crimes against the honor of one's god(s).[60]
Holy war is thus an affair of honor. As the Syrians insulted God
by asserting that his power was restricted to the hill country, so
Sennacherib insulted him by claiming that his conquests were his
own doing.

Now chapter 10 makes sense when it is compared with 37:23-29, even though we may not be able to solve completely the problem of the original form of the oracles contained in it. As it now stands, vss. 15-16 fit the same reason-judgment form with which the other passage ended:

> Does the axe glorify itself over the one that hews with it?
> Or the saw magnify itself over the one that wields it?
> As if a staff could wield those who lift it,
> Or a rod could lift what is not wood?
> Therefore the Lord, Yahweh of Hosts will send
> leanness to his stout men,
> and in place of his glory a burning will burn,
> like the burning of fire.

Many scholars question whether vs. 16 and those which follow it can have formed the original conclusion of the oracle, but that some such conclusion is required was recognized already by G. B. Gray,[61] and modern form critical studies support that.[62] It seems fair to assume, then, that the oracle beginning in 10:5 was originally an expanded type of the reason-judgment form, but one ought not to have too much confidence that vss. 16-19 represent the original form of the judgment speech.

This is a passage which is comparable in form and thought to 37:23-29, but it goes deeper than the latter. Great emphasis is put on the theme which was central and yet not stated as explicitly in the accusation against Sennacherib: that he is the instrument chosen by Yahweh to carry out a certain work (vss. 6, 15). An additional theme, not present in chapter 37, strengthens the moral judgment which is made: the king has not only put himself in the place of the One who has appointed him, but his ambition and cruelty have overstepped the limits authorized by God (vss. 7-11).

An extensive exegetical study of these two passages cannot be included in this context. The attempt has been made only to clarify their major themes by showing how they are rooted in Israel's traditions concerning the holy war, and to offer some reasons for considering them to be the work of the prophet Isaiah. The latter was done primarily so that we may be justified in setting the oracles in the Assyrian period and in comparing what they say with other messages of Isaiah. If the setting is the late eighth century it is one in which Assyria's world-shaking power, unrestrained by any internal moral force or externally by force of arms, was threatening Isaiah's people. He saw his own government reacting with what Smith called the atheism of fear. His oracles addressed to Ahaz (chaps. 7-8) and Hezekiah (chaps. 36-39), as well as to others (chaps. 28-31) deal with the reaction to overwhelming power by those

against whom it is used.[63] But he also dealt with the other side
of the question, the atheism of force, the response to the possession
of overwhelming power by Assyria. This raises some serious questions
in our minds, questions almost never discussed by the commentators.

Can we assume Sennacherib ever heard these words? It seems
unlikely, and so we cannot help asking what is the point of all this?
Why address, admonish, and condemn someone who never hears you? This
is a problem with nearly all the oracles against foreign nations
(exception, Jer. 27), and it is usually answered by saying that such
words are in effect oracles of salvation for Israel. That is clearly
true on some occasions, and Isa. 37 is probably one of them, but at
others it is clearly not true, e.g., Amos 1:2-2:8 and Isa. 10:5ff.,
where God's judgment of Israel is included with the judgment of other
nations. Nevertheless, we assume the oracles were _heard_ by Israelites,
not Assyrians, so must have been intended to say something to the
former. It seems to have been necessary to deal with the atheism of
force in order to make it possible to cope with the atheism of fear;
to assure the panic-striken that brute force was not indeed the _only_
factor which makes any difference in international affairs. Furthermore, as one who believed that he had been commissioned to declare
God's truth, Isaiah may have believed he ought to put the truth into
words whether or not they were obeyed (6:9-10) or even heard. Compare Deutero-Isaiah's affirmation about the power of the Word of God
in itself (55:10-11; cf. 40:8).

But what right did Isaiah have to condemn Sennacherib for failing to recognize that he was only an instrument carrying out the
plans of the God of Israel? No one had ever told Sennacherib that,
so how could he deny it? He said of himself that he was carrying
out the will of God--i.e., Ashur, his god--although we have seen
that he and not Ashur tends to occupy the center of the stage. Isaiah
says nothing about other gods; to him there is only one worth mentioning, Yahweh, and he believes Sennacherib acknowledges no other god but
himself, since he disdains the gods of the nations as weaklings. We
do not know whether or not a given Assyrian king was really a pious
man who devoutly believed in Ashur, but to Isaiah that question was
quite beside the point. For he says that to grasp, then flaunt gross
power without conditions or moral limitations is wrong under any circumstances, no matter what one's religion or what he knows of Yahwism.
It is wrong because it gives to man a degree of power which he cannot
rightfully or properly use (we might say). It is wrong (Isaiah says)
because there is one God to whom world power belongs, and any man or
government that wields it is responsible to that God. To use such
power without acknowledging such restraint is to defy that God.
Isaiah faced a nation which confidently, arrogantly, almost jovially
asserted its intention to do anything it pleased, and he could

scarcely deny that it was doing it. The alternative to knuckling under was to believe that there existed a God to whom this was hybris, who would have the last word.

Pride's Future

That "last word" is described in a terrifying fashion in the second chapter of Isaiah (vss. 6-22). Here the coming of the Day of the Lord is depicted as a judgment of everything which might in any sense be raised up in defiance against God, and idolatry is introduced as the epitome of human presumption. It is a very forceful and impressive passage despite the fact that its structure has been the despair of modern scholars. Almost all agree that the present arrangement has a thematic unity, so that if it is the work of an editor he did an effective job. There is general agreement that the nucleus of the section is Isaianic, but as to the analysis of its structure there is no agreement at all. Scholars may be grouped according to three opinions: 1) those who believe the present unity to be original;[64] 2) those who sort out parts of what they consider to have been several originally separate units;[65] 3) those who despair of determining the original form.[66] Fortunately, the problem need not be solved conclusively before one can feel he understands the basic intent of the passage. All agree that its theme is clear, and we can shed a great deal of light on it through the history of the traditions it uses.[67] A tentative suggestion about its structure will be made, however, and the translation and interpretation will be based on it.

It is clear that in its present form our text has as its center vss. 12-16, a powerful, unified description of the destructive effect of the Day of the Lord. Next, it may be observed that sentences which have been called refrains bracket this center in chiastic fashion; vss. 11 and 17 are almost identical, as are vss. 10 and 19. Our hypothetical chiastic structure is interrupted by vs. 18, but outside of 10 and 19 we encounter material dealing with idolatry (vss. 6b-8 and 20), which leaves to be accounted for the first and last sentence (vss. 6a and 22) and two "refrains" (vss. 9 and 21) which do not fit the structure. One needs to be aware of the danger of finding chiasm which exist only in the mind of the exegete, but the general arrangement of the passage fits the pattern so well that the following tentative conclusions may be suggested:

a) Efforts to divide the passage into strophes by using the "refrains" (9, 10, 11, 17, 19, 21) have not been convincing. They assume either very irregular strophes or a seriously damaged text, either of which is, of course, possible.

b) Efforts to isolate two separate poems have not persuaded
either. Conflation may well have taken place but there is no way
to demonstrate that it did.

c) The section is generally chiastic in structure.

d) The exceptional verses 9, 18, and 21 may be explained as
the refusal of an author or editor to be strictly bound by chiasm;
as dittography; or, in the case of 18, either as a line misplaced
from after 20 or as a marginal note.

e) There is both repetition and development when the passage
is read in this way. One cannot affirm with much conviction that
vss. 6a and 22 were its original introduction and conclusion, but
it is possible to read them as parallel to a certain extent. Both
have to do with rejection, neither is explicit as to whom it is
addressed, and there is development from denigration of Jacob to
that of mankind in general. Idolatry now forms the framework for
a description of the Day of Yahweh (6b-8, 20) giving the latter a
new significance. There is movement from condemnation of idolators
in traditional fashion (6b-8) to a prediction of an end to all
dependence on idols (20). There is also movement at the next level
of the structure, from command to hide oneself (10) to a description
of how men hide when the glory of the Lord is revealed (19).

> For you have forsaken your people, the house of Jacob. 6
>> For they are full of Easterners,
>>> and soothsayers like the Philistines,
>>> and they make bargains with foreigners.
>> And his land is full of silver and gold, 7
>>> and there is no end to his treasures,
>> And his land is full of horses,
>>> and there is no end to his chariots,
>> And his land is full of idols, 8
>>> they bow down to the works of his hands,
>>> to what his fingers have made.
>>>> Come into the rock and hide yourself 10
>>>>> in dust
>>>> From the terror of Yahweh and
>>>>> the splendor of his majesty.
>>>> The proud eyes of man shall be abased, 11
>>>>> and the haughtiness of men
>>>>>> shall bow down.
>>>> And Yahweh alone shall be exalted
>>>>> in that day.
>>>>> For Yahweh of Hosts has a day-- 12
>>>>> Against all arrogance and
>>>>>> haughtiness,
>>>>> And against everything exalted
>>>>>> and proud,

And against all the cedars of Lebanon 13
(haughty and exalted),
And against all the oaks of Bashan,
And against all the high mountains, 14
And against all the exalted hills,
And against every high tower, 15
And against every fortified wall,
And against all the ships of 16
Tarshish,
And against all the boats of
pleasure.
And the pride of man shall bow down, 17
And the haughtiness of men shall be
abased,
And Yahweh alone shall be exalted in that
day.
And they shall come into caves in the rocks, 19
and into holes in the dust,
From the terror of Yahweh,
and the splendor of his majesty,
when he rises to shake the earth.
In that day man will cast his 20
idols of silver and gold
which he made for bowing down
to the mice and the bats.
Leave man alone, in whose nostrils is breath, 22
for of what account is he?

This is a complex work, bringing together in original ways
several of the themes of Israelite tradition, the most obvious of
which is the Day of Yahweh. This is referred to by Amos (5:18-20) as
a popular belief in his time and it is used by the prophets and later
in apocalyptic as a standard eschatological symbol. Although there
are competing theories in modern scholarship as to the origin of the
concept, its connections with the ideology of holy war are indisput-
able.[68] "The Day" was the day of Yahweh's victory over his enemies
and so Amos' contemporaries looked forward to it as the time when
their God would give them hegemony over their neighbors. Amos said,
but you are included among God's enemies (2:4-8). Now Isaiah makes
the Day even broader in scope, for he includes as enemies everything
which is arrayed against the uniqueness of God. As we have seen
earlier, the use of themes which had their origin in the holy war
was appropriate when dealing with God-denying self-aggrandizement,
for the holy war was an affair of honor in which God settled an insult
which he took to be the result of hybris. So the Day of Yahweh can

readily become the central theme of a passage in which pride and
self-glorification are condemned.

Often associated with the Day of the Lord was a theophany of
some kind. Yahweh is said to go out to battle himself (Isa. 13:5,
34:6; Ezek. 30:12,13), and various frightening natural phenomena
are described (Isa. 13:10,13, 34:4,9; Ezek. 30:3). Most scholars
speak of such a theophany in this passage, and explain vss. 12-16
as an account of a terrible windstorm (or earthquake, or fiery
apparition), but it should be observed that the text itself is
scarcely that explicit. There can be no doubt that the terrifying
theophany known to Israelite tradition lies behind the present
words, but it should be emphasized as an important feature of this
text that none of the usual details is included except one; no
clouds, smoke, fire, wind or earthquake, no description of damage,
only the terror in men's hearts is mentioned. While the terrifying
features of the theophany were indications of the immediate presence
of God, Isaiah has gone a step further; he has done away with the
signs of his presence and now God is not only central, he is All.

Some commentators find traces of Wisdom influence in the
passage, in the references to 'ādām and 'īš, i.e. to man in general
rather than the Israelite in particular; and in the use of terms
for pride which occur with some prominence in Wisdom. We have
observed how these terms for pride are used, and are discovering
that the most significant passages are not in the Wisdom literature;
but this is not to deny that they are a favorite part of that vocabulary. An important parallel to our text occurs in Job 40:10-14, re-
vealing that these are terms which are properly divine attributes
and which only wanton pride will ascribe to man.[69] The universal
scope of the passage, produced by the use of 'ādām and 'īš, among
other things, is one of its most important features and it may well
be that the influence of Wisdom is to be detected here.

Finally, the anti-idolatry traditions which are to be found in
the second commandment, and especially in Deuteronomic material and
in certain prophets (e.g. Hosea, Jeremiah), have been brought in as
examples of that self-sufficient human ingenuity which usurps the
rightful place of God. This is an unusual emphasis for Isaiah, but
is not to be excised simply because it is unusual.

Now that we have sketched a bit of the pre-history of the
passage, let us approach it from the other way. What immediate
impression does it make upon us? The first time I can remember
reading it, it struck me as describing nothing so well as an atomic
war in which the surface of the earth is utterly desolated and the
only hope of survival is to hide underground. It sounds like
realism now but must have seemed utter fantasy before the bomb--
and in Isaiah's time! The only other effort to imagine a comparable

scene which I have encountered is in the story of a man who used
his miraculous powers to stop the earth's rotation.[70] The earth
stopped, but everything on it kept going, leaving the hero on a
thoroughly desolate planet. My point is that this is a disturbing
mixture of realism (terror, hiding underground) and mystery, for
there is no natural agent described, only the unveiled presence of
God himself. We shall not accept the eisegesis of the commentators
who speak of windstorms, for no such thing is described. It is
Yahweh rising to terrify the earth with whom we must cope. And in
this book such language will not be called mythology, assuming to
call it that has explained something (see the Excursus).

The extremism of this passage will not be easily explained
away. It involves mankind in general which has been judged to be
proud and haughty, devoted to its own works and wealth, worthy of
being brought low. So we learn that when the God of Israel judges
Mankind, it is that sin which we have been studying of which he is
found guilty. But it is worse than that. Yahweh has a day against
everything that is proud and lofty; the works of man: towers, walls,
and ships; but also God's own works: trees and mountains, which he
made and called good. The extremism of this passage has taken the
Hebrew terms for pride so literally that everything "high" comes
under condemnation. "Height" may belong to God alone. So this is
not a statement merely against hybris, in the sense we found it in
Isa. 10:5ff. It affirms there is no rival to God anywhere; not in
human-kind, not in the works of men's hands, not in nature; and so
real hybris is put completely out of the picture. It so concentrates
on God in his magnificence that man and nature become nothing by
comparison. Man--"of what account is he?" (vs. 22).

Let us return to the questions raised by the appearance of the
Assyrians in Syria-Palestine. How could Isaiah, or anyone else,
believe what he said in 10:5ff. and 37:22ff.? The Assyrian went
on doing as he pleased. What good did it do to say those words
and what basis could he have for claiming their truth? His basis
was the future, as this passage makes clear. It asserts, what one
cannot in truth prove but can only believe, that human time does not
go on forever, but has an end. It asserts that God is not confined
to a time and a place of his own, but that he breaks into our time.
He has a Day.[71]

Ancient Israel understood pride to be a universal characteristic of man without any special relationship to the peculiar demands
of Yahweh upon his covenant people. So the most prominent occurrence
of references to pride are in the Wisdom literature (and Psalms),
which speaks of man in general, and in the primordial history, which
deals with the whole human race. That pride may verge upon hybris
is recognized again and again, but hybris itself is scarcely conceivable unless one possesses great power over men so that he can

become virtually a god to them. Hence the full-fledged <u>hybris</u>
passages in the Old Testament deal with political power as it is
concentrated in the great nations of the earth, normally in the
person of the king.[72]

Now it is all very well to talk about how pride of power has
adversely affected the history of the human race, and to give
advice to individuals about avoiding prideful behavior. The truth
and usefulness of this we acknowledge. But what good does it do
to speak to or about a man or an institution which has all the
power to do just as it pleases, and to say, "You are making a
great mistake."? Whether it does any good may depend on whether
the party involved is really guilty of <u>hybris</u> yet, but why should
he bother to listen to moralizing advice when he can do as he
pleases? This applies now not only to governments but also to
the private citizen of the secular world, who feels no supernatural
constraints on his freedom, who no longer fears judgment by disease
or accident or in a hell after death. We have learned from Isa. 2
that if there is no future which is in God's hands there is no
Biblical answer to that attitude. The Old Testament passages which
will concern us in the succeeding chapters not only take with the
utmost seriousness the human effort to replace God in the world's
economy, but also struggle to find a realistic position from which
such efforts may be shown to be absurd.

CHAPTER III

REBELLION AND FALL

One of the key passages in our study of hybris in the Old
Testament is the magnificent poem contained in Isa. 14:4b-21. It
is a mock funeral song composed for a now unknown king. The introduction which is provided for the poem, vss. 1-4a, sets it in the
exilic period and addresses it to the king of Babylon, but it is
clear that these verses are not the work of the author of 4b-21,
so that the date and subject remain open. Most modern scholars
have denied that Isaiah can have been its author; however the
arguments against Isaianic authorship are not particularly strong
and there has continued to be a minority which favors it.[1] There
can be no question, however, that the passage fits in the book of
Isaiah better than anywhere else, no matter who its author was, for
in no other book will we find a passage so nearly parallel in
thought to Isa. 10:5ff. and 37:22ff. If it does belong to the
same period as these texts then the subject will have been an
Assyrian king, but the historical allusions in the poem are not
unequivocal, and it is not possible to say with much confidence
whether it was Sargon or Sennacherib, or some later king. But the
identification of the poem's author and subject is not of prime
importance for our purposes, so we shall not go into details. What
is important is the unusual similarity between the poem and Isa.
10:5ff.; 37:22ff., and it is from this point that we shall approach
our text.

This is another text which condemns a mighty, world-conquering
king for his attitude of hybris against the God of all the nations,
but it does so in a very different way from the passages we studied
earlier. The ideas are similar but the form and the materials used
are entirely different. The form has been mentioned before; it is
a pseudo-funeral song, and the materials are "mythological". (What
I mean by this is explained in the Excursus.) Now the question is,
Does that mean anything special? Is it saying the same thing in a
new way, or do the different materials make it say something
slightly different from the passages studied earlier?

Some conservative scholars have said that such language could
not possibly refer to a human being, so that the real subject of
the poem must be a supernatural creature, viz. Satan.[2] This view-
point has a long tradition behind it, going back at least to
Tertullian;[3] but at least since Calvin's time it has been under fire

from those who believe the passage should be interpreted in strictly historical terms.[4] But if the latter is the correct approach, in the sense that it gets at what the Old Testament intended to say (i.e., not something about Satan but about man), then why the mythological stuff? Why call a real king Helel ("Brilliant One") ben Shahar ("son of the Dawn") and speak of his plan to ascend into heaven? The conclusion of Childs' study of myth in the Old Testament is that this kind of thing is for illustrative purposes only;[5] and that is very probably so; but why such bizarre illustrations? Are they necessary in order to say what the author intended, or could we "de-mythologize"? It is my conclusion that the author found these peculiar materials indispensible, for the poem's meaning is not identical to the other passages we have considered.

Form

The structure of this text is remarkably regular for Hebrew poetry. It divides very neatly into three strophes of seven lines each, then concludes with twelve or thirteen lines which do not follow the preceding pattern. The meter, which is 3:2 with very few exceptions down to vs. 19, also becomes less regular in the last few verses. Many different efforts have been made to solve the double problem of irregularity of structure and obscurity of meaning in vss. 17b-21, and it seems likely that there has been some textual corruption at this point.[6] However: 1) Minor changes do not solve the problem, and it is hard to put much confidence in drastic revisions of the text. One has the feeling that a good modern poem has been produced by some of these efforts, but probably not the one which originated in antiquity. 2) Changes based on our theories about metric or strophic regularity always ought to be suspect. The Ras Shamra texts are illustrations of what I believe to be a general truth; that Semitic poets never considered themselves rigidly bound by strict metric and strophic rules. 3) To make an arbitrary division between 19b and 19c to produce a fourth strophe of seven lines, as is often done, cannot be accepted for it interrupts a thought which is begun in 19a. Each of the preceding strophes is a closed thought unit, not merely a fixed number of lines. Hence, we may be faced with (a) a long concluding unit of twelve or thirteen lines, (b) two strophes of seven lines each, both of which have been damaged, (c) a strophe of eight (vss. 16-19) or ten (vss. 16-20b) lines followed by a short concluding section of three lines, or (d) a poem the end of which is completely uncertain (if we suspect the originality of vss. 20-21). I do not believe that we possess the equipment to do any more than guess at

which of these possibilities (or others) is likely to be correct,
so with the exception of a few textual alterations which seem
well grounded, the translation which follows will be an attempt to
make sense of the passage as it is (though admitting that certain
lines may very well be corrupt).

The poem is introduced as a <u>mashal</u>, which most often means
"proverb" but which is used sometimes in the prophetic books to
indicate that a type of literature is being used for a purpose
different from its normal one (Mic. 2:4; Hab. 2:6), and that is
true here.[7] The poet has used one of the forms of speech which
the prophets most liked to borrow and put to their own use, the
dirge. There are a few examples of true laments for the dead in
the Old Testament (especially David's laments for Saul and Jonathan,
2 Sam. 1:19-27, and for Abner, 2 Sam. 3:33-34), but we know the form
best from the ways the prophets put it to use. It appears in Amos
5:1, sung to mourn the death, not of an individual but of the nation
Israel, and sung before the death occurred! (Most impolite.) When
used in such a way it obviously has become one of the methods which
a prophet could use to announce the coming of God's judgment. It
still conveys the feeling of real grief. Similar uses are found
elsewhere, e.g., Jer. 9:17-21; Ezek. 19; but frequently the form
is converted into a taunt, a funeral song from the lips of those
who are glad to be rid of the deceased.[8] Our poem is the finest
known example of this type.

Here we find many of the same motifs which are used in the
true funeral song with a sometimes subtle, sometimes blunt reversal
of meaning. The meter is the limping, so-called <u>Qina</u> type, with
the latter half of each verse shorter than the former half, a meter
frequently used in dirges.[9] Two strophes begin with 'ēk, "How!",
an introductory particle very common in the dirge (2 Sam. 1:19,25,
27; Lam. 1:1, 2:1, 4:1). The funeral song may introduce as one of
the factors aggravating one's grief the rejoicing of the deceased's
enemies now that he is out of the way. But here it is the singers
of the mock-dirge who rejoice, and indeed there are no mourners at
all for the whole earth is relieved (vss. 7,8). A common, mournful
strain is "no more . . .," (Ezek. 19:9,14), expressing one's sense
of loss, but now "no more" means release and relief (vs. 8b). The
tendency to eulogize naturally affects Semitic dirges and it often
took the form of stressing the incomparability of the deceased,
which made his fate the more poignant and the mourners' loss all
the greater (2 Sam. 1:23; Ezek. 26:17f.; Lam. 1:1). The subject
of our poem was incomparably powerful (vss. 6,10,16,17) and that
is stressed because it makes the sense of relief at his death all
the greater. One way of expressing the enormity of the change
from strength and vitality to the stillness of death is the wonder-
ing, incredulous question; and this we also find in vss. 16-17, but

now in order to mock rather than mourn. Finally, two of the
factors which made death really tragic for the Hebrews are introduced. Death and burial far from home or worse, non-burial, was
a curse of the worst sort (Gen. 47:29f.; 1 Sam. 31:11-13; 2 Kings
9:10; Ps. 79:2ff.; Jer. 14:16; Amos 5:1), and the mourning for such
an unfortunate would be especially intense. Now it is a cause for
satisfaction (vss. 19f.). If a man left no children behind so that
his name and reputation would soon be forgotten there was, again,
real cause for grief (Ps. 109:13); but where the tyrant is concerned,
it is fervently to be hoped that remembrance and progeny will be
denied him (vs. 21).

More could be said about the rhetorical skill of the author of
this poem, but only one additional characteristic will be noted.
It is the artful way in which four scenes are set for us with the
introduction of a speaker in each of them. In the first strophe
the poet envisions the whole earth rejoicing and since the tyrant
has afflicted not only man but the natural world also, the trees of
Lebanon, which had been preyed upon by Mesopotamian kings since the
third millenium B.C., speak to express the relief of the world. In
the second the scene has shifted to Sheol; the dead king has entered
and the inhabitants of Sheol now speak to make the poet's point--
in death this world-conqueror is no different from any other dead
man. In the third strophe we have entered the realm of the gods,
of "myth", for in the mind of the king we range the heavens to learn
from his own words the extent of his self-exaltation. Then we are
brought back to earth with a thump, to the reality of an unburied
corpse stared at by the curious who marvel at how they once trembled
before him.

Translation[10]

How the taskmaster has ceased,   4b
    Ceased is the tyranny!
Yahweh has smashed the staff of the wicked,   5
    The scepter of rulers
        Which smote peoples with fury,   6
            Smiting without end;
        Which trampled with anger the nations,
            Trampling without restraint.
At rest, undisturbed is all the earth--   7
    They cry out with joy!
Even the junipers rejoice at you,   8
    The cedars of Lebanon:
"Since you lay down no axeman
    comes up against us."

* * *

Below, Sheol is perturbed about you,   9
    To meet your coming;
Rousing for you the shades,
    All the leaders of the earth;
Raising up from their thrones
    All the kings of the nations.
All of them speak up   10
    And say to you:
"You too are made weak as we,
    Have become like us.
"Brought down to Sheol is your pomp,   11
    The sound of your harps.
"Beneath you maggots are a bed,
    And your cover is worms."

* * *

How you are fallen from heaven,   12
    Helel ben Shahar!
Felled to the earth,
    Reaper of nations!
And you said to yourself,   13
    "I will go up to heaven!
"Above the stars of God
    I will exalt my throne,
"And I will sit in the Mount of Assembly,
    In the recesses of the North!
"I will ascend upon the backs of the clouds,   14
    Make myself like Elyon!"
Instead you are brought down to Sheol,   15
    To the recesses of the pit.

* * *

Those who see you will stare at you,   16
    Will peer at you:
"Is this the man who perturbed the earth,
    Who shook kingdoms,
"Who made the world like the wilderness   17
    And ruined its cities?

> "His prisoners he did not free to their homes,   18
>   All the kings of the nations."
> All of them lie down in splendor,
>   Each in his house,
> But you are cast out, without sepulchre,   19
>   Like a loathsome shoot,
> Clothed with the slain,
>   Those pierced by the sword,
> Who go down to the stones of the pit
>   Like a trampled corpse.
> You shall not be united with them in burial,   20
> For you ruined your land,
>   you killed your people.
> Nevermore let there be mentioned
>   The offspring of evildoers!
> Prepare for his sons a slaughtering-place   21
>   Because of their fathers' guilt,
> So they do not arise and possess the earth.
> Then the face of the world will be full of cities.

Mythological Themes in Isaiah 14

Until late in the nineteenth century interpreters of this passage took vss. 12-15 either as examples of the unbridled imagination of the man of _hybris_ or as literal statements about a supernatural creature, Satan. But as early as the 1880's the similarity between this text and the Greek myth of Phaethon were being discussed.[11] This was an era, however, when Old Testament scholarship was being dominated by the new discoveries of Mesopotamian civilization, so that it was assumed for some time that our passage was based on a Babylonian myth, although several features could not be adequately explained in this way.[12] As would be expected, Hermann Gunkel was ahead of his time in suggesting that it could be of Phoenician origin, while also pointing out its similarity to the Phaethon myth.[13] Since the discoveries at Ras Shamra began in 1929 there has been a tendency to replace the old Pan-Babylonian approach with a Pan-Ugaritism, and with some justification here, at any rate, for several of the words and phrases in vss. 12-15 do appear in the Ugaritic texts.[14] These coincidences have led some to affirm that this is a quotation of a Canaanite myth, or at least that we now can be sure that the materials are of Canaanite origin.[15] We can agree with the latter statement without reservation because of the close verbal similarities which exist and because it is only natural to expect Israelite literature to be more like that of the Canaanites than of any, more distant peoples. But the proof of the former affirmation has not yet been provided, and it does

require some proof. As yet no Ugaritic text describing the fall
of a rebellious king or god from heaven has been found, so that
we do not presently possess a full parallel to the plot of vss.
12-15.

However, valiant efforts have been made to reconstruct the
"original myth" which it is assumed must lie behind these verses,
by drawing together South Arabic, Ugaritic, Hittite and Greek
materials.[16] The evidence may be surveyed as briefly as possible
in the following manner:

a) The name in vs. 12, Helel ben Shahar, means "Brilliant One,
son of Dawn," and very probably refers to the morning star, Venus.[17]

b) The name Phaethon means "Gleaming One", so is similar to
Helel; and this character is sometimes said to be the son of Eos,
the dawn (but elsewhere is the son of Helios, the Sun).[18]

c) There is a myth in which Phaethon falls from heaven (but,
it is the wrong Phaethon, not the son of the dawn; and it involves
no grab for kingship of the gods, nor probably hybris of any kind).
The young Phaethon went to his father the Sun to ask permission to
drive his heavenly chariot for a day. This was reluctantly granted,
and he was cautioned to keep the fiery steeds in check and not to
drive too high or too low. But he let them get out of control,
scorching earth and heaven, so that finally Zeus had to intervene
and kill him with a thunderbolt. His smoldering body fell into
the river Eridanus.[19]

d) Other evidence for the existence of a star-deity related
to the dawn is sought in South Arabia, Ugarit and Mesopotamia. In
South Arabic texts there is a high god named Athtar, who is equated
with Venus, sometimes as both morning and evening star but other
times only as the latter.[20] Now, this divine name is a common one
throughout the Semitic world, in both male and female forms. It
appears in Mesopotamia as Ishtar, who is the goddess of fertility
and is equated with the planet Venus, in Canaan as Astarte, the
fertility goddess, and in Ugarit as Athirat, the wife of El and
mother of the gods.[21] The masculine form, Athtar, also appears
at Ugarit, but it cannot be determined whether he is primarily an
astral figure.[22] The deity Shahar appears both in South Arabia
and at Ugarit, but nowhere is Athtar said to be his son.[23]

e) No "fall" of any of the deities bearing the 'ttr name is
recorded anywhere. It has been assumed that behind Isa. 14:12-15
is a nature myth telling how the morning star appears, then is
vanquished by the rising sun,[24] but it should be emphasized that
we do not possess the text of any such myth. In one of the Ras
Shamra texts (49:I, 11-37) Athtar is set upon Baal's throne to take
his place while he is in the netherworld, but there is no rebellion
and fall here; he is legally appointed by El and Athirat and is not

deposed but steps down of his own accord because he is not great enough to occupy the throne.[25]

The "reconstructed myth", then, of the unseemly and unsuccessful effort of the morning star to grasp the kingship of the gods is one for which there is clear evidence only in Isa. 14, and the value of the efforts to trace such hypothetical migrating myths is rather small for one who is attempting to understand the meaning of the Biblical text.

But there is another way. The problem with the approach just described is not only that it presently lacks adequate evidence to answer the questions asked (we cannot criticize it for that), but that it is not asking the most significant questions, and it is making unnecessary assumptions. It assumes that Isa. 14:12-15 is a fragment of or a quotation from some "original myth" and asks what the "original form" was and from whence it was borrowed by the author. And there is a feeling of considerable triumph when affinities with Ugarit are discovered; the problem of derivation is solved--it was Canaanite. But as I have already indicated, that is no surprise and might well have been assumed without evidence. The next step might be more meaningful, to find out how the comparative material (here, especially the Ugaritic) helps us to understand the meaning of the Hebrew work. The Ras Shamra texts have shed new light on a good many of the terms which occur in Isa. 14, e.g., rephaim and ṣaphon, to mention only two; but where the myth as a whole is concerned the assumption has been that there must have existed a Canaanite myth like Isa. 14:12-15 from which the latter could be derived; and since we do not possess the hypothetical prototype a process of reconstruction, using elements which appear to be related, no matter what their source, is called for.

Why assume that a myth recounting the attempt of a lesser deity, apparently an astral figure, to usurp the throne of the high god, resulting in his being cast into the netherworld, ever existed among the Canaanites when we have no evidence for it except in the Old Testament? Consider the elements which have been traced from Isa. 14:12-15 into Ugaritic, Greek, Hittite and Mesopotamian mythology. They are: the morning star, Venus; the dawn; the fall of a heavenly body; death and the concept of a netherworld; the concept of rivalry among the gods. Now, Venus, the dawn, falling stars and death are parts of the experience of everyone on earth and are basically the same no matter where one lives. So it is not surprising to encounter similar myths about the morning star all over the world, for the planet Venus is seen everywhere.[26] On another level myths about rivalry among the gods may also be found all over the world.[27] Now we are approaching an area of dispute among folklorists and anthropologists which, fortunately, need not become a critical issue for us; i.e., the debate over diffusion.[28]

Are the common elements in myths and customs of different peoples
due to common circumstances or something basic to human nature, or
are they to be explained as the result of diffusion from an original source somewhere? The preoccupation of Old Testament scholars
with borrowing would appear to put them in the latter camp while
my de-emphasis of borrowing appears to put me in the former, but
it must be observed that the problem does not have the same magnitude for one who concentrates on the ancient Near East as it does
for the anthropologist who compares cultures which are widely
separated geographically. For it is clear to everyone that within
the Middle East there was effective diffusion, so that the same
symbols can be traced in Mesopotamia, the Levant, Asia Minor, and
even on into Greece.[29] And the intriguing problem of tracing these
diffusions of cultural and religious symbols, then of making de-
ductions about the movements and interactions of peoples, has very
properly occupied archaeologists and historians. But what I am
emphasizing is that to establish areas of cultural continuity is
not necessarily to determine the meaning of the symbols involved
for the people who used them. To discover the derivation of a
symbol is not to reveal its meaning, unless we assume that the
same symbol means the same thing in every time and place.[30] This
cannot be assumed, and indeed we shall find evidence that it is
false even as the closely related cultures of the ancient Near East
are compared.[31] Our basic method, then, in dealing with mythological themes, is to search for the meaning of a theme by comparing
how it is used in different cultural contexts. It can be shown
that: a) a given symbol can mean anything, even exact opposites,
as one moves from culture to culture;[32] b) but that in closely
related cultures such as those of the Middle East there is likely
to be considerable continuity of meaning;[33] c) however, each of
these cultures has its own integrity and is not to be considered
as simply a mirror of a single pattern,[34] so that the precise
significance of a given theme can be determined only by the way it
is used in the myths of a certain culture.[35]

The study which follows, then, will not deal with terms, such
as saphon, but with the great mythological themes which appear
here and elsewhere. In order to determine what they mean in Isa.
14 it must be learned where they occur in related cultures, and by
studying how they are related to one another and to other themes
to set up a series of structures with which the use of the themes
in Isa. 14 may be compared. We shall proceed simply by naming the
themes in the order that they occur in vss. 12-15, then by gathering other examples of each for comparison.

A) <u>Fall from Heaven</u>:

> How you are fallen from heaven,
> Helel ben Shaḥar!

A fall from heaven may appear in two broadly different contexts, either in the expulsion of one who originally belonged there, or in the failure of an effort to gain heaven by one who belongs below. Let us retain this scheme even though it brings together materials widely separated in space and time.

1) Lamaštu: In an Old-Assyrian incantation from Kultepe the existence of the female demon Lamaštu is accounted for by recounting her rebellion against Anu, the god of heaven, and her consequent expulsion from heaven:

> One is she, "pure" is she, late-born of the type
> of Muštabbabbum-demons is she,
> <u>Utukkum</u>-ish is she, . . . is she, the child
> of a god, the daughter of Anum.
> Because of her poor sense, her vulgar counsel,
> Anum, her father, has dashed her down upon
> the earth.
> Because of her poor sense, her rebellious counsel,
> her hair hangs down loose, her body is un-
> covered.
> She makes straight for a godless man.
> The sinews of a lion she has made weak,
> the sinews of children and infants she . . . ![36]

2) Ate: In the Iliad there is also an account of a goddess who is banished from heaven, Ate, the eldest of Zeus' daughters, the personification of mental blindness. She once fooled even Zeus himself, for he was tricked by Hera into swearing an oath that the child to be born on that day would be lord over all that were of Zeus' lineage, thinking the child would be Alcmena's son, Hercules. But Hera then held back the birth of Hercules and had Sthenelus bring forth Eurystheus a month early. Zeus was enraged at this, caught Ate by the hair and, swearing that she should never again invade heaven, whirled her around and flung her down from heaven to earth, where she now hovers over the heads of men to make them stumble.[37] There is clearly no rebellion against the high god in the case of Ate; whether there is in the Lamaštu text we cannot be certain. In both, however, one of the spiritual sources of evil on earth is said to have fallen from her original place in the heavenly court precisely because her evil nature made her unwelcome there.[38]

3) Two fragments may be added here, although little can be said about either. There is a Hittite text which tells of the Moon-god falling from heaven, without, however, any indication of the reasons or consequences except that several other deities are stirred up by it.[39] Also there is a reference in a bilingual Sumerian and Akkadian text to a mysterious man of the distant past (an apkallu) named Nunpiriggaldim, who is said to have "brought down Istar from heaven into Eanna," but the meaning of this reference remains obscure.[40]

4) The failure of an effort to reach heaven is well exemplified by the Etana myth from Mesopotamia.[41] Etana is the first king on earth but he lacks an heir. Having befriended an eagle, he is offered a trip to heaven by the bird so that he may obtain the needed "plant of birth". Their ascent is described graphically, then, just before the text breaks off, he and the eagle are falling. We lack the most important part of the story (for us), since we do not know the reason for the fall or whether he ever reached heaven. A recently published text does make it clear, however, that he eventually obtained the plant of birth and had an heir.[42]

This is the first of several texts in which both an ascent and fall appears, as men (in every case) attempt to break their ties with earth and are unsuccessful in doing so. It should be noted that in what we possess of the Etana myth his effort is not described as a sin, and it certainly is not an attempt to usurp heavenly privilege.

5) Icarus fell from heaven after an attempt to fly with wings of his own, made by his father Daedalus.[43] But this involves no effort to reach heaven; the wings were used to escape the labyrinth and Icarus simply made the mistake of flying too close to the heat of the sun, which melted the wax of his wings. This barely qualifies as a fall from heaven, then, but we include it because it is often mentioned in connection with Etana.[44]

6) Phaëthon also fell from heaven because of youthful indiscretion. The myth has been summarized earlier so let us simply compare it with our other materials. He is semi-divine, the son of Helios, gets permission to drive the sun-chariot for one day but because he is unable to handle it must be struck down by Zeus' thunderbolt in order to save earth and heaven from destruction. Unlike Etana and Bellerophon, he has nothing to do with an attempt to reach the realm of the gods; the house of the sun-god, at any rate, is readily available to him.[45]

7)   Our final example is the story of Bellerophon who, in
Euripides and later writers is said to have rebelled against the
injustice of life and to have decided to ascend into heaven on
his winged steed Pegasus in order to prove that there are no gods.
According to one tradition Pegasus threw him down when Bellerophon
ordered him to fly higher; according to another Zeus sent a gadfly
to sting the horse and cause the atheist to fall, but in either
he survived the fall although badly mutilated.[46]
     In this story a rebellious motive is clearly present, leading
a mortal to attempt to storm heaven. It is unusual in that it involves a denial that the gods exist rather than an effort to over-
throw the rule of a high god or to grasp something which the gods
possess.[47]   Hence it sounds very much like the use of traditional
mythological themes under the influence of the philosophical atheism
of fifth-century Greece.

     The theme of fall from heaven is used, then, sometimes to
account for the presence of evil, spiritual powers on earth and at
other times to express man's sense of being earthbound. In the
material available to us it nowhere is used in connection with the
desire to usurp the power of the high god for oneself (either as
god or mortal) except in Isa. 14:12ff. (with certain forms of the
Bellerophon story being the closest parallel we can find).

B) Ascent into Heaven:

                 And you said to yourself,
                      "I will go up to heaven!
                 Above the stars of God
                      I will exalt my throne."

     The subject of all efforts to ascend into heaven will naturally
be human, since heaven is always considered to be the dwelling place
of the gods.[48]   This theme overlaps a very common theme in folklore,
that of flying heroes, but we can eliminate from our listing all
flight which is basically horizontal, and in addition will find some
references to ascent toward heaven which do not involve flight, so
that the two themes do not coincide completely.[49]

     1) Icarus and parallels: Let us begin with a group of materials
which can quickly be set aside as not being true examples of our
theme. Icarus flew too close to the sun, but there is no reason to
take this as an effort to ascend into heaven. The same can be said
of numerous other examples of unsuccessful flight,[50] and we can at
the same time see that the Phaëthon myth, which does contain a fall,

does not use the theme of ascent into heaven in any significant way.

2) Etana: Both themes do occur in this myth and we know a bit more about the significance of Etana's ascent than we do about his fall. Even though he is a great king he suffers a severe deprivation, the lack of an heir; and that need can be met only by obtaining the plant of birth. How he knows this and learns that he might be able to obtain it by making a trip to heaven we do not know, because of the fragmentary nature of the text. But the flight expresses certain convictions which will be found elsewhere: that there are certain essentials to man's life and happiness which are denied him, but that they must exist in some realm, access to which is difficult if not impossible.

3) Bellerophon contains many of the same elements found in other myths of flight, the one distinctive feature being the intent, in some versions of the story, of proving that the gods do not exist. This is a kind of "storming the heaven", then, which we assume would not have been present in the full text of Etana, although we cannot be positive of it.

4) Elijah: We must not omit Old Testament uses of this theme. Elijah was carried off to heaven by a fiery chariot (2 Kings 2:11), which represents a different use of the theme from those we have seen previously, since it represents a kind of permanent translation of man from earth to heaven, taking the place of death. It involves no human effort but is an expression of the belief that the divine initiative may occasionally disrupt the normal earth-bound, death-anticipating existence of man.

5) Finally, we include some poetic uses of the theme in the Old Testament: "If they break through into Sheol, from there my hand will take them; and if they go up to heaven, from there I will bring them down" (Amos 9:2). "If I ascend to heaven, you are there, and if I make a bed of Sheol, there you are" (Ps. 139:8). Both of these are hyperbolae, not raising the question whether such actions are possible for men, but emphasizing that there is no place in the cosmos which is inaccessible to Yahweh. "For this commandment which I am commanding you today is not too hard for you and is not far off. It is not in heaven, that you should say, 'Who will go up to heaven for us and bring it to us, so we may hear it and do it?'" (Deut. 30:11-12). In this passage the theme is used with man's normal sense of incredulity at the idea that any-one could ascend into heaven (cf. also Job 20:6).[51]

6) Adapa: One human hero does go to heaven, however, on an official visit. He is described as the "model man", a kind of "first man" figure, who plays an important role in the service of the temples of Eridu.[52] But one day while he was out in a boat the south wind angered him and he broke its wing. This was a serious crime, which can be explained by reference to the role the south wind plays in date palm culture in Iraq,[53] so he was summoned to appear before Anu to account for himself. He then takes "the road to heaven", ascends and approaches the gate of Anu,[54] as simply as that! This is the only case we have found where the ascent to heaven is described without reference to flight of some kind, which may possibly be explained by its purely incidental place in the plot, although why it could be accepted as incidental is not so clear.

We have found no example in ancient Near Eastern literature of an ascent into heaven by a rebellious deity or by a mortal set on storming heaven (again with Bellerophon the closest case).[55] Those who do make an ascent of some sort are mortals, and the very necessity of ascent always emphasizes their subordination to and separation from the heavenly.[56]

C) War in Heaven:

"Above the stars of God
        I will exalt my throne,
And I will sit in the Mount of Assembly,
        In the recesses of the North!
I will ascend upon the backs of the clouds,
        Make myself like Elyon!"

The title chosen for this theme permits us to include all kinds of heavenly conflicts so that, as we classify them, we may find out precisely how these verses from Isaiah are related to other texts. First we ought to look at the Old Testament text, however, in order to be as clear as possible about what is being said. The middle statement seems to be the mildest. It is a claim to the privilege of sitting in the council of the gods, an institution which is well known in Mesopotamian and Ugaritic myths,[57] and which appears in the Old Testament as well (1 Kings 22:19-23; Job 1-2; Ps. 82:1). Presumably all gods (except those of the netherworld) had the privilege of sitting in the council, in polytheistic mythologies, and the divine council included various spiritual beings in the Old Testament, so that the ambition expressed in Isa. 14:13c would not make sense in the mouth of a god but must have originally been attributed to a man. This represents a kind of human presumption

which is repudiated elsewhere in the Old Testament (so is somewhat analagous to the poetic uses of ascent to heaven). Eliphaz
put down Job with these words:

> Are you the first man to be born?
> And were you brought forth before the hills?
> Do you listen in the council of God?
> And do you take for yourself all wisdom?
> What do you know that we do not know,
> Understand that is inaccessible to us?
>
> (Job 15:7-9)

Also Jeremiah asserted that those whom he condemned as false
prophets had certainly not stood in the council of Yahweh, for if
they had they would have received a far different message from the
one they were proclaiming (Jer. 23:18,22).[58] So this sentence of
the Isa. 14 passage represents a human claim to a right to partici-
pate in divine affairs which is normally considered to be impossible
for men. We do not find any examples of men making such claims for
themselves elsewhere.[59]

Several different readings of vss. 13b and 14a are possible,
but they do not involve drastic differences in meaning. "Stars of
God" is taken by some to refer to deities,[60] while others would
take it as a superlative, "highest stars".[61] The king may be
claiming to ascend "above the heights of the clouds", simply a
reference to height, or he may say that he will ascend "upon the
backs of the clouds", i.e., he will ride upon them as did Baal and
Yahweh (Ps. 68:4; 104:3).[62] But in any case these expressions are
subsidiary to "I will exalt my throne", and "I will make myself like
Elyon", for the word 'elyon means "most high" and these statements
cannot be taken as just a claim to the right of participation in
divine affairs; they represent a grab for primacy, the kingship of
the gods. Let us now see how the theme of conflict over kingship
of the gods is used in the ancient Near East.

This is a very common theme which has been divided by Kapelrud
into three types: 1) a young god against the old god (e.g.,
Kumarbi), 2) a young god saves the old (e.g., Enuma Elish), 3) the
old god against the young (e.g., The Song of Ullikummi).[63] We
shall find a different division more enlightening for our purposes,
however, although it will leave out most of the material in Kapelrud's
second category:

1) A Rebel is Unsuccessful in his Attempt to Grasp the Kingship
of the Gods.
2) A Rebel Succeeds in Grasping Kingship.
3) The Deposed Incumbent Attempts to Regain Kingship.

Isa. 14 leads us to be interested in cases of usurpation only,
which means that where a young god has been legally appointed to
the kingship, as with Marduk in Enuma Elish, we shall feel justified in ignoring such texts. This will clearly apply to the
Zagreus-Dionysus myth, where Zeus puts his infant son upon the
throne and gives him his thunderbolt, but the baby is attacked and
killed by the Titans.[64] It also probably includes the Hittite
KAL-text, although its fragmentary state makes the decision uncertain.[65] KAL is an inept and/or wicked king, is called rebellious
and is eventually deposed, but it is clear that he was legally
appointed to the throne by Ea, so that he cannot be considerd a
usurper. The Baal-cycle from Ras Shamra probably also should be
excluded from our collection of usurper texts, since Baal apparently
achieved his pre-eminence by legal means, since he did not depose El,
even though there was some tension and fighting involved.[66] It will
be maintained that the figure of Athtar in Ras Shamra text 49 also
belongs in this category, although since some scholars have interpreted his role as an example of our first type, we shall discuss
him there.

1) A Rebel is Unsuccessful in his Attempt to Grasp the Kingship
of the Gods: Remarkable as it may seem, we can find only one good
example of this theme in the ancient Near East (outside the Old
Testament), the Myth of Zu.[67] Zu is a divine figure mentioned in
passing in several Mesopotamian texts, apparently partly bird-like
in appearance, probably connected with the netherworld, and always
described as an evil being.[68] But only from the Myth of Zu do we
learn anything about his grand gesture. He apparently held a
subordinate position in the court of Enlil, king of the gods, and
as he witnessed the exercise of kingship began to covet that power
for himself.

> I will take the divine tablets of destinies, I,
> And the decrees of all the gods I will rule!
> I will make firm my throne and be the master
> of the norms,
> I will direct the totality of all the Igigi.[69]

The similarity to Isa. 14:13b-14 need not be emphasized. Once when
Enlil had removed his crown to wash, Zu seized the tablets of
destinies and flew away with them. The result was chaos; Zu did
not rule but became a fugitive from the wrath of the other gods, so
there was no rule at all. Finally, the last of a series of would-be
champions succeeded in vanquishing him and sovereignty was restored
to its proper place.

It is unfortunate that we do not know more about the relationship of this text to other myths for as it is we understand little
about the meaning of this interregnum in heaven for Mesopotamian
thought. Since Zu is always an evil character it may be that we
should see analogies with the Lamastu text described earlier. If
so, the text might be expressing convictions about the magnitude
of the evil powers with which men are now confronted, but this can
only be conjectured at present.

Earlier we discussed the possibility that Athtar may have been
an astral deity of the type presumably referred to by the terms
Helel ben Shahar. The attempt has been made to find a further
parallel to Isa. 14 by interpreting Ras Shamra text 49.I, ll. 15-37
as the account of an effort by Athtar to usurp the throne of Baal.[70]
In order to support such a reading of the text, line 34, which is
ambiguous in itself must be read, "I will surely be king in the
recesses of Ṣaphon" (cf. Isa. 14:13c), rather than "I may not be
king . . . " Either reading is theoretically possible, but most
translators have rendered the line in the latter way because the
context seems to indicate that Athtar is immediately found to be
inadequate to fill Baal's throne and that he steps down of his own
accord. Grelot, however, believes that he is done away with by
Baal in the lacuna that immediately follows his stepping down.
Most of the scholars who have commented on Grelot's reconstruction
indicate that they see no evidence of usurpation in this text, however.[71] It seems clear that Athtar is legally named king to replace the missing Baal by those competent to bestow kingship, El
in consultation with his wife Athirat.[72] So it must be concluded
that we do not have evidence in the Ugaritic texts presently known
of an unsuccessful attempt by a rebel to grasp the kingship of the
gods.

2) A Rebel Succeeds in Grasping Kingship: In contrast to the
materials which we know from Mesopotamia and Ugarit, which describe
the transfer of power from one god to another as occurring with
reference to some legal structure (though including some battles,
certainly), there are Hittite and Greek myths which tell of completely uncontrolled, intra-family struggles for supreme power.
The Hittite Kumarbi and Ullikummi texts and the Greek Titanomachia,
known from Hesiod's Theogony and later sources, have such remarkable
similarities that they may indeed be a true case of derivation,
although the discussions of that question have not yet ceased.[73]
For our purposes it will be adequate to summarize the material
briefly. In the Kumarbi myth, which is known to be of Hurrian
origin, Alalu is said to have ruled for nine years then to have
been overcome by Anu, his cupbearer, so that he fled to the dark
earth.[74] After nine years of rule Anu's cupbearer Kumarbi attacked

him, "bit his knees" (a euphemism for castration), banished him
to heaven, but was himself impregnated with three dreadful gods,
one of which is the Storm-god, whom we know will eventually
succeed to the throne. But the accounts of the eventual fate
of Kumarbi and the accession of the Storm-god have been lost.

A remarkably similar story is found in the Theogony, as
Güterbock has pointed out.[75] Ouranos and Gaia (sky and earth)
produce a series of children (the Titans) but Ouranos refuses to
permit any of them to emerge from Gaia until she instructs one of
her sons, Kronos, to castrate his father. Kronos then becomes
chief of the gods, but he swallows all of his children except Zeus
who, after a terrific battle with Kronos and all the Titans,
eventually becomes king of the gods. A similar "succession history"
is given in Philo Byblos, and we may compare the three texts as
follows:

Hurrian	Theogony	Philo
Alalu	Aither	Eliun = Hypsistos
Anu	Ouranos	Ouranos
Kumarbi	Kronos	El = Kronos
Weather-god (Teshub)	Zeus	Demarus = Zeus

The most significant points of comparison are that the god of heaven
(Anu, Ouranos) is castrated by a god who succeeds him and who, in
turn, is overthrown by the weather god (Teshub, Zeus). In every
generation the younger god defeats the older, which means that we
are here dealing with a quite different use of the theme of kingship
over the gods from what occurs in Isa. 14, where the rebel is turned
back.

3) The Deposed Incumbent Attempts to Regain Kingship: This
theme is found in the Song of Ullikummi, which presumably recounts
the history of Kumarbi and Teshub after the latter becomes king.
The deposed Kumarbi created the monster Ullikummi to threaten Teshub,
but he was thwarted with the help of Ea.[76] There appears to be a
parallel to this in the Theogony, in a passage which several scholars
have excised as not part of the original work,[77] in which just after
Zeus has banished the Titans to Tartarus he is confronted by the
monster Typhoeus, whom he must defeat before his kingship is secure.

Some scholars have interpreted large sections of the Ugaritic
myths in accordance with this theme.[78] They see El, as the old god
who has been deposed by Baal, calling upon Yam (the sea monster) in
a futile effort to regain the throne. It seems wise to use caution
in reading the texts in this way, however, as El's attitude does not

always appear to be hostile to Baal, and in one sense El continues
as chief of the gods throughout the texts.[79] Some scholars do
believe that there is a lengthy conflict between Baal and the
deposed El in which first Yam, then Mot, and finally Athtar attempt
to regain his throne for him.[80]

These texts have some surface resemblance to Isa. 14 in that
they deal with unsuccessful efforts to grasp kingship of the gods,
but they have their peculiar meaning only in the context of a
successful palace revolt, which is completely missing from the
Biblical text, so that this may be seen to be a quite different
use of the same theme.

Now it must be observed that no human being appears in any of
these myths of war in heaven, so that Isa. 14 is truly unique in
ascribing to a man the ambition to grasp the kingship of the gods.[81]
It is not easy to decide whether this use of the theme is to be
ascribed originally to the author of the poem or whether we ought
to think it had been treated this way in Israelite popular mythology,
but in either case it will be seen (very shortly) that this is a use
fully in keeping with the Israelite understanding of God and man.

D) The Attempt by a Mortal to Grasp Equality with the Gods:

Having seen that the contests for supremacy in heaven do not
involve human beings in other myths, we must now try to discover
whether and how a slightly different, but related theme, which does
involve mortals is used outside the Old Testament. We have found
no examples of a grasp for supremacy on man's part, but our earlier
survey of ideas related to hybris in the Near East may lead us to
think that attempts to grasp equality could be found, and we would
expect them to appear for the most part in Greek myths.

1) Contests between mortals and gods: This is a rather popular
theme in Greek stories; we shall list some examples and no doubt
there are more: Niobe dared to boast that she had many children and
the goddess Leto but two, all hers were killed by the two; Eurytus
challenged Apollo to an archery contest, was killed for it; Thamyris
challenged the Muses to a musical contest, lost and was blinded;
Marsyas challenged Apollo to a musical contest, lost and was killed;
Kadmos vanquished Apollo (!) in a musical contest, Zeus destroyed
his lyre strings to satisfy Apollo; having stormed the walls of
Thebes Capaneus dared Zeus to smite him, and Zeus did.[82] It should
be noted that the Prometheus myth does not seem to use any of the
themes which concern us. He is a rebel in a sense, but for the sake
of man rather than for his own sake. There is no struggle for power,

he gets things by trickery; kingship is never at stake, and men
are by no means raised to equality with the gods by Prometheus'
gifts but only just above the level of the beasts, where they had
been.[83]

2) The search for immortality: If to become immortal would
not make man fully equal to the gods it would at least give him
one of the qualities which is so far reserved for deity and denied
to man. "When the gods created mankind, death for mankind they set
aside, life in their own hands retaining."[84] Two of the great works
of literature from Mesopotamia, the epics of Gilgamesh and Adapa,
deal with man's unsatisfied longing for immortality, and this is a
theme to which we shall return later in this book, for it is the
key to much of the material with which we are working. For the
present, however, we must be content to observe that the search for
immortality is not at all the theme which appears in vss. 12-14 of
Isa. 14, even though it is as close as we can come to an effort by
man to grasp equality with the gods in Mesopotamian mythology.
Man's mortality does, however, provide the entire framework for
these verses, in that they are set in a funeral song where the contrast between man's ambition and the conditions of his death is the
central emphasis.

E) <u>Descent into the Netherworld</u>:

> Instead you are brought down to Sheol,
> To the recesses of the pit.

One immediately encounters a problem in formulating this theme.
In our text it refers to the death of a human king; should our theme
then be restricted to death and the state of the dead? Or, since
the usual subject of the other themes in vss. 12-15 is divine, shoul
those myths in which a deity descends into the netherworld be considered relevant? We must look at some of the latter in order to
decide.

1) Inanna, Ishtar, Kore and company: These are all deities
who descend into the netherworld but return from it, so they obvious
represent a unique theme, related to the cycle of the earth's fertility and in no way related to our text except in some of the incident
details of the description of the world below.[85]

2) Nergal, Tammuz and company: These are gods of the netherworld, and we possess myths which describe how several of them
attained that position. Nergal was originally a celestial deity but

because of an insult to Ereshkigal, goddess of the netherworld, he had to make a journey there. Since he slept with the goddess while in her domain he was forced to make it his permanent residence.[86] In the Sumerian myth of the descent of Inanna, she is insulted by Dumuzi (Tammuz in Semitic languages), a deity ruling on earth, when she returns, and because of this he is carried off to the netherworld.[87] He appears as a god of that region in many texts. Other myths concerning gods of the lower regions could be added here, but they would contribute little to our understanding of Isa. 14. It does appear possible that the king's entry into Sheol in vss. 9-11 may have some relationship with the humiliation suffered by deities who must descend into the netherworld, although any hint of divinity is missing from the passage.

3) Other references to descent: Earlier we noted the poetic use of the contrasts, heaven-Sheol, in Amos 9:2 and Ps. 139:8 (also in Amarna letter 264), where the descent has a quite different meaning, to express the conviction that no place is inaccessible to God.

4) Sheol as the abode of dead men: In its present context the descent into Sheol simply refers to the death of a human being, and we could cite numerous descriptions of what happens to a mortal when he goes down to the grave. One of the most instructive is to be found in the Gilgamesh Epic, tablet VII, col. iv and Tablet XII,[88] where the nature of the world below and the fates of various kinds of mortals are described.[89] Another is Ezek. 32:17-32, the closest Old Testament parallel to our present text, about which more will be said later.

This section should have demonstrated fairly clearly how many different meanings can be conveyed by a mythological term such as "descent into the netherworld", depending on the context in which it is used. It may be a central theme in a fertility cult or it may have nothing whatever to do with fertility. It means something quite different in Isa. 14 from what it means in Amos 9. So although there may be some overtones of myths concerning the descent of deities in Isa. 14, it is the present context which tells us what the theme means, and we ought to compare it with the accounts of the death of mortals in preference to other materials.

These are the major mythological themes which occur in Isa. 14:12-15. This study of their use in other contexts makes it possible to draw certain conclusions about their meaning in this passage:

1) No one has yet discovered a close parallel to the myth recounted in Isaiah 14. Even though each of the elements in it appears

in other literatures they are always combined in significantly different ways. Now, as stated earlier, the thesis of this study is that what is really significant is not parallels of terms or themes but of structure, for that will reveal the unique outlook of a given culture on the subjects denoted by the themes.

2) The structure of Isa. 14:4-21 makes a human being the subject of all these themes. Let us compare it with other texts in this respect:

a) One sense of the Descent into Sheol is properly and exclusively used of mortals, to describe death. Here the parallel is exact.

b) The Ascent to and Fall from Heaven may be used of mortals, but generally in contexts rather different from Isa. 14 (e.g., Etana, Adapa, Icarus, Bellerophon). The structures most similar to Isa. 14 in which we find it involve divine figures (Lamaštu, Ate).

c) The theme of Usurpation is confined to divine subjects when equality with the high god or kingship of the gods is involved. Those passages which might be called human efforts to usurp some divine privilege are so different from Isa. 14 that they help to demonstrate the closeness of its structure to myths about a type of rebellion which is totally within the divine realm.

3) This leads us to the following understanding of the intent of Isa. 14:4-21:

a) In materials which normally would deal with gods all have been deposed except one.

b) Yet the myth of a rebellious god is still told, with the subject changed; now it is a human being.

c) The implications of this are tremendous. It was not enough to depose the gods; man has been promoted to take their place and it is assumed that it is legitimate to speak of him in terms which would be used of the gods elsewhere. So an Israelite has exalted man almost to heaven, at least to the point that he can dream of equality with the Most High. And this means that he dares to make man the kind of danger to God that divine rebels are to the high god elsewhere. Nietzsche went further, but in the same direction, it would appear, blazed by the author of Isa. 14!

We must say more about this, especially about the use of foreign kings as subjects and about the emphasis put on death, but first we shall reinforce the statements just made by examining several other Old Testament passages in the same way. We especially need to show that the words of self-exaltation put in the king's mouth were not considered to be utter folly by the author of the poem, but that he took them seriously. This we can do.

CHAPTER IV

THE GARDEN OF GOD

There are several ways to take the extravagant claims which are attributed to the king in Isa. 14:12-15. They may be taken with the utmost seriousness, as a literal description of the fall of Satan.[1] They may be considered utter nonsense, the kind of thing only a fool or madman would dream.[2] They may be called a "mythological" form of the sometimes expressed humanistic claim that man is the only god who needs to be taken into account.[3] Or, it may be thought the author of the poem never intended to represent by these words the conscious aspiration of any man, but that they are his judgment as to the real effect and the spiritual implications of an empire builder's acts and words. The interpretation given at the conclusion of the preceding chapter suggests that the quotation is not to be taken as something which its author judged to be utter nonsense on the face of it, something no sane man could comprehend, but that he meant it seriously. This means either that he knew or believed that some men (or institutions) intentionally claim the rights and powers of gods for themselves, or that the actions of some overtly religious men (or institutions) must be judged as being in truth lèse majesty.

Such a decision is based not so much on the text of Isa. 14 itself as on its apparent agreement with the general Israelite conceptions of man and of government. The correctness of this interpretation can be verified, then, by studying a series of passages which can be shown to be based on the same beliefs about man and which make it clear that there was in Israel so high a conception of man that his creature, government, must be judged a potential rival to God himself.

The theology of Ezek. 28:1-19 will be shown to be essentially the same as that of Isa. 14:4-21 and it also resembles the taunt song in using "mythological" material, but the themes which are employed and the tone of the passage are quite different. It deals with a foreign king, this time the king of Tyre, and accuses him of self-deification. But the central mythological theme is not war in heaven, but the beauties of Paradise. The emphasis in vss. 11-19 is on the genuine glory of the king of Tyre as he is equated with the First Man in the Garden of Eden, and the tone is one of lamentation rather than rejoicing at his fall. It is the closest parallel to Gen. 3 which can be found and so it provides a link

with the Yahwistic writer's statements about the general human
predicament as a result of sin. In addition, other affinities
with Israelite literature may be found. The vocabulary is remarkably similar to that of the Priestly writer in Exodus, while
vss. 1-10 are composed of typically prophetic forms. So this
passage could be of key importance for helping us to understand
the place of Gen. 3 in Israelite thought (since that text, so
important in later theology, is seldom alluded to in any way in
the rest of the Old Testament), and the relationship of the foreign
nations to Israel and her God, but if it has not entirely fulfilled
this promise it is probably because of the extreme difficulties it
presents to the interpreter. The first oracle (vss. 1-10) can be
translated, although the syntax is awkward, but the second (vss.
11-19) is still impossible to understand in places. An effort will
be made to translate it, with apologies for the failure to solve
many of its problems, but here, as in the preceding chapter, the
greatest attention will be paid to the gathering and interpreting
of the traditions from within and outside of Israel which lie behind
the present work.

Form

There are two well-defined oracles contained in Ezek. 28:1-19;
each introduced by the formula which is so common in Ezekiel, "And
the word of Yahweh came to me saying, 'Son of man, . . . , "Thus
says the Lord Yahweh."'" The first unit also has a concluding
formula, "For I have spoken; an oracle of the Lord Yahweh." Its
genre is the reason-announcement form,[4] which has been expanded in
a way which has damaged the syntax considerably. Instead of the
well-defined structure usually found in sentences which contain a
ya'an ("because")-clause[5] the sentence rambles on, introducing a
quotation of the prince's words followed by a contradiction of them
(vss. 2b-5), finally coming to, "Therefore thus says the Lord Yahweh
(vs. 6a) and beginning all over again with a well-structured "because . . . therefore" sentence (6b-8). This strongly suggests that
the original oracle has been expanded so as to produce something
resembling a disputation or diatribe form,[6] but this has confused
the structure so that it can best be represented by an anacoluthon
in English.

While the first oracle is a word addressed to the prince (nāgīd
of Tyre, the second is introduced as a kīnā (lament) to be raised
over the king (melek). The lament is used with considerable skill
in the book of Ezekiel (e.g., chaps. 19, 27:32ff.) but we cannot
be positive of the extent to which this passage was originally intended to fit the kīnā pattern. It is metrically uneven and only a

few lines presently fit the so-called kinā-meter of 3:2, but the
efforts which have been made to produce a poem with this meter
throughout have involved such extensive changes that one must have
strong reservations about them.[7] Although it bears some resemblance
to the funeral song genre this is greatly attenuated and it cannot
be analyzed as a parody of the genre, as could Isa. 14:4-21.[8]

Questions have been raised about whether these two oracles
belong together, with some claiming that they have different subjects
and entirely different messages,[9] while others merely believe they
were produced at different times.[10] This is a matter of some importance to us, since it is the first part which speaks explicitly of
the sin of self-deification while the second contains the mythological material, so that we really need both to get a good parallel to
Isa. 14. The main argument for saying the two oracles do not shed
light on one another is the occurrence of different terms for the
subject: nāgīd (prince) in vs. 2 and melek (king) in vs. 12. However, the conclusion that melek ṣōr really refers to Melqart, patron
god of Tyre, does not seem warranted by the material in the oracle
which follows. Several factors suggest that the two oracles do help
to interpret one another, even though they may not have been produced
at the same time. There are coincidences of vocabulary between the
two and also between chapter 27 and each of the passages in 28.[11]
More important is the fact that in chapters 29 and 31 a similar relationship between a poem full of mythological imagery and a reason-
announcement oracle dealing with the same subject has been created;
whether by the prophet himself or by an editor it really matters not,
although I incline to think it is the prophet's work. The presence
of a song equating the king of Egypt with a dragon (tannim) in the
Nile followed by "because . . . therefore" in 29:3b-6a, 6b-9a, 9b-12,
and a song in which the Pharaoh is likened to a great tree followed
by "because . . . therefore" in 31:3-9, 10ff. surely indicates that
these passages and also the analogous ones in chapter 28 have been
intentionally joined.

Setting

These oracles are almost certainly the work of the prophet
Ezekiel. They make better sense in his time than any other, for
after Jerusalem fell to Nebuchadrezzar in 597 and some Judeans,
Ezekiel included, were exiled, the king of Babylon laid seige to
Tyre; a seige which continued for thirteen years. Tyre probably
became a symbol of resistance for the Judeans as news came to them
of her stubbornness, and hence it became a symbol to Ezekiel of the
misplaced faith of his compatriots. This may be why so much is
said about so small a state(three chapters, 26-28), for not only

did he find it necessary to try to undermine a faith inadequately based on the inviolability of Jerusalem,[12] but he also had to set the celebrated impregnability, wealth and pride of Tyre in its proper perspective.[13]

The setting of chapter 28 within the book of Ezekiel is of some interest to us also. It appears that there once may have existed a series of seven oracles against the nations surrounding Judah, probably patterned after the series in chapters 1 and 2 of Amos, for we can locate within chapters 25-29 seven oracles of the reason-announcement type, each with the reason clause introduced by ya'an ("because") plus an infinitive (with one exception; 26:2-6 uses a perfect), and with the judgment of each nation based on its behavior with respect to Judah when Jerusalem fell. This series, if it once existed separately, would have contained the following oracles: 25:3-5, Ammon; 25:6-7, Ammon; 25:8-11, Moab; 25:12-14, Edom; 25:15-17, Philistia; 26:2-6, Tyre; and 29:6b-9a, Egypt. The present dislocation of the Egypt oracle could be explained by assuming that an editor wished to include all the Tyre material in one place so that 26:7-28:19 was inserted in the midst of an earlier series.[14]

These seven oracles express a point which is unique in the book of Ezekiel, for only here is the relationship between Israel and her neighbors discussed with reference to the fall of Jerusalem and only here is their attitude toward Judah made the basis for God's judgment of the nations.[15] It was shown earlier (chap. II) how oracles of the same genre were used by early Israelite prophets to justify warfare and how in Amos and Isaiah the forms and ideology of these holy war oracles were put to new uses. Now, at the end of Israel's national history we encounter similar material, probably deliberately patterned after the series in Amos, but with an outlook closer to that of the old, holy war prophets than we find in the earlier prophetic books. Here the sins which are described have been committed against Judah and it is assumed that a sin against Judah is a sin against God. Rather than describing world-wide judgment, as in Amos, the series seems to be intended as a prelude to the restoration of Israel.

But there is now associated with these oracles a body of material partly similar and partly very different in genre: three times, in chapters 28, 29 and 31, a reason-announcement oracle (always using ya'an) is associated with a mythological poem; in chapter 27 a long, allegorical poem appears; two other oracles of a type that might be called mythological are found in chapter 32; and chapter 30 contains a rambling poem filled with holy war terminology.[16] The three reason-announcement oracles in chapters 28, 29 and 31 differ from the series of seven just described in being directed to a king instead of a nation, in saying nothing about the

fall of Jerusalem or sins against Judah, and in accusing the
kings of hybris.

Now we are reminded of the Isaiah passages discussed in
chapter II. In 10:5ff. and 37:22ff. we found reason-announcement
oracles addressed to foreign kings accusing them of hybris and
strongly flavored with reminiscences of the holy war. The same
features are to be found in Ezek. 28, 29 and 31 but also in
association with poems of a type that reminds us of Isa. 14:4-21.
Surely the evidence now makes it clear that the subject of the
hybris of nations, although not dealt with at great length in the
Old Testament, was one which was taken up at various times in the
history of Israel and which made use of a traditional body of
materials of a very impressive type.[17]

Translation[18]

And the word of Yahweh came to me saying, "Son of man,
say to the Prince of Tyre, 'Thus says the Lord Yahweh:
"Because your heart is haughty
and you said, 'I am a god;
'I live in the dwelling of God
'in the midst of the sea'
"---but you are man and no god,
though you consider yourself like a god.

"Yes, you are wiser than Danel,   3
no secret is a match for you;
"In your wisdom and perception   4
you made yourself rich,
"And you got gold and silver
for your treasuries.
"In your great wisdom, by your trade,   5
you increased your wealth,
and your heart became haughty
because of your wealth---"'

'Therefore thus says the Lord Yahweh: 6
"Because you consider yourself like a god,
"Therefore behold I am bringing against you   7
strangers, the most terrible of nations;
"And they shall draw their swords against the beauty
of your wisdom,
and they shall profane your splendor.
"They shall send you down to the pit   8
and you shall die the death of the slain
in the heart of the seas.

"Will you really say, 'I am God,'　　　　　　　9
　　　before those who kill you?
"For you are man and no god
　　　in the hands of those who slay you.
"You shall die the death of the uncircumcised　　10
　　　by the hands of strangers.
"For I have spoken."'"
Oracle of the Lord Yahweh.
And the word of Yahweh came to me saying, "Son of man,
raise up a lament over the king of Tyre, and you shall
say to him, 'Thus says the Lord Yahweh:
"You were a seal of perfection,
　　　full of wisdom
　　　and perfect in beauty.
"You were in Eden, the garden of God;　　　　　13
　　　every precious stone enclosed you:
　　　sardonyx, topaz and jasper,
　　　chrysolite, beryl and onyx,
　　　sapphire, carbuncle and emerald;
　　　and the work was of gold.
"Your tuppīm and neqābīm were on you;
　　　on the day you were created they were prepared.
"With an anointed, guardian cherub　　　　　　14
　　　I placed you;
"On the holy mountain of God you were,
　　　in the midst of stones of fire you walked.
"You were perfect in your ways　　　　　　　　15
　　　from the day of your creation
　　　until iniquity was found in you;
"In the abundance of your trade you filled your-　16
　　　self with violence
　　　and you sinned,
"And I cast you down from the mountain of God,
　　　and the guardian cherub destroyed you
　　　from the midst of the stones of fire.
"Your heart was haughty in your beauty,　　　　17
　　　you spoiled your wisdom because of your
　　　　　splendor,
"Upon the earth I cast you,
　　　in front of kings I put you
　　　so they might see you.
"By your many crimes and the iniquity of your trade　18
　　　you profaned your sanctuaries,
"And I sent fire out from your midst---
　　　it consumed you;

    "And I put you like dust upon the ground,
        in the sight of all the onlookers.
    "All who know you among the nations   19
        were appalled on your account.
    "You became a sudden terror---
        and you were no more."'"

Mythological Themes in Ezekiel 28

    Although some scholars have believed there are reminiscences of Phoenician myths in vss. 1-10 the traces are too slight to be of much interest to us, so we shall concentrate on the relationships which vss. 11-19 have with ancient Near Eastern myth.[19] The same issues concerning the interpretation of myth which faced us as we dealt with Isa. 14 appear here, and the question of the sources of Ezekiel's material has been even more frequently discussed. The passage has been called a variant of the Hebrew creation myth,[20] a Phoenician myth,[21] and a myth originally of Babylonian origin.[22] But Gunkel has said that although the traditions are originally non-Israelite (since mythological), direct borrowing need not be postulated since they were traditions common to the whole region;[23] and Fohrer observes that whatever the original myth was it has not been left in one piece by Ezekiel,[24] which indicates that the way has already been left open for us to use the approach tried on Isa. 14, leaving to one side, at the beginning at least, questions of source and original form in order to study the elements of the myth and how they are structured wherever they occur. The delineation of the themes will not be quite as straightforward as it was in the preceding chapter due to the allusive character of the poem and the difficulty of the text, but we shall attempt to cover some broad areas which will hopefully include all the major allusions.

A) The First Man:

    Although some interpreters believe that the figure in the garden of God is an angelic, not a human one, we shall see that a strong case can be made for believing that Ezekiel depicted the king of Tyre as an "Adam", the first man on earth. Since vss. 11-19 speak of a figure who walks in the Garden of Eden, otherwise known to have been inhabited only by the first created couple, and since the word "create" (bārā') is used twice (vss. 13 and 17) and perfection is emphasized (vss. 12 and 15) it seems logical to assume the author intended us to think of the primordial age, immediately after the

creation of man.[25] Some scholars have spoken of an Urmensch
(primordial man)-concept in dealing with this passage but recent
debate over that subject has made it clear that the term should
be avoided in this context.[26] The Urmensch is a cosmological
figure whose earliest manifestations are found only in Indo-Aryan
texts.[27] He is macrocosm represented as microcosm, the cosmos in
human form. The world was either made from the dead body of the
Urmensch or somehow emanated from him, and he is also the Urseele
from which all other souls proceed.[28] He is thus quite a different
figure from the first created man, who appears in many Semitic
texts, and indeed he represents an idea which does not appear in
Mesopotamia or the Levant until very late in ancient history.[29]
Hence, throughout our discussion we shall mean by "first man" a
figure like Adam in Genesis and not one like Gayomart, the Urmensch
in Iranian religion.

As we found other mythological themes to vary greatly in meaning and importance from region to region, so we shall find it to
be with the creation of man.[30] In Egyptian mythology creation is a
subject of considerable importance,[31] and yet man's appearance is
mentioned only in passing. The most explicit account of it ascribes
man's origin to the tears which came from Re's eye in a story about
the origins of the gods: "I wept over them [Re's limbs]---and thus
mankind came into existence from the tears that sprang from my Eye."[3]

In contrast to the Egyptian's casual acceptance of the existence
of man, the inhabitants of Mesopotamia showed a considerable interest
in man's origin and nature. One Sumerian text containing a flood
story makes a brief reference to creation:

> After Anu, Enlil, Enki, and Ninhursag
> Had fashioned the black-headed (people),
> Vegetation luxuriated from the earth,
> Animals, four-legged (creatures) of the plain,
> were brought artfully into existence.[33]

Another text indicates that man was created for the service of the
gods, and that he was made of clay, while also giving an explanation
of the existence of non-typical individuals (e.g., the sterile).[34]
The myth which Kramer calls "Cattle and Grain" also reveals that man
exists for the welfare of the gods.[35]

Akkadian literature continued to express the ideas about man
found in Sumerian writings. In the Babylonian Creation Epic, Marduk
announces:

> I will establish a savage, "man" shall be his name,
> Verily, savage-man I will create.
> He shall be charged with the service of the gods
> That they might be at ease![36]

In this case, man is made from the blood of one of the gods,
Kingu, rather than from clay, but another Akkadian text reads:
"He who shall serve all the gods, Let him be formed out of clay,
be animated with blood!"[37] The blood of the slain god is mixed
with clay to form man.[38]

One other Akkadian text is of importance here, since it is
the only one to give names to the first human beings. The myths
which have been discussed up to this point deal with the creation
of the race of men, and show no sign of being aware of the concept
of a First Man. But this account says, after the description of
the creation of man, "Ulligarra (and) Zalgarra thou shalt call their
names."[39] This is the first indication we have found that there may
have existed in Mesopotamia the concept of a First Man, somewhat
similar to that found in the Bible. Heidel points out that the
determinative for "deity" is placed before each of the names of the
first couple, apparently indicating that the ancestors of men were
thought to be divine to some degree, since divine blood was used
in their creation.[40] However, despite this, none of the creation
stories cited thus far shows any tendency to give man an exalted
position in the cosmos because of his divine blood. This may be
because everything in these cosmogonies has been made from parts
of the gods. However, the relatively inferior position of man in
these creation stories stands in some contrast to the exaltation
of the First Man in texts which will be dealt with shortly.

Phoenician mythology, as described by Sanchuniathon, also contains an account of the appearance on earth of the first mortal
couple. It is not quite as discrete an event as the creation of
Adam and Eve in the Old Testament, but is still significantly
different from stories of the creation of the race of men. Sanchuniathon is quoted by Eusebius as follows: "Then he says that
from the wind Colpius and his wife Baau (which he translates
"Night") were born Aeon and Protogonus, mortal men, so called: and
that Aeon discovered the food obtained from trees. That their offspring were called Genos and Genea, and inhabited Phoenicia: and
that when droughts occurred, they stretched out their hands to
heaven towards the sun."[41]

The material presently available from Ugarit does not provide
any support for this late version of a Phoenician creation myth,
since it does not contain a creation story of any kind. Quite unlike Sanchuniathon's great interest in the origins of things, the
Ras Shamra texts do not make any reference to the creation of man,
unless it be in the title given to El: 'ab 'adm, Father of Mankind.[42] This suggests that if El is to be considered a creator god,
it must be in the sense of progenitor.[43] This at least is in accord
with Sanchuniathon's account of beginnings, which is to a great extent a lengthy geneology. It is to be noted that the first mortal

couple come in rather early in the geneology, and do not play
nearly as prominent a role as some of the later figures, so they
also do not represent a good example of the concept of the First
Man.

We must turn to the Old Testament to find a good description
of the First Created Man as part of a creation story. The "demythologized" Israelite approach to cosmogony in Gen. 1-3 has deprived us of any revelations concerning what went on in heaven before the earth came into being, and concentrates instead on the
creation of the earth and its inhabitants. Man is no afterthought,
as the Babylonian Genesis would suggest, but is the climax of
Yahweh's creative intent. Since the creation of man is the most
important part of the Hebrew creation story, we can understand why
there was a greater emphasis on the qualities of the First Man,
who is the prototype for all humanity. We shall discuss these
qualities more fully in a later section.

B) Eden:

1) The Garden of God: One of the details which has led interpreters to compare the king of Tyre in Ezek. 28 with Adam in Gen. 2-3
is that both dwell in Eden, the garden of God (Gen. 2:15; Ezek. 28:13)
This is another feature of Ezekiel's work which has some parallels in
the mythology of the ancient Near East, but since the parallels are
not clear and straightforward, they need to be given careful analysis.
Since there is no Egyptian material which is useful here, we
turn immediately to Sumerian literature. The text called "Enki and
Ninhursag" begins with a well-known passage describing Dilmun, the
habitation of the gods, in paradisiacal terms:

> In Dilmun the raven utters no cries,
> The ittidu-bird utters not the cry of the ittidu-bird,
> The lion kills not,
> The wolf snatches not the lamb,
> Unknown is the kid-devouring wild dog,
> Unknown is the grain-devouring . . . ,
> [Unknown] is the . . . widow,
> The bird on high . . . s not its . . . ,
> The dove droops not the head,
> The sick-eyed says not "I am sick-eyed,"
> The sick-headed (says) not "I am sick-headed,"
> Its old woman (says) not "I am an old woman,"
> Its old man (says) not "I am an old man."[44]

Only fresh, sweet water is missing in Dilmun, and this Enki soon
supplies. It will be noted that this text makes no explicit
reference to Dilmun as a garden; but its fertility after water
is provided, and Enki's designation of himself as a "gardener"
later in the story,[45] suggest that Dilmun may have been thought
of in this way.

Widengren has shown that it was probably customary for the
Mesopotamian temple to have a garden or grove of some sort associated with it, and that the king was its builder, its owner, and
its caretaker.[46] There can be little doubt that such gardens were
assimilated to a mythological paradise such as Dilmun, the abode
of the gods. Some passages which refer to these sacred gardens
may be quoted:

> To Nin-Isin, lady of his . . . his lady for the
> life of Sumu-ilu king of Ur, Abbadugga, the digni-
> tary, son of Urukagina, chief priest of Girsu, the
> fine garden (?) which produces the plant, the plant
> of life in the year of power, the year of glory,
> presented.[47]

> [Of him to whom] Ashur, in view of his priest-
> hood, . . . the celebration of the holy New-Year's-
> Festival-in-the-Plain, in the Garden of Plenty, the
> image of Lebanon, forever [decr]eed.[48]

> Date formula: The year in which the garden of the
> gods was made.[49]

Widengren offers the following passages as evidence that the king
functioned in some sense as the caretaker of these sacred gardens:

> Akki, the drawer of water, (took me) as his son
>   (and) reared me.
> Akki, the drawer of water, appointed me as his
>   gardener.
> While I was a gardener, Ishtar granted me (her) love,
> And for four and (. . .) years I exercised kingship.[50]

> Irra-imitti, the king, installed Bel-ibni, the
> gardener, on his throne as a "substitute king" and
> he (even) placed his own royal crown on his head.[51]

> Then thou lovest Ishullanu, thy father's gardener,
> Who baskets of dates ever did bring to thee,
> And daily did brighten thy table.[52]

The problem with these references is that in each case, the text
may well be referring to a real gardener. Sargon and Bel-ibni
are called gardeners before they become kings, and Ishullanu is
not called a king. Böhl has noted the occurrence of the title
"gardener" in royal letters and inscriptions, however, and
theorizes that it was one of the sacral titles of the king.[53]

Sacred gardens or groves play a fairly prominent part in
the Gilgamesh Epic. In both the Sumerian and Akkadian versions,
Gilgamesh makes a long and hazardous journey to the "Land of the
Living" (so called in the Sumerian version) to cut the sacred
cedars. Later, in the Akkadian version, he travels for twelve
double-hours underground, arriving at length in the garden of the
gods. Oppenheim's translation of the badly damaged passage is
quoted here in full:

> He went directly to the [   ] of the Garden
>   (Ḫissu-enclosure)
> of the gods in order to admire (it),
> as its fruit it carries carnelians,
> vines are climbing (there)--beautiful to look at--
> (with a) foliage (made) of lapis-lazuli.
> The(ir) grapes (lit. fruits)--a pleasure to behold--
> [are made of . . . stones].
> (break of about 23 lines)
> [   ] cedar [   ]
> its [. . . are made of] white ston[es] . . .
> The sea-_larus_ [its . . . are made of] _sasu_-stones.
> Instead of thistles (?) and thorny shrubs
>   [their . . . are made of]
> (red) AN. GUG-stones,
> (and) the _harubu_-thorns [their . . . are made of]
>   _abarummu_-stones.
> Sabu-stones and haematite [are   ],
> [   ]-_ri-e_ and pearls (?) [are   ].
> Instead of [are made of] agate (?),
> of the [   ] sea
> [   ]
> While/when Gilgamesh was walking [through the . . . of]
>   this [garden?]
> he looked up [and   ] this [   ].[54]

This passage is of considerable interest for the student of Ezek. 28,
since it describes a garden of the gods adorned with precious stones,
just as in 28:13. Unfortunately the fragmentary state of the tablet
makes it impossible to determine what happened there. Oppenheim
suggests it probably was the scene of another attempt by Gilgamesh

to achieve immortality.[55] But neither the cedar grove nor the
garden of precious stones is inhabited by any human being, as
far as we can tell. The cedar mountain is explicitly called the
abode of the gods.[56] And Gilgamesh is warned that to attempt to
reach either area is extremely dangerous for a human being. So
while we have abundant evidence for the existence of a garden of
the gods, we still lack any sure indication that the king or the
First Man was supposed to dwell there.

The writers of the Old Testament knew of a garden of God and
referred to it in a variety of contexts, but with reasonable consistency about its characteristics. It was located in the land
of Eden, to the east of Palestine (Gen. 2:8,10,15; 3:23,24; 4:16;
Isa. 51:3; Ezek. 28:13; 31:9,16,18; 36:35, and Joel 2:3); it was
a place of great fruitfulness, so that Eden could be a byword for
fertility and prosperity (Isa. 51:3; Ezek. 36:35; Joel 2:3); and
it is always mentioned in connection with some tragic event.[57]
In Gen. 2-3 and Ezek. 28:13 it is a "Fall"; in the other passages
it is some natural disaster.

2) The Mountain of God: Ezekiel 28:14 locates Eden on the
holy mountain of God, and so we need to add a few remarks about
the concept of the holy mountain in Mesopotamia and in Ugarit.
The Cedar mountain, which is called the abode of the gods in
Gilgamesh, has just been mentioned. It has often been suggested
that the ziggurat is a visible representation of the mountain of
the gods.[58] That the king might be thought to have his dwelling
on the mountain of the gods is revealed by a prism of Tiglath-
Pileser I:

> To him have ye granted majesty, glory, and power,
> and ye have decreed that his rule should be mighty,
> and that his priestly seed should have a place in
> Eharsagkurkurra forever.[59]

A mountain which is the dwelling place of the gods is also
prominent in the Ugaritic texts, and by now it has been recognized
that the fact that Mount Saphon is the mountain of god in the Baal
epic is probably responsible for the Israelite use of the term
saphon to refer to the mountain of Yahweh, Zion (Ps. 48:3; Isa.
14:13).[60] But in these texts only the gods appear, so they provide no parallel to the idea of king or First Man on the mountain
of god.

While the Old Testament knows that the First Man lived in the
garden of God, to say that he had access to the mountain of God is
a bit more unusual (note especially Isa. 14:13). The concept of

the mountain of God is a familiar one in the ancient Near East,
as we have seen, but it is normally the divine abode exclusively.
That this might be conceived of as a garden is shown by Gilgamesh
V. 1. 6, where the cedar mountain is called the abode of the gods.
We have seen that the way in which the king might be associated
with the ziggurat gives us some indication that the appearance of
a mortal on the mountain of the gods might not be completely
foreign to ancient Near Eastern thought. But for Ezekiel to locate
the garden in which the First Man dwells on the mountain of God is
to give the Man a place unequalled elsewhere in the Old Testament.

3) Jewels: It has been traditional for commentators to observe
that the gardens in Gen. 3 and Ezek. 28 differ from one another most
obviously in that the latter one is full of precious stones. We
have already found a description of a similar garden in the Gilgamesh
Epic but have been disappointed that its fragmentary nature made it
of little help in understanding our text. There are no other
parallels as close as that one, so we shall have to look for other
types of material which may help to explain the prominence of jewels
in the divine garden.

In addition to the reference to "precious stones" in Ezek.
28:13, followed by a list of nine gem-stones, there also occurs an
expression "stones of fire" in vs. 14 which has long puzzled commentators. In addition to numerous emendations several different interpretations of the existing words have been proposed, of which
three recent theories may be mentioned. Pope believes this term
refers to a palace made of fused precious stones, such as the one
which seems to have been made for Baal in Ras Shamra text 51:VI,
22-35.[61] Fensham suggests the term should be translated "thunder-
stones", meaning flint, along with abn brq in Ras Shamra text ˈnt:
III, 41 and abnᵉᵐᵉˢbirqu in Akkadian.[62] He believes flints were
called thunderstones because they produced fire and because men
believed the flint artifacts they found to have been projectiles
hurtled by the gods in lightning. Yaron prefers to compare the
term to the "coals of fire" which are associated with the throne-
chariot of God in the visions of Ezekiel (1:13, etc.) and to assume
that both are based on a tradition that in the Garden of God there
were coals of fire which emitted lightning.[63] None of these explanations seems quite as probable as the assumption that "stones
of fire" was a natural expression to choose to describe the
brilliancy of the gem-stones in the garden.[64] We may well be
dealing with a tradition about a garden filled with trees bearing
precious stones which so far is known from two sources: Ezekiel
and the Gilgamesh Epic.

The list of nine stones in vs. 13 has suggested another
referent for these terms, however, viz. the bejeweled garments of

the Israelite high priest. In Exod. 28:15-30 there is described
the breastplate to be worn by the high priest, made of gold and
fine fabric, with a pocket in which Urim and Thummim were kept,
and set with twelve precious stones, in four rows, inscribed with
the names of the tribes of Israel. Two features of Ezek. 28
bring this passage to mind. First, all nine precious stones
listed in Ezek. 28:13 are also found on the high priest's breastplate and there are certain coincidences of order. If the twelve
stones in Exod. 28 are numbered consecutively, then the order in
Ezek. 28:13 is, by comparison: 1, 2, 6, 10, 11, 12, 5, 4, 3.
Since there are only about seventeen precious stones mentioned
in the Old Testament one may wonder whether the occurrence here
of nine of the twelve breastplate stones may not be pure coincidence. However, the probability of selecting at random nine stones
out of a group of seventeen and getting none but stones which are
among the twelve in Exod. 28 is only about 1/120. Also four of
the nine stones are mentioned only in these two places in the Old
Testament.[65] Most commentators, then, have concluded that the list
of stones on the high priest's breastplate was copied into the
Ezekiel text some time after it was written, and they believe that
the fact the Septuagint contains a list of twelve stones just as
in Exod. 28 confirms this.

What is left unexplained by this theory is why on earth a
glossator would think of adding such a list of stones to a description of the king of Tyre. That the list (either of nine or twelve
stones) is more likely to have been originally part of the text is
supported both by this consideration and by the observation, which
is the second feature of Ezek. 28 mentioned above, that the vocabulary of the entire poem shows a certain relationship to Exod. 28.[66]
When this is added to the well-known affinities between the language
of the book of Ezekiel and that of the Priestly document, it seems
most likely that this priestly vocabulary including the names of
gem stones is Ezekiel's own contribution to the formulation of the
material. We shall return shortly to the question of why the First
Man, or king of Tyre, should have been described in terms reminiscent of the Israelite high priest, having for the time being concluded that the precious stones may properly belong to the description of the garden of God.

4) The Cherub: The cherub is the one remaining figure in the
garden to be discussed. The matter is partly a textual problem,
since the pointing of the Massoretic Text identifies the cherub
with the king in verse 14, while the Septuagint and Syriac versions
distinguish king from cherub. It has been observed above that some
scholars accept the Massoretic pointing as correct;[67] however, there
seem to be good reasons for favoring the versions in this case, and

hence for interpreting the cherub as a figure subsidiary to the king in this passage. Wherever the cherub appears in the Old Testament it plays the role of a guardian figure, and is neither identified with a king nor considered to be a rival of God. In Gen. 3:24 the cherubim are God's servants who guard the garden of Eden. In Exod. 25:18-22 (and 37:6-9; Num. 7:89; I Sam. 4:4) they are attendants on either side of the "mercy seat", and in I Kings 6:23-28; 8:6-7 they perform the same function for the whole ark. In Pss. 80:1; 99:1; Isa. 37:16 God is said to be enthroned upon the cherubim, and in II Sam. 22:11; Ps. 18:10 he is said to ride upon the cherubim. The same idea is reflected in Ezek. 10.

Similar figures are found in Mesopotamia, bearing the name _karibu_ (or _kuribu_).[68] They are represented as guardians of the sacred tree and as figures flanking royal thrones. So the cherub plays the role of a guardian spirit without exception in the Mesopotamian material, as well.[69] This means that either to identify the cherub with the king or to make the cherub the original rebellious subject of the myth would be to make a unique case of Ezek. 28. It seems preferable to give the cherub the function of a guardian spirit who finally excludes the First Man from the garden, as in Gen. 3:24.

To summarize what has been learned about the garden of God:

(a) The concept is a familiar one in Mesopotamian myths and may have corresponded to actual gardens which existed in sanctuaries.

(b) To associate the garden with the mountain of God is unusual for the Old Testament but might not seem strange in Mesopotamia where there may have been temple gardens and ziggurats (thought of as mountains) in propinquity to one another.

(c) Although the king was certainly associated with the temple in a special sense in Mesopotamia, there are no mythological texts which clearly link king or First Man with the garden or mountain of the gods.[70] In the Old Testament the garden seems to have been planted by God specifically as an abode for the First Man (explicit in Gen. 2, possible in other references), but there is no hint outside of Ezek. 28 that he had access to the mountain of God.

Since we are faced more with descriptive material than with "plot" material in this passage it raises questions about whether it is based on a myth or is rather describing the precincts of a sanctuary, or the king as he was idealized in oriental ideology. In neither of the last two options would there be a logical place for a "Fall", however, and it is to this aspect of our text that we must turn before attempting to make a judgment about its true nature.

C) The Fate of the First Man:

It has already been noted that the Garden of Eden in the Old
Testament is always related to some sort of tragic event. In
Ezek. 28 it is the expulsion and death of the king of Tyre because
of his sins. In general terms the fate of Adam in Gen. 3 is the
same. Now it has often been stated that there is no parallel to
the Old Testament concept of the Fall of Man in the mythologies of
the nations surrounding Israel, and this cannot be denied.[71] We
have seen that the first created men in other religions play relatively insignificant roles, but there are other figures who, in
their prototypical functions bear a certain relationship to Adam,
and, although there is no Fall story, their fate does partly
parallel his. We must consider the role of the prototype more
fully, then, before we can draw any conclusions about the Old
Testament stories of a Fall of Man. Our materials will come from
the Epics of Adapa and Gilgamesh, and from the ideologies of kingship in the ancient Near East.

1) "Adam"--The Typical Man: The legendary figure, Adapa, was
thought of as a prototype of humanity, and it is probable that he
was a king. At the beginning of one tablet containing the Adapa
Epic we read, "His command was indeed . . . like the command of
[Ea]."[72] His duties as the chief servant of the gods are also
probably to be considered those ascribed to the king (in theory
if not in practice).[73] Two facts point to the equation of this
legendary king with the First Man. In lines 5-6 of the same tablet
we read, "In those days, in those years, the sage from Eridu, Ea,
created him as the model of men," and the translator informs us
that the word "model" is to be taken in the sense of "something to
be followed".[74] Also, Ebeling found the word a-da-ap in an unpublished syllabary, where it was equated with "man".[75] Adapa, then,
seems to have been a king who was conceived of as a real Adam; a
prototype so that his fate is the fate of all men.
Gilgamesh is nowhere described as an Adam, but in several
respects he did play the role of a prototype for mankind. That is
especially true where his fate is concerned, but we shall discuss
that later. One function which is ascribed to him makes him something of a prototype for humanity in the Babylonian, though not in
the Hebrew sense. He is one of the judges of the dead. Bousset
has noted that the First Man, since the first to die, often becomes
the prince of the underworld and judge of the dead.[76] This is true
of Yama in India and Yima in Iran. Now, Gilgamesh plays the same
role in the Sumerian poem of Ur-Nammu, where he is called lugal-
kur-ra, "king of the nether world" (col. 3, l. 11), and where it is
said of him, "Gilgamesh, his beloved brother [pronounces] to him the

judgment of the nether world; defines to him, the rules of the nether world."[77] Another text translated by Kramer probably refers to Gilgamesh's distribution of offerings in the nether world.[78] A magical text published by Ebeling addresses him as perfect king; regent of the earth; more exalted, wiser, and greater than men; before whom kings, viceroys, and princes kneel; who has been appointed judge by Shamash; and whose judgment is discerning and unchangeable.[79] In Judaism we find something resembling this only late in the post-exilic period, where the Son of Man is king of Paradise (I Enoch 61:12). Ezekiel's picture of the fate of the great king when he reaches the nether world is quite a different one, as we shall see in a subsequent section.

In certain ideologies of kingship the monarch himself might be thought of as the First Created Man. There can be no doubt that Mesopotamian kings functioned in a very literal sense as the representatives of their people so that their welfare in all respects was immediately dependent on the king. To this extent, at least, the king could be considered the prototype of humanity.

> The king is the typical man. What concerns him
> also concerns his subjects eventually. For since
> the king was considered not only as the repre-
> sentative of deity, but also above all as that of
> humanity (the typical man), everything which con-
> cerned him or which he, as the representative of
> the people had to perform in the cult, eventually
> was ascribed to the common man.[80]

When we turn to Israelite kingship, once more it seems that the concept of the First Man plays a more prominent part than in the surrounding cultures. Aage Bentzen has dealt with the equation of the king with the First Man in his book King and Messiah, and the main points of his argument may be noted here briefly.[81] The clearest evidence for this identity would seem to be Ezek. 28:1-10, 11-19, the passage we are most concerned about, but there are others which point in the same direction. The First Man in Gen. 1, 2, and Ps. 8 is also the First King, since he is represented as ruler over the animals.[82] Job 15:7ff. which Gunkel had long ago described as based on a myth of the Urmensch, Bentzen also believes may refer to a king.[83] Then there are passages in which the Messiah, the future king, is described as the king of paradise; esp. Isa. 9, 11 and Mic. 5; also cf. Ps. 72. Although this king is not called "First Man", the term in "days of old" in Mic. 5 is equivalent to "the primeval age".[84] Not only are Man and King identified in Ps. 8, but also the king is called Son of Man in Ps. 80:18.[85] So Bentzen concluded that the original concept of kingship was best described in terms of the Primordial Man from whom stemmed the institutions of king, prophet, and priest.[86] Engnell has also stressed the identity of the king with the First Man by describing Adam as an <u>Urkönig</u>, whose royalty is indicated by several features.[87] He is made in the image of God, is the caretaker of the garden of God, aids in creation and participates in the <u>hieros gamos</u>.

The idea that the present, reigning king might be identified with the First Created Man, is one which is strange to our ways of thinking, but this was not true for the people of the ancient East. As Pedersen and others have shown, the concept of corporate personality made it normal to think of the ancestor, or the chief, or the king as the visible embodiment of the community and created such a sense of identity with the members of one's family, present, past, and future, that one's ancestors could be said to live on through oneself, and in particular through the king.[88] This also suggests that Ezekiel's identification of a king with the First Man was not a new idea but already had its basis in traditional beliefs.

Now let us compare what has been said about these figures who in some sense have been considered prototypes of humanity as we prepare to discuss their fate. They are kings (granting that Adam's only subjects are the animals, at least at first). They hold a special position in the sight of the gods; Adapa and Adam are clearly represented as being in the service of God, Gilgamesh is so robust physically that he is called two-thirds god and one-third man, while the exalted position of the king of Tyre is given great stress. Gilgamesh, in some texts, functions as a deity in the nether world, several of the rulers in the Sumerian king list were believed to have become gods,[89] while in Sanchuniathon's mythology the first men and first kings are worshipped as gods. In the Old Testament Adam is made "in the image of God" and the king can be addressed as "God" (Ps. 45:6).

The prototype possesses great wisdom. Of Adapa it was said, "Wide understanding he had perfected for him to disclose the designs of the land. To him he had given wisdom; . . . The capable, the most wise among the Anunnaki is he."[90] Of Gilgamesh: "Anu, Enlil, and Ea have broadened his wisdom."[91] Of the king of Tyre: "You are indeed wiser than Danel . . . You were the signet of perfection, full of wisdom and perfect in beauty." Adam is no exception, although some scholars have depicted him in contrast to the First Man in Ezek. 28 and Job 15 because of his supposed lack of wisdom.[92] Gordis seems to be correct in his affirmation that Adam is presented as a paragon of wisdom in Gen. 2, for he named every living creature, hence, knowing their names he understood their natures (Gen. 2:19-20).[93]

2) The Loss of Immortality: Indeed it seems appropriate
to say, as Ezek. does in 28:12, 15, that the First Man in Old
Testament thought is perfect, but the same cannot be said of
Adapa and Gilgamesh. They lack something which makes life less
than it ought to be. "To him (Adapa) he had given wisdom;
eternal life he had not given him."[94] "Enlil . . . has destined
thy fate, O Gilgamesh, for kingship, for eternal life he has not
destined it."[95] This lack and the attempt to remedy it are the
main themes of the Adapa and Gilgamesh epics, but they are missing
from the Old Testament stories. Adapa and Gilgamesh are cheated
in their efforts to find eternal life, and it escapes them either
by chance or by a subterfuge of the gods. In contrast, the
activity of the First Man which forms the main theme of the Old
Testament stories is a rebellious act which results in the loss of
something he had. This has no parallel in Babylonian mythology.
The heroes offend the gods, it is true; but those offenses are not
described as the reason for their failure to obtain immortality,
indeed Adapa lost his chance because of his strict obedience to
the orders of Ea.[96]

While men were taught by the great Mesopotamian epics that
death is natural for humanity, in the Old Testament it is considered
to be a punishment for sin. Since Adam is punished by being denied
further access to the tree of life,[97] and since the self-deification
of the kings in Isa. 14 and Ezek. 28 is properly recompensed by
death, it seems logical to deduce that in Hebrew thought God intended man to be immortal until he sinned. Whereas in Babylonia Adapa
and Gilgamesh are prototypes of humanity in that they, like everyone else, had to die, in the Old Testament death is the result of
denying one's humanity by trying to become a god.

We have found that most of the elements from which Ezek. 28:
1-19 was composed appear to have been well known to the peoples of
the ancient Near East. Two aspects of Ezekiel's combination of
these elements stand out as the key to the meaning of the passage;
the glorification of the first man and the explanation of his death
as the result of hybris. The former is emphasized in vss. 11-19
and the latter in vss. 1-10; but it has been maintained earlier
that it is proper to read both oracles together, so that hybris,
self-deification, may be inferred for the subject of both; and there
is support for this in what is said of the First Man. His pride is
mentioned in vs. 17 and in Gen. 3 his sin is to want to become
"like God" (or "as gods"). He is thus a figure who surpasses other
prototypes of humanity in the high honor which is paid him (presence
in the garden on the mountain of God), and whose fate provides a
different explanation for human mortality--it is due to sin, the
sin of attempting to go beyond even the exalted position he rightfully holds.

Conclusions

After all this it is not difficult to determine the intention
of the author of this passage, and once that is understood a series
of "Why?" questions can be answered with a fair degree of certainty.

>"Yes, you are wiser than Danel,
>   No secret is a match for you;
>"In your wisdom and perception
>   you made yourself rich."

>"You were a seal of perfection,
>   full of wisdom
>   and perfect in beauty."

Surely there can be no doubt that the strongest emphasis in both
these passages is on the genuine glory of the king of Tyre (as is
true also of the emphasis in chap. 27). There is no sarcasm here,
as in Isa. 14; the beauty, wisdom and wealth of the subject are
real and marvelous. For the divine source and approval of the king's
glory is made clear by making him a rightful resident of the garden
of God!
Ezekiel could never have been satisfied with saying, "You are
very clever and very rich." That would not have said it effectively
and would not have said enough. This prophet's rhetorical device
is allegory (chapters 16, 17, 19, 23, 27) and to choose his metaphors
from mythological sources enabled him to say more than merely to
describe a wealthy trading city (as he did in chap. 27). Where
could better materials be found for an idyllic picture of. human perfection than in the myths of paradise? This would be an even more
obvious choice if, as seems likely, the ideal of kingship throughout
Mesopotamia and the Levant was regularly assimilated to the idea of
the archetypal man.
Once we emphasize the main intention of these two oracles the
kinds of materials used are seen to be natural choices. It would
probably be no novelty to describe a king as the first created man,
although we cannot demonstrate that precisely this kind of thing
was said in oriental kingship ideology. And, granting the desire
to emphasize all that was genuinely good about kingship, the idea
of paradise is most appropriate. Of course the ultimate purpose of
each oracle is to announce God's condemnation of this glorious
figure, and to this the Hebrew version of the myth of paradise lent
itself perfectly, for it included the sin and expulsion of the First
Man.
This suggests that vss. 11-19 do not represent a description of
the temple at Tyre with its priest-king, nor of the Jerusalem temple

and its precincts, as others have thought.[98] If some of the
details resemble parts of oriental sanctuaries that is coinci-
dental, since a description of a sanctuary would scarcely serve
the purpose of the author in the way that the adaptation of a
myth of paradise would. We may add that if details of the passage
correspond to the expositions of divine kingship which have
appeared in recent scholarship,[99] that is fortuitous. The ideology
of kingship would not account for the materials in the poem as
adequately as the paradise concept but, as has been shown, the
two do overlap to some extent. A further point may be made. It
was the paradise myth in its peculiar Hebrew form which was the
principle source of all the materials used here, as a comparison
of paralleled with non-paralleled themes will show. Common to the
ancient East are: first created man, king as typical man, the
garden of the gods, the mountain of the gods, and details such as
gem-stones and the cherub. Without parallels outside of Israel are:
Eden as the dwelling place of the First Man, the sin of the First
Man, the expulsion of someone from the garden of the gods. Certainly it is these latter elements which give the whole complex of
materials their meaning as Ezekiel uses them, and since Gen. 3
enables us to identify them as having been used earlier in the
history of Israel, it seems pointless to claim that Ezekiel is
quoting a lost Phoenician myth.[100]

Now the why questions. Why apply materials of this kind to
Tyre and its king? And why the intent which we have emphasized,
to glorify a pagan king? We have just alluded to an answer which
has often been given to the first question, that the materials were
naturally used for this subject because they were of Tyrian origin;
but we have rejected that solution. It appears, rather, that the
paradise theme, and not war in heaven or some other theme, was used
because it provided the most natural means of making Ezekiel's
point, as the preceding paragraphs have shown.

But why does he give a pagan king so exalted a role, as the
first created man, put by God in the garden of Eden and endowed by
him with beauty, wisdom and wealth? Why the absence of any charge
of attempting to usurp something not rightly his (as in Isa. 14)
but instead a description of the loss of one's rightful place? And
why the consequent tone of lamentation in a word which concerns a
foreigner, a rival, a pagan?

Let us consider Tyre. It was a rival of Jerusalem, to be
envied because far more successful in trade, but not a bitter enemy
and never a serious danger politically. For long periods Tyre had
been an ally, and Israel and Phoenicia had much in common culturally
Workers from Tyre built Solomon's temple for him and much of the
commercial activity of Israel was probably carried on via Phoenician

merchants. They were famous for their wealth and their skill
as traders, and for both reasons must have been hated at times,
but envy would usually have been a more appropriate emotion than
hate. Their cruelty to slaves was denounced (Amos 1:9-10) but
in most of the oracles concerning Tyre and Sidon in the prophetic
books the dominant themes are the description of wealth and the
tone of lamentation (Isa. 23; Zech. 9:2-4; Ezek. 26-28). Wealth
itself is not denounced, the successes of Tyre are described in
tones of admiration; the glories which the prophets believed God
has made it possible for men to get for themselves are real and
God is to be thanked for them. The basis for Tyre's condemnation
was her cruelty to men and her attitude of self-sufficiency as she
waited out every seige on her fortified island, an attitude which
to a Hebrew prophet was an insult to the God on whom all things
depend. But that the punishment of Tyre's hybris meant the destruction of wealth, wisdom and beauty was cause for lament.[101]

It could only have been possible for Ezekiel to have spoken
this way if our earlier descriptions of the Hebrew doctrine of man
are correct (chapters I, III). It is the first created man who
appears in this passage and he is not a mere servant of the gods
made of blood and clay, as in Mesopotamia, nor a brutish creature
lacking natural gifts, as in some Greek myths. He belongs to a
Golden Age, as other myths of origins have depicted primordial man.
He is no wretch but a magnificent being, beautiful to look at, and
with a mind. He is cause for wonder, for he has peopled earth with
godlike beings (Gen. 1:27f.; Ps. 8:5). Paradise is not utterly lost,
for in the great kingdoms of the earth may be seen the magnificence
which the brains and hands of these almost divine beings have created.
But the same kingdoms are also evidence of the Fall, for in them are
to be found violence and iniquity (28:15f.), and they die in flames
(vs. 18). And why is that? It is because men are not gods ultimately,
not fully able to be masters of their futures nor even to act always
in their own best interests. It is because they attempt to act as
independent rather than dependent beings and create little "kingdoms
of god" which are inadequate to be the gods of men. "Your heart was
haughty in your beauty, you spoiled your wisdom because of your
splendor" (28:17).

The Hebrew view of man is thus profoundly humanistic; tremendously
enthusiastic about the man God made and the gifts God gave him. But
it is also profoundly theistic, for the Israelite was convinced there
is one thing that man cannot do, and that is replace the God who made
him. Further, he was convinced that all the ills of human life are to
be traced to the effort to do just that, and he saw in the successes
and failures of the great governments of his time the evidence for
man's near divinity, man's instinct to make himself a god over his
fellows, and the brutalizing effect of man-made "kingdoms of god".

CHAPTER V

THE COSMIC TREE

The vigorous nature of Isa. 14, which describes a struggle over
divine kingship, stands in considerable contrast to the largely descriptive passage just studied in Ezek. 28 and to the virtually
static picture to be found when the cosmic tree becomes the central
symbol. A tree, after all, is not capable of much activity and we
shall find that its symbolic value is in setting two contrasting
pictures side by side; one of the true magnificence of human achievement and the other of degradation and decay.

Twice in the Old Testament the tree, which is a common enough
source of metaphors in ordinary speech, is used as a symbol of
hybris in a way which can be explained only by reference to clearly
mythological concepts, and so once again we shall be led on a
search through the myths of the ancient Near East to attempt to
determine what meanings the tree could have as a religious symbol.[1]
The two Old Testament passages which will concern us are chapter 31
of Ezekiel and chapter 4 of Daniel. The Ezekiel text has much in
common with the Tyre oracles discussed in the preceding chapter.
It brings together a poem with mythological content and a prophetic
judgment oracle, so that some of the forms are familiar to us, and
there is some continuity of content, but much of the latter will be
new. The chapter in Daniel which interests us is harder to date
(Ezekiel 31 was almost certainly produced in June of 587, as vs. 1
says) but must be from 250 to 400 years younger, and its literary
characteristics are quite different; yet we shall find it to have
some remarkable similarities to Ezek. 31 in its theological outlook
and its use of mythological themes.

The question might be raised at this point whether there is
really more to be said about the Old Testament concept of hybris
or whether additional texts will merely say the same thing in different ways. I believe that these two passages do have something to
add, both in reinforcing some things which have been said before and
in emphasizing an aspect of hybris which has not been stressed elsewhere. One thing they will do is to raise again the question which
faced us as we discussed Isa. 2: What, after all, can anyone do
about the tyrants of the earth, and is there really anything to be
gained by talking about hybris? Our texts tend to emphasize the
ultimate tragedy of hybris, and although that is not always answer
enough for us, it is one answer. We shall examine it from the

Biblical perspective in this chapter and from the modern in the
Epilogue. But first it will be necessary to set forth the texts
of Ezek. 31 and Dan. 4 and to evaluate the nature of the mythological materials which are used in them.

Ezekiel 31

Form

This chapter may be divided into two parts consisting of an
allegorical poem (vss. 2-9) followed by its interpretation, but the
presence of introductory formulas in vss. 1, 10 and 15 shows that
it actually has three parts. Older literary analysis of the chapter
(e.g., Hölscher, Irwin) automatically considered the prose portions
to be secondary; recent commentators (e.g., Fohrer, Zimmerli) have
observed, however, that at least vss. 10-14 must be included with
the poem for it to have any prophetic meaning. The poem is purely
descriptive, with no development of any kind; it is not naturalistic
nor is it influenced in any way by the political world it symbolizes,
but it is based entirely on the mythological concept of the cosmic
tree, as will be demonstarted shortly. It is thus a single metaphor
developed at some length. The introduction, vs. 2, provides the key
to its interpretation; the magnificence of the world tree is to be
taken as a suitable way of describing the glories of Egyptian kingship. This passage differs from Isa. 14 and Ezek. 28 in that the
mythological materials offer no basis for saying anything about sin
or judgment; the poem is wholly positive in tone.

The element of judgment is introduced in vs. 10 by a reason-
announcement oracle beginning with ya'an, a feature which the
chapter has in common with chapters 28 and 29 as noted earlier.
The traditional form of the oracle ends with vs. 11 and the remainder
of the passage is to be taken as a prosy "interpretation" of the
poem, a type of material which is common in the book of Ezekiel.
The explanation of his symbolic acts given in chap. 5 may be compared
with the material here, to cite one example. But this goes far beyond interpretation in that it actually produces two sequels to the
description of the great tree. In the first, vss. 12-14, the tree
has been cut down and it lies sprawled across an earth which is a
fit habitation only for the beasts (12b-13). That this is not
originally part of the myth is shown by the introduction of
"foreigners" who cut down the tree, an oddity when one is dealing
with a cosmic concept. The somewhat unexpected turn at the end of
the segment (vs. 14), in which a descent into the netherworld is
described, may have been suggested by the close connections the cosmic
tree had with the world below, to be documented later.

The development of the same idea in the second segment (vss. 15-18) is less easy to explain, however. Here the tree is said to have descended to Sheol, to join the trees of Eden, the uncircumcised and those slain by the sword. This appears to be a rather strange mixture of metaphors, but it will lead us to consider the prominence of Sheol in each of the sections which have been treated in depth, and so it will prove to be a passage of some value to us.

Setting

This chapter is provided with a date, June of 587, and whether or not the dates in Ezekiel are thought to come from the prophet himself, this does point to the most likely time in history for such a text to have been produced. The second Judean revolt against Nebuchadrezzar began in 589 and resulted in an eighteen-month seige of Jerusalem by the Babylonian army (Jer. 39:1-2), a seige which was lifted once when an Egyptian force threatened to enter Palestine. A new king, Apries (Hophra) came to the throne of Egypt in 588/87 and in his first year made a two-pronged attack on Western Asia. Herodotus (II, 161) and Diodorus Siculus (I, 68) tell of his attack by sea on Tyre and Sidon, and although they do not give a date, it most probably occurred at the same time as his land attack on Palestine.[2] His timing and strategy were good since Nebuchadrezzar was occupied with the seige of Jerusalem, but the latter wisely broke off the seige and went to meet the Egyptian army directly, forcing it out of Palestine (Jer. 37).

These developments, which would have been known to the exiles in Babylonia eventually, must have raised their hopes temporarily and would have offered support to those whose faith in God was based on a belief in the inviolability of Jerusalem, so that the series of prophetic words against Egypt which the book of Ezekiel contains provided an important corrective to a popular misinterpretation of what God was doing in the affairs of nations. Egypt had been a source of false hope before in Israel's history and Isaiah had found it necessary to warn against depending on her help (30:1-7; 31:1-3). Ezekiel did so at even greater length, for the chapter which concerns us is one of four devoted to the subject (29-32). Some of the materials in the chapters may come from a slightly later time, but most of them appear to be the work of the exilic prophet himself.

Translation:[3]

And it happened in the eleventh year, on the first of
the third month, that the word of Yahweh came to me
saying:
"Son of man, say to Pharaoh, king of Egypt, and to
his multitude,

'To whom shall you be likened in your greatness?
      ---Lo, a cedar in Lebanon!   3
Beautiful of bough and haughty of stature,
And amongst the clouds is its crown!
Waters nourished it, Tehom made it grow;   4
Tehom's streams flowed around the place
      it was planted,
And it sent its channels to all the trees
      of the field.
So its stature towered above all the trees   5
      of the field,
And its branches were many and it extended
      its shoots.

In its boughs nested every bird of the heavens,   6
And under its branches every beast of the field
      gave birth,
And in its shade dwelt all the many nations.
And it was beautiful in its size, in the extent   7
      of its foliage,
For its roots stretched to abundant waters.
Cedars were no match for it, in the Garden of God;   8
Junipers could not compare to its boughs,
And plane-trees were not like its branches.
No tree in the Garden of God could compare to it
      in its beauty.
I made it beautiful in its abundant foliage   9
And it was envied by all the trees of Eden
      which were in the Garden of God.'"

Therefore thus says the Lord Yahweh, "Because it was   10
haughty in its stature and it put its crown among the
clouds, and lifted up its heart in its haughtiness,
then I will put it into the hand of a despot of nations   11
who will surely deal with it according to its wickedness. I have cast it out, and foreigners, the ruth-   12
less of the nations, have cut it down and abandoned
it. Upon the mountains and into every valley its
foliage fell, and its branches were broken in every

stream-bed of the land, and all the peoples of the
earth left its shadow and abandoned it.

> Upon its remains all the birds of the heavens   13
>> dwelt,
> And among its branches was every beast of the
>> field.

----So that none of the trees of water will be   14
haughty in its stature nor put its crown among the
clouds, and none that drink water shall reach up to
them in height,

> for all of them shall be given to death,
>> to the land below,
> in the midst of the sons of man,
>> to those who descend to the pit."

Thus says the Lord Yahweh, "On the day when it de-   15
scended to Sheol I caused Tehom to mourn over it,
and I held back her streams and the many waters
were restrained, and I darkened Lebanon because of
it, and all the trees of the field fainted because
of it. With the sound of its falling I terrified   16
the nations, when I brought it down to Sheol, with
those who descend to the pit; and all the trees of
Eden were comforted in the land below, the choice
and best of Lebanon, all that drink water. They   17
also descended to Sheol with you, to those slain
by the sword; and those who dwelt in its shadow,
in the midst of nations, were scattered. To whom   18
shall you be likened in glory and greatness among
the trees of Eden?---but you shall be brought down
with the trees of Eden to the land below; in the
midst of the uncircumcised you shall lie down, with
those slain by the sword. This is the Pharaoh and
all his multitude." Oracle of the Lord Yahweh.

Daniel 4

Form

This chapter is composed of a complex set of literary types
which have been worked together into a unified whole. The result
might be called a short story or possibly a legend. It is introduced
as a royal proclamation (MT: 3:31-33; English versions: 4:1-3) with
a formula which may be compared with the beginnings of the decrees
and letters of the Persian period which are quoted in Ezra (1:2; 4:11,

17; 5:7; 7:12).[4] The contents of the proclamation are quite surprising, however. Although kings have been known to describe their dreams for public benefit,[5] the humiliating nature of what follows this introduction shows that we are dealing here with an artful combination of literary types and not with a real royal proclamation. The same thing is revealed by vss. 32-33 (English 4:2-3), which would be unexpected in the proclamation of a king, but which are actually the theme verses for the present composition since they declare in hymnic form the aim of the entire work: to demonstrate that God Most High is King of kings.

The next major section (4:1-24; English 4:4-27) follows the familiar pattern of the court-wise-man story which, in its barest outline, goes as follows: a king poses a problem to the wise men of his court which proves to be an enigma to all but one who, because of his special gifts in discerning mysteries, is highly rewarded. The closest parallels to our story are to be found in Dan. 2, 5 and Gen. 41, although there are many others.[6] This section continues to use the familiar royal style at the beginning with, "I, Nebuchadnezzar . . . ," but strangely enough the first person form of the narrative is lost in the midst of it. Daniel's interpretation of the dream and its fulfillment are recounted in the third person.[7] It is the dream and interpretation which are of the greatest interest to us, since the dream's subject is the cosmic tree in a form which is in obvious dependence on Ezek. 31. The sequel to the "wise man episode" (vss. 25-34; English 28-37) depicts the affliction of the king by a malady which turns him into a beast for a limited period of time. We now know that this portion of the chapter was based on a defamatory legend about king Nabonidus, since a partial parallel to it has been found at Qumran.[8] The Qumran text tells how Nabonidus was afflicted for seven years and was led to the truth about his sins and the need to honor God by a Jewish "magician" (gzr). In our text the restoration of the king to rule calls for another hymn (vss. 31b-32; English 34b-35) in which the theme introduced in the hymn at the beginning is reiterate and in which the narrative also returns to the first person.

It may be seen, then, that this chapter has been produced by someone who has made a very skillful use of a variety of materials with only one apparent lapse, the inconsistency in the use of first and third persons. The materials which are used date from the Persi period at the latest, while the tree myth is timeless.

Setting

There can be no question that the book of Daniel was put into its present form in the second century B.C., around 165, and that it took that final shape under the impress of the persecution of the Jews by Antiochus IV Epiphanes.[9] However, it is possible and even probable that the stories in chapters 1-6 came into being long before the time of Antiochus. They are set in the Neo-Babylonian or early Persian period and preserve in distorted form some memories of those times. The kings are not depicted on the pattern of Antiochus, as unreasonable tyrants, persecuting without mercy, but as rulers who are not entirely ill-disposed toward the Jews and who are as reasonable as any absolute monarch could be expected to be. The situation of the Jews under these kings is not depicted as a desperate one; certainly Daniel and his friends are threatened because of their faith in chapters 3 and 6 (and in a milder way in chapter 1), but the dominant picture is of Jews who have become very successful in a pagan court and who can expect to remain that way, not by giving up their religion, but precisely because the God they worship is able to help them. Hence, these stories appear to represent a positive reaction to the challenge of trying to maintain one's Jewishness while living in an alien culture. Some of them may have first been told in the diaspora during the Persian period, and after Hellenism swept across the ancient East (third century B.C. and later) they would have made sense to Jews in Palestine who, under the Ptolemies and Seleucids, found themselves confronted by a cultural revolution.[10]

We can conclude that the story of Nebuchadnezzar's dream took shape during the post-exilic period in a time when it was still possible for Jews to speak of pagan kingship in relatively favorable terms. It probably grew out of a derogatory story about Nabonidus which was improved by making the subject a more famous king and by making the wiseman a Jew,[11] and was artistically elaborated by using the court wiseman genre, the symbol of the cosmic tree and other literary genres. Thus it, along with the similar stories in Dan. 1-6, became one of the classical expressions of the conviction that it is possible for a monotheist to live in a non-supportive culture both faithfully and successfully.

Translation:[12]

Nebuchadnezzar the king to all peoples, nations and tongues who are dwelling in all the earth: May your peace be multiplied! Signs and wonders which God Most High has done with me he has been pleased to make known to me.
            His portents, how great they are!
                and his signs, how mighty!
            His kingdom is an eternal kingdom,
                and his rule with all generations.

I, Nebuchadnezzar, was at ease in my house and
flourishing in my palace. I saw a dream which made
me afraid, and the imaginings upon my bed and the
visions of my head frightened me. And a decree
went forth from me to bring in to me all the wisemen
of Babylon so that they might tell me the interpretation of the dream. Then the soothsayers, the con-
jurers, the Chaldeans and the diviners came in and I
told them the dream, but its interpretation they did
not make known to me. At last there came in to me
Daniel, whose name is Belteshazzar after the name of
my god, in whom is the spirit of the holy gods, and I
told the dream to him: "Belteshazzar, chief of the
soothsayers, I know that the spirit of the holy gods
is in you and that no mystery troubles you; behold my
dream which I saw, and tell its interpretation. Upon
my bed I was beholding the visions of my head:
> And lo, a tree in the midst of the earth,
>> and its height was great.
> The tree became large and strong,
>> and its height reached to the heavens,
>> and it was visible to the end of all
>>> the earth.
> Its foliage was lovely and its fruit much,
>> and food for all was in it;
> Under it was sheltered every beast of the field,
>> and in its boughs dwelt the birds
>>> of the heavens,
>> and all flesh was nourished by it.

I was beholding in the visions of my head, upon my bed,
and lo, a watcher and a holy one came down from the
heavens. He cried with a loud voice and thus he spoke:
> 'Cut down the tree and cut off its boughs,
>> shake off its foliage and scatter its fruit.
> Let the beasts flee from under it
>> and the birds from its boughs.
> But leave the stump of its roots in the earth,
>> and with a band of iron and bronze
>> in the grass of the field,
>> and by the dew of heaven let him be wet,
>> and with the beast be his share in the herbs
>>> of the earth.
> His heart shall be changed from human
>> and the heart of a beast shall be given him,
>> and seven times shall pass over him.

By the decree of the watchers is the command,
     and the word of the holy ones is the
          decision,
in order that the living may learn that the Most High
is ruler in the kingdom of man and to whomever he
wishes he gives it, and raises up the humblest of men
over it.' This dream I, king Nebuchadnezzar, saw, and
you, Belteshazzar, tell the interpretation, because
none of the wisemen of my kingdom is able to make known
the interpretation to me, but you are able, for the
spirit of the holy gods is in you."

Then Daniel, whose name was Belteshazzar, was appalled
for a moment and his thoughts were troubling him. The
king responded, "Belteshazzar, do not let the dream and
its interpretation trouble you!" Belteshazzar responded,
"My lord, may the dream be for those who hate you and its
interpretation for your adversaries! The tree which you
saw, which became big and strong and its height reached
to the heavens and it was visible to all the earth and
its foliage was lovely and its fruit much and food for
all was in it; under it dwelt the beasts of the field
and in its boughs lived the birds of the heavens---it
is you, O king, who have become great and strong, and
your greatness has increased and reached the heavens and
your rule to the end of the earth. And what you saw, O
king: a watcher and a holy one coming down from the
heavens and saying, 'Cut down the tree and destroy it,
but the stump of its roots leave in the earth and with
a band of iron and bronze in the grass of the field and
with the dew of the heavens be wet and with the beast
of the field be his share until seven times pass over
him---this is the interpretation, O king, and it is the
decree of the Most High which has befallen my lord the
king: They will drive you away from mankind and with
the beasts of the field will be your dwelling, and they
shall give you grass to eat like oxen and you shall be
wet with the dew of the heavens, and seven times will
pass over you until you learn that the Most High is
ruler in the kingdom of man and he gives it to whomever
he wishes. And that they said to leave the stump of
its roots---of the tree: your kingdom endures for you
after you learn that the heavens rule. Therefore, O
king, let my counsel seem good to you: remove your
sins by righteousness and your iniquities by mercy to
the afflicted, if there may be a lengthening of your
prosperity."

It all happened to Nebuchadnezzar the king. At the
end of twelve months he was walking upon the royal
palace of Babylon. The king said, "Is this not
Babylon the great, which I have built for a royal
house with the strength of my might and the dignity
of my majesty?" The word was still in the mouth of
the king when a voice fell from the heavens, "To you
it is said, O Nebuchadnezzar the king, the kingdom
is taken from you. And from mankind they will drive
you away and with the beasts of the field will be
your dwelling and they will give you grass to eat like
oxen and seven times will pass over you until you
learn that the Most High is ruler in the kingdom of
man and he gives it to whomever he wishes." In that
moment the thing was fulfilled upon Nebuchadnezzar,
and he was driven away from man and he ate grass like
oxen and his body was wet with the dew of the heavens
until his hair became long like eagles' and his nails
like birds'. And at the end of days I, Nebuchadnezzar,
lifted my eyes to the heavens and my understanding was
given to me and I blessed the Most High and praised
and glorified him who lives forever:

> His dominion is an everlasting dominion
> > and his kingdom with all generations,
> And all who dwell on earth are counted as nought,
> > and he works according to his will with the
> > > army of the heavens,
> and there is no one who can check his hand,
> > or say to him, "What are you doing?"

At that time knowledge was given to me and the dignity
of my kingdom, my majesty and my countenance were given
to me, and my officials and chiefs were searching eager-
ly for me, and I was re-established in my kingdom and
extraordinary greatness was added to me. Now I, Nebuchadnezzar, praise and extol and glorify the King of
the Heavens, for all his works are true and his ways
are just and those who walk in pride he is able to abase.

Mythological Themes

These chapters have one dominant mythological motif, unlike
those discussed earlier, where a variety of themes appeared. In
Ezek. 31 it does get combined with another concept which might be
called mythological, that of Sheol; and we shall discuss the significance of that in time. But first the meaning of the sacred tree in

religion must be surveyed. The tree is one of the most common of all religious symbols. It appears in prehistoric art and is to be found in one form or another in every historic religion. In Christianity, for example, not only has the Tree of Life been a subject of continuing interest but the cross has been poetically called "the Tree". Extensive studies of the many meanings of the sacred tree have been published and we need not make an effort to summarize them here, for it can be shown that it is one type, the cosmic tree or world tree, which is the sole basis for the imagery in Ezek. 31 and Dan. 4.[13]

The cosmic tree is properly a way of imagining the entire cosmos. In its height and with the depth of its roots it comprehends heaven and hell, while the shade of its branches is depicted as the place of habitation of all living things. However, it is understandable that such a concept could be closely related to a slightly different one, that of the sacred pole (sometimes actually represented as a tree) which connects heaven, earth and hell. The latter object is understood as providing a means of contact between the earth and other realms. It is related to the concept of the "world mountain", which also serves to connect the three realms of the cosmos.[14] But although the cosmic tree proper and the sacred pole do have certain elements in common, it is the former concept which is clearly in mind in the Biblical texts which concern us.

Often the world tree has been related to the "tree of life", or the two have been equated.[15] To the extent that the world tree is depicted as the source of nourishment for all living things, that might be justified (cf. Dan. 4:9 H; 4:12 E); but since the tree of life as a source of immortality (or healing) is in itself a much disputed subject it would seem best not to use that term for the world tree, since the evidence provides little reason for associating the two concepts.[16] We shall be concerned not with a plant which bestows immortality (like the tree in Gen. 2-3 or the plant of life in the Gilgamesh Epic) nor with a plant which has magical healing powers (like the kishkanu tree[17]), but with the representation of the whole world in the form of a tree.

Since the best examples of the cosmic tree are to be found in Indo-European mythology we shall begin there, although it will be shown that the concept is also common in Semitic myth. The classic example is the tree Yggdrasill in Norse mythology.[18] It was the center of the divine world, where the gods sat in council every day. It rose to the sky and upheld the universe as pillars uphold a house, while its branches spread over the whole world. It was supported by three roots; one of which went to the world of death, one to the world of the frost-giants and one to the world of men. There was a well under each root; the Well of Mimir in which lay Odin's eye, pledged in exchange for knowledge, Hvergelmir (roaring

kettle?), and Urdharbrunnr (well of fate). In its branches sat
the cock Vidhofnir. This tree was probably represented by an
evergreen which stood beside the great pagan temple at Uppsala
which was described by Adam of Bremen.[19] It was associated with
a sacred well and a sacred grove. In myth the Yggdrasill is
already past its prime when it first appears.[20] A hart is
devouring its foliage, its trunk is rotting and a serpent is
gnawing it from below. This represents the pervasive sense of
the decay of the earth and diminishment of vitality even of the
gods which appears in Norse mythology, leading to the Ragnarök,
at which time the old tree will shiver and creak.[21] But it must
be noted that the tree is not cut down and is not destroyed so
that Yggdrasill is not treated as severely as the tree in Ezek.
31 and Dan. 4.

A variant of this northern form of the world tree may be
mentioned in passing. In Siberia the tree extends from the
netherworld to heaven, and since heaven has seven realms the
tree has seven branches.[22] It is commonly associated with some
source of water. Sometimes two or three trees are spoken of, to
correspond to heaven and the netherworld or to these regions plus
earth.[23]

Although they tend to be less explicit, similar references to
the cosmic tree occur in Mesopotamian literature. For example, a
tree whose function is not clear is described in the Erra Epic as
follows:

> Where is the mes-tree, the flesh of the gods, the
> adornment of kings [. . .] The holy timber
> (the surpassing?), the sublime, which is fit for
> lord[ship,] whose foundation(?) in the wide sea
> 100 double hours of water, . . . the bottom of the
> netherworld [covers (?)] Whose top reaches up to
> the heaven [of Anu].[24]

The text is not well-preserved, but Marduk seems to have saved this
precious tree, which Erra was seeking, by changing its location
(note column 3, line 28 of the same tablet).

One of the Shurpu-texts also praises several kinds of trees,
which evidently were used in magic rites, in terms strongly reminiscent of the world tree:

> Incantation. Tamarisk, lone tree, growing in the
>   high plain!
> Your crown above--your root below--
> your crown, above, is a tree releasing everything,
> your root, below, is a . . . terrace,
> your trunk is the gods.

. . . with bathed head,
you cleanse, you purify the mouth of the humans,
may the evil tongue stand aside![25]

Incantation. Tall cedar, growing in the high
      mountain!
Whose fate was determined in the mountain,
      the pure place,
whose fragrance drifts over the fields,
who day and night, on a resplendent day,
a favorable day, fit for sprinkling water,
has come from the mountain,
you cleanse, you purify the mouth of the humans,
may the evil tongue stand aside![26]

Incantation. Juniper, growing from the sprout!
Young juniper, growing from the sprout,
juniper whose boughs (and) intertwining branches
      are precious,
great pillar of heaven, great foundation of the
      earth,
resplendent doorpost of Enlil, strong lock of the
      temple of Enlil,
who on a day fit for . . . has come from the
      mountain, etc.[27]

Each of these trees is described as being of tremendous size, with
its top reaching heaven and its roots deep in the earth, while they
are also usually associated with the waters of the abyss, and sometimes with the "mountain" (kur).

Just what is meant by the trees which appear so frequently in
central positions in Mesopotamian art remains an unsolved problem,[28]
but certain uses of the symbol appear to be related to the cosmic
tree notion. Frankfort showed that the use of a tree or pole with
the sun disk hovering above is related to the concept of the pillar
of heaven and first appears in Western Asia in Mitannian (an Indo-
European people) cylinder seals.[29] In Central Asia the pillar of
heaven is surmounted by a great bird; on the seals the bird has
been replaced by the Egyptian sun-disk, long a familiar symbol in
Western Asia.[30] And usually the bare pillar has been replaced by
the traditional Mesopotamian sacred tree.[31] Precisely what ideas
lie behind these combinations of symbols cannot be determined,
since there are no texts which correlate with them, but their in-
terchangeability seems to indicate that there was a similarity between the cosmic conceptions of Indo-European peoples such as the

Mitanni and earlier inhabitants of Mesopotamia, as these conceptions were expressed in terms of a pillar of heaven or world tree.

There is some evidence that the Egyptians had a concept of a world tree although it was not a prominent idea among them. They sometimes referred to the celestial pole around which the stars moved (invisible, since our Pole Star was in a different location then) as a tree, and regarded the circumpolar stars as souls perching on its branches.[32] At other times it was thought of as a tower or pole, with guide ropes. The Pyramid Texts also describe a tree with cosmic connotations, "that high sycamore east of the sky," on which the gods sat.[33] In the Book of the Dead this tree was connected with the sun-god.[34]

The preceding paragraphs should suffice to show that cosmic speculations lie behind the imagery used in Ezekiel and Daniel.[35] The height of the tree, the depth of its roots, its association with subterranean streams, its provision of dwelling places and nourishment for all creatures--these are ways of representing the life-sustaining properties of the whole earth. Only the references to the subterranean regions are missing in the Daniel passage.

But this tree gets cut down! Elsewhere it appears in connection with astral speculations (Egypt), convictions about the relations between the three realms of the cosmos and about the life-giving powers of the cosmos, but none of these uses could make any sense of cutting down such a tree. So we must look further to see whether that is a theme peculiar to Israelite literature.

There are trees which get cut down here and there in mythology, but since most of these fellings obviously have no relation to our subject we shall simply mention them briefly. In a Sumerian text, "Gilgamesh and the Huluppu-Tree", the named tree is raised by Inanna in her garden in order to provide wood for a chair and a bed.[36] But she was unable to cut it because the snake who knows no charm had built a nest at its base, the Zu-bird had placed its young in its crown and Lilith, the demon of destruction, had built a house in its midst. Gilgamesh then came to the rescue, smote the snake so that the other two fled, and was given the tree in gratitude by Inanna. From it he made a pukku and a mikkû, the significance of which remains uncertain.[37] Except for the various kinds of beasts which dwelt in the tree, this text has no similarity to ours and is probably a myth to accompany the construction of certain wooden objects.

Gilgamesh is elsewhere involved in cutting trees. In both the Sumerian and Akkadian versions of the Epic he makes a hazardous journey in order to fell some sacred cedars. The Sumerian text seems to indicate that his effort was connected with his search for immortality; parallels to the cutting of the cedar in Ezek. 31 are completely lacking.[38]

A scene which is depicted on several cylinder seals has been interpreted as the cutting of trees on a mountain. Both Hooke and Frankfort believed the scene to represent a tree-covered mountain with a god imprisoned inside.[39] Hooke saw a deity cutting the trees; Frankfort could see no axe and said the trees were being pulled up. In either case one might be tempted to think Ezek. 31 and Dan. 4 could have been based on a myth, pictorially represented on these seals, of a god-king represented as a cedar which was cut down and went to Sheol each year when the summer heat came. But an older interpretation, offered by Ward, saw no tree-covered mountain at all, but a slender tree with branches being bent completely over by the sun god, and it must be admitted that if the seal cutters intended to depict a mountain covered with trees they did a remarkable job of making it look like a bent-over sapling.[40] Photographs and drawings of the seals leave real doubt as to whether they can be accepted as evidence of a tree-cutting myth or ritual.

One effort has been made to explain the mysterious "bands" of iron and bronze which are mentioned in Dan..4:15, just after the felling of the tree is described, by reconstructing a ceremony which presumably involved the death and renewal of a tree during the Assyrian New Year festival.[41] Sidney Smith has suggested that a bare tree trunk stood in the gardens of Nabu's temple and that in the ceremony old fillets of green leaves which had previously been placed on the trunk were removed and replaced by fresh ones; also metal bands called "yokes" were cut off, perhaps to be replaced by new ones. This offers one conceivable explanation for the "bands" on Daniel's tree, they would be an echo of an Assyrian fertility rite; but on reflection it does not appear very convincing. The text itself, a letter, is not at all clear at the crucial points;[42] and the text of Dan. 4 is far removed chronologically from the time when the Assyrians observed their New Year's festival.

The mention of fertility suggests that we look to the materials concerning the vegetation god, Tammuz, for a tree-cutting ceremony. Once again we can summarize our search in a few words. Tammuz probably was symbolized as a tree at times and we know that the lamenting of his death (Ezek. 8:14) was connected with the seasonal wane of vegetation, but whether a tree was ever felled as a part of such rites cannot at present be determined.[43]

Since Ezek. 31 compares the king of Egypt with a cedar in Lebanon it is natural for us to investigate the Egyptian cult of Osiris, since the deceased Pharaoh was identified with Osiris, a vegetation god who was sometimes represented as a tree.[44] A late form of the Osiris myth, which does have some support from early

Egyptian texts, however, tells that after the death of the god
his enemy Set put his body into a trunk and cast it into the sea;
whereupon it floated to Byblos and caught in the branches of a
tree ("heather," ereichē).

> The heather in a short time ran up into a very
> beautiful and massive stock, and enfolded and
> embraced the chest with its growth and concealed
> it within its trunk. The king of the country
> admired the great size of the plant, and cut off
> the portion that enfolded the chest (which was
> now hidden from sight), and used it as a pillar
> to support the roof of his house. . . .[45]

Eventually Isis located the body of her husband, and asked the king
of Byblos for the pillar.

> Then, when she had wrapped up the wood in a linen
> cloth and had poured perfume upon it, she en-
> trusted it to the care of the kings; and even to
> this day the people of Byblos venerate this wood
> which is preserved in the shrine of Isis.[46]

Unfortunately, for our purposes, once again the cutting of the tree
is only incidental to the main part of the myth and its attendant
ritual.

The same thing is true of the ceremony involving the Djed-
pillar. An important part of the Osiris ceremony was the raising
of the Djed-pillar by the king or chief priest on the last day of
the festival.[47] It symbolized the rising of the Osiris soul, and
probably originated as a harvest ritual. It was commonly believed
that the grain god was killed by reaping, but his essence was kept
alive in the last sheaf, and the harvest ended with rites which re-
asserted his continuing vitality.[48] The Djed-column in historic
Egypt was probably made of wood, but it seems to represent in form
a bundle of grain; the last sheaf. Stress is not put on the cutting,
nor the laying down of the Djed-pillar, but on setting it upright in
the ritual. The word means "stable" or "durable",[49] and its significance is that the column stands firmly upright; a symbol of the
overcoming of death and decay. So it may be used in art as a cosmic
pillar or sky support as well as a symbol of revival.

The setting up of a sacred tree as part of seasonal fertility
rites is attested in other cultures as well; we need note here only
its appearance in the Hittite myth of Telepinu,[50] and in the Attis
cult as it was celebrated in Rome.[51] But in none of these is the
felling of the tree given special significance. So, although there

have existed several kinds of sacred trees which are cut down, none of them seems to provide a parallel to the meaning of the cutting of the tree in the Old Testament.

The preceding paragraphs may appear to be a kind of scholar's wastebasket into which a lot of false parallels to Ezek. 31 and Dan. 4 have been put. But it must be remembered that our method does not look for "parallels" in the traditional sense of sources from which we can say that the biblical text has been derived. When and if we locate such a source, that is fine and helpful; in this chapter we have seen that the source of parts of Ezek. 31 and Dan. 4 is a myth of the cosmic tree which appears to have been beautifully preserved in both texts. Having found no parallels to the felling of the world tree we can state the negative conclusion that to our present knowledge this is a distinctive feature of Old Testament material. The discovery of a new text could change all that, of course, and so it needs to be emphasized that our method does not need to be at the mercy of accidents of discovery. On the basis of present evidence we can do more than just conclude there are no parallels to the felling of the cosmic tree, then sweep the unrewarding material into the wastebasket. For it helps us to understand the Biblical texts better when we discover in how many different kinds of structures and for how many different purposes the cutting of a tree has been used.

Again we see that the meaning which a theme has is determined by the structures in which it appears and we can be free to consider the significance of the combination of themes which occur in these chapters without trying to import meanings from outside which do not play a role in the way the themes are presently used. And if someday a cuneiform text appears in which the felling of the world tree is described, that will add to our knowledge of the ancient world surely, but it will not necessarily change our understanding of what it means to combine those two themes, if we have, in the present, interpreted the Biblical texts correctly.

As an additional example of this, we may observe that in Hindu literature the cosmos was represented by an inverted tree, which, in the Upanishads came in addition to be a symbol for man's earthly condition.[52] Given the Hindu ideal of release from all attachment to existence, it is not surprising to find the Bhagavad Gita teaching that the tree must be cut down with the weapon of renunciation.[53] So the radically different understanding of existence found in India led to a use of the same symbols which appear in the Near East for a very different purpose.

The King as the Cosmic Tree

If we take the concept of the world tree at all seriously, to say that it is appropriate to compare a king with such an image is a bit startling. And when we consider that these are Israelite authors writing about foreign kings the combination is especially surprising. They must have taken kingship very seriously, unless they were not aware of the cosmic implications of the figure they were using. I fear they have described the world tree too fully and too accurately for us to dare to suggest they did not know what they were saying, however. We must assume they did this deliberately and because it was the way to say precisely what they believed.

Certainly the authors have appropriated some older traditions in their assimilation of king to tree, however. There is a limited amount of evidence connecting Mesopotamian kings with the tree of life, but the theory that king, vegetation deity and tree were identified with one another falls short of proof.[54] An empire might be described in terms of the world tree, as Nebuchadrezzar's inscription in the Wadi Brisa shows: "Under her everlasting shadow I gathered all men in peace."[55] But to take the next step and speak of the king himself in these terms is to produce an extremely exalted picture of kingship. It is a real glory which these authors intend to describe and they do not deny its reality when they announce God's judgment of the sins of Gentile nations. This is an emphasis which we have found elsewhere in the Old Testament (especially Ezek. 28) and it is put even more strongly here, for the materials used elsewhere have some built-in flaw; the First Man, for example, despite his excellence, always loses the chance for immortality. But the cosmic tree is simply a representation of the world as the realm of life and that is a positive concept throughout. Only in Nordic myth, with its concept of a Dämmerung, is there a threat to the tree, but we find no trace of that in the world tree materials available from the Near East. The apocalyptic conception of a destruction and re-creation of the world does not make use of the cosmic tree imagery. So the tree represents a very exalted picture of kingship, of the earthly glory of mighty nations. It almost gives to these political realities a life-supportive function.

For what is said in judgment obviously has nothing to do with the cosmos; it refers solely to the demise of political power. There is not a hint that the authors of these texts thought about the fact that presumably to cut down the world tree would mean the end of the world for each of them is clearly using this exalted language not to talk about cosmology at all, but about political entities. That is especially clear in Dan. 4:12-13 where already

in the king's dream the symbolism has nothing to do with the tree
and can only apply to the fate of a human being. It may also
account for the apparently odd feature of a tree (perhaps really
the king, in the author's mind) descending into Sheol in Ezek. 31.

What probably influenced Ezekiel most strongly in his development of these themes was native Israelite tradition. Although the
cosmic tree does not appear elsewhere in the Old Testament the use
of horticultural symbolism with reference to royalty was rather
common. The Messiah, for example, is called "the Branch" in Jer.
23:5 and Zech. 3:8, 6:12; with which we may compare the "shoot
from the stump of Jesse" in Isa. 11:1 and Ezekiel's allegorical
use of tree and vine imagery to represent royalty in chapters 17
and 19:10-14. So although chapter 31 says something about kingship
which is not said elsewhere the imagery is still closely related
to familiar language patterns. Likewise the use of a cut-down
tree as a symbol of judgment was probably drawn from prophetic
tradition. Consider Amos 2:9:

> Yet I destroyed the Amorite before them,
> whose height was like the height of the cedars,
> and who was as strong as the oaks;
> I destroyed his fruit above and his roots beneath.

Two passages which we studied earlier are in the same line; Isa. 10:
18-19 and 2:12-16. Ezekiel's precedents, however, deal with ordinary
trees; he has produced a far more radical statement by using a mythological figure which affirms something positive about the one to be
judged while also emphasizing all the more the enormity of the judgment. Daniel follows in Ezekiel's footsteps in this respect.

The effect of judgment upon hybris is not described the same
way in our two chapters, and each of them makes its own valuable
contribution. In neither of them is the nature of hybris or the
kinds of activity which it involves described at all fully; the
material being used does not lend itself to that. Ezekiel just
takes the literal height (qōmāh) of the world tree and makes use of
the fact that in Hebrew the same words (gbh, qwm) mean "height" and
"pride" in order to affirm something similar to Isaiah's judgment
"against everything proud and lofty" (2:12). Daniel is more explicit,
describing briefly Nebuchadnezzar's exultant feelings at the magnificence of his accomplishments (4:29, E), and emphasizing throughout
that it is God Most High who alone rules the kingdom of man (4:3,17,
25,26,32,34f., and note the final words of the chapter). But both
find ways to make their material deal with the kinds of judgment
which hybris brings upon itself although in both cases the tree
imagery does not lend itself naturally to that use.

Let us consider the Daniel passage first. Within the dream itself the true nature of the judgment is made plain, although it is necessary to depart from the tree imagery: "His heart shall be changed from human and the heart of a beast shall be given him" (vs. 16, E). And the story tells us that the king did become like an animal. We are being told here as plainly as can be of the de-humanizing effect of self-deification. Here is the glory and the degradation of man as the Bible reveals him—capable of so much: " . . . it is you, O king, who have become great and strong, and your greatness has increased and reached the heavens and your rule to the end of the earth," (vs. 22), created for greatness by God himself, and yet unwilling to accept a greatness which is subordinate to the creator God—grasping for more, claiming everything for self, and as a result gaining—not godhood but bestiality; losing the glory of humanity. Need I cite examples? Is the story in Dan. 4 any more bizarre than the bestial behavior of those Nazis who claimed to be a divine race? We can document from our experience that what Daniel says about the ultimate effect of self-glorification is true.

Perhaps Ezek. 31 contains a hint of the same idea. In vs. 6 the tree is said to provide a place for all the birds, beasts and nations to dwell. Some exegetes have dropped the line dealing with nations, thinking it inappropriate for the imagery, but we have found evidence that it is quite appropriate for the cosmic tree. In the judgment-section, however, all the peoples of the earth leave the shadow of the cut-down tree although it continues to provide shelter for the birds and beasts (vss. 12-13). Again, something desperate has happened to humanity. The world, which had been made to be a place for men to live and thrive (Gen. 1:28) becomes a place fit only for the beasts because of human sin; the nations, which the metaphor of the cosmic tree tells us have been designed by God to nourish human life, can no longer exist. Here we must add the because—because in their arrogation of divine powers they do not nourish humanity.

Now we return to a subject which has appeared in nearly all the material which has concerned us; the ultimate fate of man—death. The Old Testament says far more about death in its hybris passages than it does anywhere else, and this in spite of the fact that the most emphatic hybris passages deal with nations, to which the death of an individual, even a king, does not necessarily represent the end of vigorous existence. This makes these passages of special interest to us again. For while it is clear enough that a man's claim to divinity appears to be rather effectively ended when he dies, it is not so easy for us to understand what controls can be set over against the power of a government to be our god. The Old Testament seems to be concerned about that question also, and its concern leads it to speak of death and the netherworld.

But suppose we begin with Genesis 3 and man's fate before tackling the more difficult question of governments. We might have spent much more time on that chapter but have kept it in a peripheral position in this work for several reasons. The litera- ture on the chapter is so immense and its implications are so broad that to attempt to deal with it in any depth would make it overshadow all the rest. And those attempts have been made else- where, of course, while the materials chosen for detailed study here have largely been neglected. So we have had to be content with allusions to Gen. 3 and the use which has been made of it in theology, as we shall do here again. The issue at the beginning of that chapter, raised by the serpent, is man's status with respect to God--has God really given him all that he needs? Man's answer is No, but when he proceeds to take the rest for himself he learns that the ultimate issue is something else--life itself. As a re- sult of his effort to "become like gods" death comes into the world, and that chasm between man and the gods which was felt so intensely by those neighbors of Israel who produced the literature we surveyed in Chapter I is seen to be present also for one who in all other respects is "little less than the gods".

Now this in itself is basis enough for poking fun at the human tendency to make too much of oneself, and the Old Testament writers see the hybris of individuals as absurd. "Will you really say, 'I am God,' before those who kill you? For you are man and no god in the hands of those who slay you" (Ezek. 28:9). "I say, 'You are gods, sons of the Most High, all of you; nevertheless you shall die like men, and fall like any prince'" (Ps. 82:6-7). But, as we have seen, this sort of thing does not occur very often in the Old Testa- ment, for it is hybris of nations, not individuals, which is viewed as the real danger. Yet a similar response is made to the nations; descent into Sheol is threatened. In Isa. 14, Ezek. 28, 31, and now we may add chapters 26, 27, 29 and 32, death is the most consistent motif which appears.[56] Nowhere else in the Old Testament can we find a description of any length of the nature of Sheol and the state of the dead, but in these chapters there are fairly detailed accounts of Sheol plus elements of funeral songs (Isa. 14:4ff.; Ezek 26:17f., 27:2, 29-36, 28:12, 32:2,16,18), and other references to death (e.g., to corpses lying about unburied in Isa. 14:19f.; Ezek. 29:5, 30:11, 31:12-13, 32:4-6). So the final stage of our study must concern itself with the Old Testament understanding of death, and that will lead us back to our own day, about which a few words will be said in the Epilogue.

Death as Punishment

Many surveys of the Old Testament concept of the state of the
dead have been made and it does not seem necessary to repeat most
of that material here.[57] This is especially true since there is
little in common between the Isaiah and Ezekiel passages on the
one hand and the rest of the Old Testament on the other. Death in
Israel was normally considered to be the lot which could be accepted
without cavil if it came to one full of years who left children
behind to carry on his name and who was properly buried with his
fathers. The tragic death was that which occurred in youth, to one
who had not partaken richly of life, who had no offspring or who
was cut off in a dishonorable way or was left unburied.[58] Sinners
might be punished by suffering such a death, but nothing is said
about a place of reward or punishment after death.

Outside of the passages which we are dealing with the Old Testament reveals very little about what Sheol was like; it uses terms
which were but a projection of the common experience of the burial
of the dead.[59] However, Zimmerli has called attention to the fact
that two concepts of the netherworld are present in the Ezekiel
passages:[60] (1) The first appears to have been this common, Israelite
view, which was simply that the dead continued a shadowy sort of
existence in the grave (called bōr or šahat, "pit"). The second is
related to the Mesopotamian concept of a kingdom in the netherworld,
separated from this world and having its own way of "life". This
idea has been greatly demythologized in the Old Testament; there is
no trace of a realm ruled over by subterranean gods; but in Ezekiel,
especially, there does seem to be some knowledge of a cosmography
similar to that found in Babylonian descriptions of the nether world.
Ezekiel speaks of 'ereṣ tahtīyōt (land below, netherworld) in 26:20;
31:14,16,18; 32:18,24 and in each of these three contexts there is
evidence that he has in mind a real, subterranean land, with a topography of its own. These hints have not been taken seriously by
those who have written on the Hebrew belief in the afterlife because
they do not correspond with the prevailing Old Testament view, but
there are a good many reasons for thinking that Ezekiel does not
reflect the common view. In 26:19-21 he is discussing the destruction of the city of Tyre:

> For thus says the Lord God: When I make you a city
> laid waste, like the cities that are not inhabited,
> when I bring up the deep over you, and the great
> waters cover you, then I will thrust you down with
> those who descend into the Pit, to the people of old,
> and I will make you to dwell in the nether world,
> among primeval ruins, with those who go down to the

Pit, so that you will not be inhabited or have a
place in the land of the living. I will bring
you to a dreadful end, and you shall be no more;
though you be sought for, you will never be found
again, says the Lord God.

There is no trace here of a use of the city as a figure of speech
for the king or its people. Ezekiel seems really to be saying that
the city will be covered by the waters of the deep (t^{e}h$\bar{o}$m),[61] and
that it will descend into the nether world where it will exist along
with other destroyed cities (k$\bar{a}$h^{o}r$\bar{a}$b$\bar{o}$t m$\bar{e}$'$\bar{o}$l$\bar{a}$m), and the dead.
Another transfer from the land of the living ('ere$\c{s}$ hayy$\bar{i}$m; 26:20,
32:23,24,25,26,27,32) to the nether world is to be found in chapter
31. There the World Tree and the trees of Eden go down to Sheol
(verses 16, 17). We have discussed what a confused allegory this
makes; now it might be suggested that Ezekiel is not using trees
as symbols of men, directly, but is describing the translation of
Eden to the nether world.[62] Finally, in chapter 32 he informs us
that graves are to be found in the nether world; so if Sheol is
approximately equivalent to the grave, as is commonly affirmed,
then we have graves within the grave in this passage. Or, perhaps
once again this is a trace of the idea of a land of Sheol within
which the dead lie or sit (Isa. 14:9) in immobility (Isa. 14:10),
so that it is possible to describe the location of graves within it,
as in 32:23: "whose graves are set in the uttermost parts of the
Pit".[63]

The principle stress in these passages in Ezekiel seems to be
that the subject of the passage will join certain others in the
nether world. The city of Tyre will join the ruins of old, the
World Tree will join the trees of Eden, and the king of Egypt will
join the kings of past empires. In each of these passages there
are certain expressions which form a common theme. These are, "with
those who go down into the Pit" (26:20; 31:14,16; 32:18,24,25,29,30;
cf. Isa. 14:15,19), "uncircumcised" (28:10; 31:18; 32:19,20,24,25,26,
27,28,30,32), and "those slain by the sword" (31:17; 32:20,21,22,23,
24,25,26,28,29,30,31,32; cf. Isa. 14:19). Lods has provided a very
plausible explanation of the significance of the term "uncircumcised"
in this context, by showing that it is derived from the belief that
infants who died uncircumcised remained in an unfortunate state in
the afterlife.[64] Eissfeldt has used Lods' explanation to provide
a clue to the meaning of "those slain by the sword", suggesting that
this refers to those who have suffered a dishonorable death; namely,
by murder or execution.[65] There is some evidence in the Old Testament, and more in Babylonian material, to show that one's fate after
death depends, not upon having lived a good or evil life, but upon
social rank, kind of death, and burial.[66] Non-burial or exhumation

was considered a curse (I Kings 14:11-13; 16:4; 21:24; Jer. 16:4; 25:33; Ps. 79:3; Eccles. 6:3; Isa. 14:19; Jer. 8:1-2). A Babylonian incantation against evil spirits of the dead reveals that those of certain conditions in life or who had died certain kinds of deaths were believed not to rest in peace, but to return to haunt the living:

> Whether thou art a ghost that hath come from
>   the earth,
> Or a phantom of night that hath no couch,
> Or a woman (that hath died) a virgin,
> Or a man (that hath died) unmarried,
> Or one that lieth dead in the desert,
> Or one that lieth dead in the desert,
>   uncovered with earth . . .[67]

It seems clear, then, that Ezekiel has intended to say that the subjects of these passages will be associated with those who are most miserable in the afterlife. Although the firm conviction that we are judged after death on moral grounds was not stated explicitly in Jewish writings until the second century B.C. (Dan. 12:2, 2 Macc. 7, 12:43-44) the interpretation just offered would indicate that the beginnings of such an idea may be found in these texts from Isaiah and Ezekiel.[68]

Kings, cities, trees, gardens, even empires are sent to Sheol in these strange texts. The oddness of such statements must be due to their authors' efforts to apply the traditional answer to the hybris of individuals ("But you shall die like any man.") to the hybris of nations. So the glory and power of earthly kingdoms is set in stark contrast to the fate of the uncircumcised and the murdered. And we are told that as death proves the absurdity of individual claims to divinity so the self-deification of nations is self-destroying.

But we cannot help responding that some tyrants die in peace and are honored in death (Lenin); some brutal governments outlast many lives, so what good is such an affirmation? Any answer must be made diffidently. Normally the only comfort the oppressed peoples of the world have been able to find under the inescapable power of those who rule them is the assurance that in death justice will prevail. That is little enough but perhaps it is not to be sneered at. And if no government is likely to be scared into change by being told it is plotting its own destruction (perhaps quoting Ezek. 31!), perhaps there is a positive vision which might inspire. It is the vision of the grandeur, the glory and the goodness of the human kingdom which is ordained by God and which might be more nearly realized if only we would be willing to handle gingerly those powers of deity which he has let us use.

EPILOGUE

THE KINGDOM OF MAN

Our studies of the Old Testament and other ancient literatures
have shown us that the modern questions about the existence or
vitality of God are a manifestation of man's long-standing uneasiness at the thought there might be Another Being above him to whom
he must remain subordinate. We could multiply the ramifications
of that but, following the lead of the Old Testament materials, we
have moved from the personal level of pride and self-glorification
to an emphasis on the power and glory of great nations as factors
really producing rivals to God which have to be taken seriously.
In this Epilogue we shall consider again both the individual and
the nation, but shall find that the Old Testament emphasis on
corporate power has a special relevance for our present situation.

The Old Testament conviction about the remarkable gifts of
man, expressed in Gen. 1:28 and elsewhere, has been confirmed--with
a vengeance, if we may say so--by the astonishing achievements of
the technological society. Modern man has made himself master,
not only of the inanimate world and non-human creatures but has
found ways to exercise godlike powers over his fellow-men. That
he has not learned to control himself or live at peace with his
fellow-men in no way decreases the awesomeness of his power, but
makes him a god more like Zeus than Yahweh, perhaps.

The magnitude of what technological man can do has led to an
increasing concern, in various circles, about problems which are
perennial but appear now to take on new importance:

1) Intense concern has been expressed by scientists--first
atomic physicists, then those in the biological sciences, then
ecologists, about the need for establishing moral and ethical
principles to control the use of technology.[1] Although related
to our study, the ethical issue is not the explicit concern of
this book and it must be left to one side, with the hope that others
better equipped to deal with it will provide some of the guidance
we need.

2) Connected with the desire to agree on ethical principles
is the concern about finding ways to control those who have access
to such awesome power so as to prevent, or at least limit, its
misuse. The former concern centers on the gray areas where it is
not easy to decide what is right and wrong, but there are some
kinds of activities about which there is general agreement that

they are highly undesirable--those which we label "tyranny".[2]
The control and prevention of tyranny is a subject ranging far
beyond the scope of this book, but we have commented on it
earlier as the Biblical materials have prompted us, and a bit
more can be added shortly.

3) Among theologians, and perhaps nowhere else, the traditional concern of Christian theology about our temptations to aspire
to full mastery of human destiny is still present. That temptation
has been the central subject of our work; it is acceded to with
enthusiasm by certain forms of humanism, scientism and nationalism,
but we shall attempt to show in this concluding section that the
Christian identification of this tendency as the source of some of
mankind's greatest evils is a valid one, and that a theological
problem, the nature of man, lies at the bottom of the other two
concerns just mentioned.

If I Ruled the World

A few years ago a song became popular because it expressed some
of our fondest dreams and hopes, saying, "If I ruled the world"
there would be peace, love, harmony and happiness for all! A strange
manifestation of hybris!--yet the reasoning in this gentle ballad
differs little from Eve's reasoning in the Garden. Peace, love,
harmony and happiness--that is what we all want and ought to work
for, but:
    we can't help thinking God and others who have put their hands
    in have botched a job which we could do better,
and
    we wish we had the power to do it right.
So Eve doubted the goodness of God's intentions and sought the power
to make life better through acquiring the "knowledge of good and
evil". So the song writer recognized the need to rule.
    Certainly these longings of ours for a better life are not to
be denied. And it is we who must do something about them, and if we
did not have confidence in ourselves, that we can do better than has
been done before, nothing would be accomplished. Yet we have a way
of spoiling all this by our fixation on a kind of self-regard which
surpasses its proper bounds.
    Sometimes that self-regard seems innocent enough, at least in
its lack of effect on others. The doctor who thinks he could have
produced a better human body if he had been in charge does no harm
in thinking so. Nor did the farmers who used to loaf in my father's
farm equipment store on winter days and work out amongst them exactly
how the country really ought to be run.

But suppose that doctor acquires the ability to remake people, surgically or genetically? Suppose the would-be politician actually acquires political power? Then the kind of behavior which we have called <u>hybris</u> in our Old Testament studies may appear, i.e., action based on the power to be a god to other men, since it is a power which recognizes no higher authority. The pleasant ideals of "If I ruled the world" remain pleasant only so long as they are only ideals and the power actually to put them into effect, viz. <u>to rule the world</u> is unavailable.

> . . . which of us, frustrated by the inefficiency
> and muddle and unnecessary contention of government
> by consent, has not on occasion thought: 'What
> could not I do, if I had dictatorial powers? The
> problems are all so simple. Just remove a few crooks
> and incompetents. Oh no! No question of concentra-
> tion camps or secret police, let alone gas chambers
> or nuclear bombs.' Yet it only needs enough people
> to think that way at the same time for long enough
> and with sufficient ferocity, and that is where it
> would lead.[3]

Men are not wise enough nor good enough, individually or collectively, to be trusted with absolute rule over their fellows. Yet there must be rule, a kind of rule which is somehow controlled to prevent the excesses to which we are prone. For us democracy seems to be the answer; consider Niebuhr's famous statement, "Man's capacity for justice makes democracy possible; but man's inclination to injustice makes democracy necessary."[4] But we have not discovered the Old Testament suggesting democracy as the remedy for tyranny; rather, we have already puzzled over its preoccupation with death at precisely this point.

"But man dies, and is laid low" (Job 14:10)

Part of Job's complaint deals with the mortality of man. "For a tree there is hope," (14:7) it can be cut down and sprout again from the roots, but there can be no such hope for man. <u>Everything</u> dies eventually, of course, except the amoeba, and so the death of men ought to be no shock or scandal. But it is. Arnold Toynbee has commented on the incongruity which we see in our own mortality by pointing to the way certain languages (including our own) use the word "mortal" to single out one small part of all that lives and dies; the human being. Surely he is called "a mortal" only because it doesn't seem right that he should be![5] Toynbee sees it as an incongruity between the mortality and the dignity of man, then goes on to connect it (following St. Paul's lead, "Death is the wages of sin.") with the incongruity between man's intellectual ability to master nature and his moral inadequacy for dealing with himself and his fellows.[6] Our study of the Old Testament has led us to a similar conclusion. We began with the strange state of man, who has been given almost all glory, cutting himself off from its source by wanting it all. We have seen how his great powers have been used to dehumanize rather than promote human potential. And we have found the incongruity of the dignity of man vs. the most ignominious of deaths set deliberately in the starkest contrast by Old Testament authors.

We have asked about the reason for the emphasis on death in the texts we have studied and have pondered some answers already. Now perhaps we can go further. Yes, we are marvelous creatures in the sight of God, but God's estimate of us is not quite so high as our own, for we cannot really accept the idea that such a being should die. Our rebellion against the fact of death is a symptom of our rebellion against creaturehood. But in God's sight the fact of our rebellion against creaturehood means that death is a necessity Or, as Toynbee puts it, we "may also admit that death itself, even when it has not been caused by sin, may not be an outrage, but a godsend, for a creature whose nature is what man's is. Though man's sinfulness is perennial, death does at least limit mankind's and Nature's or God's liability for the wickedness and folly of any individual specimen of our species."[7]

We can easily agree with Toynbee as far as others are concerned, but where we ourselves and our loved ones are concerned, that may be another matter. I cannot resist commenting further on the modern attitude toward death in the light of the Old Testament materials we have been considering. It is a truism that present-day Western culture cannot come to terms with death and has found a variety of ways of attempting to deny it.[8] I shall not labor this point; its manifestations are too familiar to us, but want only to show how this denial of death is connected with the whole success-oriented, man-affirming, God-ignoring temper of a time which seems to be set on fulfilling Ezek. 31 and its parallels. In an era when man can do anything he sets his mind to, can plot his own destiny and needs no other to help him, death is really a scandal. It is no wonder that we disguise it in mortuaries and cemeteries and in the language we use. And the kind of dreaming we do about the victories science may one day win over death is another symptom of that old hybris that lurks within each of us.

To enable each person born to this earth to live a full and useful life is a goal no one would quarrel with; I am not referring to that kind of fight against death. But to prolong the life-span to 200 years, or indefinitely, why should that be done? (Why should it be done for others, that is; for oneself the answer is obvious!) At the same time that one science writer is bemoaning the disastrous combination of a rising birth rate with a lowering death rate, another science writer talks about making life spans longer still or doing away with the death rate entirely. (At least for himself, that is.) The speculation that science might one day enable us to cheat death, centering presently about spare parts for those that wear out and about cryonics,[9] obviously involves rebellion against the fact of death, and that is quite natural for man. To prolong life as long as possible is instinctive with us and to dream of cheating death entirely was no novelty even in the earliest civilizations we know about. Mummification, the tombs of the kings and the Book of the Dead sought to assure Egypt that death was not real; the alchemists tried to find the key to prolonging life indefinitely; and their ideal has become a goal of modern science. Although one modern author has said the goal is now only prolongation, not real immortality,[10] that may be questioned by the advocates of cryonics, since they do not hesitate to use the word "immortality" of the future they seek for themselves.

A contrasting, and equally old strand of tradition has confessed all along that mortality is inescapable and has explained it by affirming that it is this which distinguishes men from gods. It began at least as early as Gilgamesh and appears throughout Judeo-Christian thought. This point of view sees the attempt to deny or cheat death as a denial of creaturehood or a denial of the deity, and it is unlikely that cryonics and similar hopes for a man-made, blissful future can escape the same judgment. Enthusiasts for cryonics speak of "immortal supermen,"[11] of a future time when man will be infinitely wise and will live forever—they speak of the tree of knowledge and the tree of life!

Are not Gen. 3 and Isa. 14 the most accurate descriptions of modern man, his potential and the dangers he faces, that we can imagine? Wisdom—death—human restiveness—the perennial themes of human achievement and tragedy; if they are described in extravagant language in the Old Testament—why, human behavior is extravagant!

But we must speak once more about the state.

"The Most High is ruler in the Kingdom of Man and he gives it to whomever he wishes." (Dan. 4)

Reinhold Niebuhr is reported to have said in a lecture, "Our question is, Does the state belong to God or to the devil? And the answer is that the state belongs to God, but it is in danger of

becoming the devil by imagining that it is God."[12] That is another
way of describing the kind of concern with the state which is
prominent in the Old Testament. We have seen that the tendency
for individuals to think too highly of themselves is recognized as
a danger which ought to be avoided in all of the literatures which
we have examined, and that warnings against it are a regular part
of proverbial wisdom. But we observed that only rarely does the
Old Testament show intense concern about excessive pride in the
individual private citizen. Certainly there is a basis in the Old
Testament for the emphasis in Christian theology on pride as the
root of the human predicament.[13] But we have found that it expresses
a special concern for that peculiar form of pride which involves a
rebellion against God so thoroughgoing that it can scarcely occur
except at the level of national government.[14] This is a theme which
comes over into the New Testament in a few passages but which has
never been taken quite so seriously as the writers of the Old Testament have taken it. We may think of Acts 12:21-23:

> And on an appointed day, Herod, having dressed himself
> in royal garb, sat upon the throne and delivered an
> address to them [the people of Tyre and Sidon]; and
> the crowd cried out loudly, "The voice of a god and not
> of a man!" At once a messenger of the Lord struck him
> because he did not give the glory to God, and being
> eaten by worms he died.

The theme is taken up into eschatology in 2 Thess. 2:3-4:

> Do not let anyone deceive you in any way; for the
> apostasy comes first [before the Day of the Lord]
> and the man of lawlessness is revealed, the son of
> destruction and the one who opposes and exalts him-
> self over every so-called god or object of worship,
> so as to seat himself in the temple of God, proclaim-
> ing himself to be God.

In these texts such exaltation of a human being merely forms
the prelude to a sudden downfall. What worries us more is the
existence of successful tyrants and the future possibility of government so powerful that it will be as god to us all.

I follow Pine Creek all the way to the Allegheny River as I
drive to work. The creek itself is seldom visible, hidden by
industrial and commercial development, but above the buildings the
wooded hills still rise, marred only in places by new housing.
One morning I began to ponder what life in western Pennsylvania
may be like for our descendents. I thought, at least the beauties

of these hills will be recorded on film, so that coming generations can see what it was like when the atmosphere was still breatheable and the earth could still support vegetation. Perhaps, I thought, they will have to live under domes, in a completely artificial environment. Certainly men won't die out no matter what they do to themselves and their environment, for they are infinitely adaptable and invincibly clever.

But what sort of men will they be? Being a clergyman, I soon began to wonder whether there would be churches under those domes. Would Christianity be an appropriate religion for such people? Other religions in human history have died out; can we be sure Christianity won't be replaced some day by a religion more appropriate to the future? In so regimented a life as that must be, will men find refuge in superstitions such as astrology, or in world-denying religions such as the Far East offers? Can it be imagined that secular humanism might triumph completely? I ask these hypothetical questions because of concern about how full humanity can be maintained under the highly restrictive type of government which the technological society is bound to bring upon us.

The validity of the concern does not stand or fall with the imaginary environmental disaster I have just described. Suppose we solve the present environmental crisis; in what way is that likely to be done? One theory is that we can insure the continuation of human life on this earth only be establishing a "steady-state" economy, in which our American by-word, "growth", is no longer possible or permitted since a balance has been reached between population and resources. This might well involve a somewhat reduced standard of living from what we now enjoy and would certainly call for a kind of austerity which modern Americans are not used to, for it would be a society in which no waste could be permitted, growth would be impossible because of the absence of new natural resources, and the emphasis would be on quality rather than quantity.

Now, if that kind of solution does become the only way to avoid an environmental disaster of the type imagined earlier, it will call for heavy restrictions on human freedom. We shall be limited in what we can buy and in what we can do with what we buy. And the gist of my description of these two hypothetical futures is that in any kind of viable future we can project for ourselves the key role is played by a government with more power over the lives of individuals than men have ever known before. This frightens us because we know that such power is seldom found outside of tyrannical states.

The Bible speaks of tyranny as the most radical kind of hybris, as a usurpation of the prerogatives which ought to be God's alone. That concept of totalitarian government is not confined to the Bible but has appeared again in the works of scholars and in the words of tyrants themselves. Thomas Hobbes spoke of the power of life and

death as the only real power in the world, which meant that when
this power was concentrated into the hands of one man or a government, then one could without exaggeration speak of a "mortal
God".[15] We may conceive of power in broader terms but our approach
to government has been similar; we have seen that it is potentially
a god to those it rules.

Another term which resonates with our concerns is found in
Toynbee's A Study of History where he speaks of "The Mirage of
Immortality" which affects those who live in and believe in a
universal state.[16] Ironically, he notes, the concept of the
immortality of the universal state usually arises after it has
begun its decline and the signs of the end have appeared. The fact
that these two authors have used the terms mortal and immortal bring
to mind our own discussions of the Biblical emphasis on death in
connection with the state, and to that connection we shall return in
a moment.

The closeness to reality of those seemingly bizarre Old Testame
materials on which we have concentrated becomes apparent when we get
acquainted with some of the world's great tyrants. Bizarre--indeed;
mythological--yes; surpassing reason with its talk of a human being
becoming a god! And very realistic--for tyranny is bizarre, has
its mythology and offends the rational mind. Frederick II Hohen-
staufen said of himself, at the beginning of the 13th century, "The
subjects, under God, draw breath only by the force of the illustriou
Caesar,"[17] referred to his birthplace as Bethlehem and his mother as
the Virgin Mary, and sought to impose totalitarian rule on the
crumbling Holy Roman Empire.[18] His courtiers said of him, "Thy
power, O Caesar, hath no bounds; it excelleth the power of man like
unto a god," and "This Emperor, the true ruler of the world, whose
fame extends through the whole circuit of the earth was convinced
that he could approximate his own nature to the heavenly nature,
perhaps by his experience of mathematics."[19]

Is it a madman who makes such claims? If so, we have had mad-
men aplenty forcing their will on the peoples of the earth. We shal
not cite the depressing facts at length; after Frederick came Napole
then Stalin, Hitler and Mao. And with men who claimed virtual divin
for themselves came the perfection of the technology of totalitarian
so that even Frederick the Great's arrangement: "My people and I ha
come to an agreement which satisfies us both. They are to say what
they please, and I am to do what I please,"[20] has become unnecessari
liberal. Now thought and speech can be controlled through mass-
communication, propaganda, control of education, informers and brain
washing. So the question which was raised in Isaiah's time, in the
face of Assyrian power, is more pertinent and more distressing than
ever before: What does God do to help his people when they are confronted by these earthly gods? No glib answers will suffice, but we

can find some help in the history of Christianity before we try to
summarize the message of Scripture.

Although Latey's book, Patterns of Tyranny, presents no
sanguine picture of Christian influence on society in the future,[21]
it does provide an instructive series of examples of the ways the
Christian Church has helped to restrain tyranny in the past. Although religion provided almost no internal defense against the
hybris of Napoleon, the Pope and the power of the church at Rome
did offer serious opposition to his pretensions from without.[22]
The Pope no longer had the material resources of his predecessors
with which to enter the lists against civil rulers, but his
spiritual power was still real enough that Napoleon recognized it
to be a factor with which he must deal. The powers of the Church
have been even more greatly eroded since that time. Stalin, Hitler,
even Mussolini had little to fear from organized religion. Yet
Christianity remained as almost the only spiritual bulwark against
the ideologies on which the modern tyrants have based their claims
to power. That it has been so ineffective is tragic, but if it
had not existed--and endured--the victories of totalitarian ideologies over men's minds might have been more nearly complete. The
futile though valiant struggle of the German Confessional Church
against Hitler is well known by now,[23] and the continuing vitality
of Christianity in Soviet Russia after decades of repression remains
a matter at which to marvel.[24]

Latey also comments on the way that the Christian faith preserved at least one man who had the opportunity to become a tyrant
from succumbing to that temptation.[25] Calvin's Geneva was very
nearly a totalitarian state, yet the man himself was probably saved
from the corrupting influence of power by those religious convictions
which led him to govern his own life as severely as those of his
fellow citizens. Needless to say, more examples can be cited of
"Christian" rulers whose faith was not strong enough to save them
from hybris, which means that to secure a "Christian government" by
some means is not the answer to the threat of tyranny which we seek.
But we do see that for certain individuals, either wielding power
or oppressed by it, belief in God has provided salvation from those
mortal gods whose power on earth rivals the power of the God of
Heaven.

Religion has often been cited as a source of tyranny over men's
minds and bodies, of course, so that we cannot remain satisfied with
what has been said thus far. Regardless of one's opinions of organized
religion, the issue raised by tyranny is a religious one, for it deals
with the nature of man. "We cannot, in fact, obliterate Nietzsche's
vision of the Superman--and its debased elaboration in Nazi and Fascist
and racist society--by the argument of power, but only by a different
view of man, of human dignity and of society; . . ."[26] Now the

Biblical religion has offered such a "different view", the view against which Nietzsche ranted, and it was a view which both explained the existence of tyranny by emphasizing the mighty powers which are men's, and offered a better way of depicting the ideal of the first created man, crowned with glory and honor, ruling over nature without perverting it or himself--an ideal realizable only when man lives in perfect obedience to his Maker. Christian theology has little impact on the secularized world of today and yet never has the Biblical doctrine of man been more crucial to the future of man on earth, for more than ever before he has acquired the power over the universe which God has said may be his. But what will become of us if that power is untempered by an awareness of the necessity of obedience to One greater than man? Isaiah, Ezekiel and Daniel have provided answers to that question which can scarcely be denied from contemporary evidence. We shall become less than fully human, like the wolverine that kills and destroys for sheer cussedness or like the victim of torture who has only a bit of animal life left in him.

How to avoid this has been made clear by the passages we have studied. The key word is "mortality"; we have been reminded time and again that men die and all that they accomplish is perishable. That is most obvious for the individual, efforts to cheat death in some science-created future notwithstanding. All men die, and what they were and have done perishes or is distorted after their lives end. The same is true of institutions, although it is often less obvious, for some of them do not pass away peacefully when their time has come. But they all stagnate and cease to be useful, and then some die, some are reborn to a new life, while others continue in a mummified condition as efforts to deny the reality of death. This effort to deny the inevitability of death is more effective for nations than it could ever be for individuals or institutions, for great nations endure for centuries. A bit earlier we referred to Toynbee's discussion of that illusion of immortality which affects universal states just when the vital signs are beginning to weaken. And all states do perish. They may gain almost absolute power but it is a gross error to imagine thereby that they are absolutes. They are the products of contingencies and so they must not be offered absolute obedience, the dignity of man must continually be held above the dignity of the state, and they ought to be viewed by their citizens as things that are passing away.

We spoke of radical humanism at the beginning of this book, and among the radically humanistic documents belongs the Bible. But it offers us a realistic humanism, which admits unblinking both the glory and the scandal of man and all his works, with the nation seen as the greatest of men's works. It can be realistic about man and his institutions because there is a God in the picture

When the nature of man is evaluated without the perspective provided by a God in the picture it either becomes falsely optimistic,
refusing to acknowledge the inevitability of sin and the enormity
of what men do, or falsely pessimistic, downgrading the real good
that men do. We have dealt with Biblical materials which are
rather strange kinds of literature, for the most part--"mythological". Now it becomes clear; the Biblical religion can speak of
nature without myth (and a great deal has been made of that), and
it tends to speak of God without myth, since what we know of him
he has revealed by intervening in human history. The rest that
might be known of God, which could have produced myths, remains a
mystery to us. But when the Bible speaks of man it uses myths,
for the mystery of humanity is revealed to us, and that requires
mythological language. The myths are true; they have been verified
throughout history by the deeds of world rulers, in whom the extent
and direction of man's potential is most evident. And they are
myths by which men and nations ought to learn to live, for their
other option is dehumanization and death.

    We may summarize the theology of these Biblical materials and
the contribution they could make to contemporary life in this way:
    A) They affirm a very high conception of man, against both
the naturalistic view which sees him as only another form of animal
and the kind of religious view which believes that man must be
downgraded in order to exalt God. They agree largely with the
humanists but hold to a theistic humanism, finding that the greatness of man and the greatness of God are somehow inseparable. They
praise God for what he has given us but do not celebrate it over-
much because of the awareness that we can do great harm with what
we have been given, for it has given us the potential for true hybris.
    B) Hybris as we have defined its Old Testament sense is full
rebellion against God; the effort to take control of the world and
all of life and to do without any God but oneself. Now, it is to
be suggested that at our place in world history we can see that the
truth of the Bible's high doctrine of man and its conception of
hybris have both been confirmed. We can truly do magnificent things,
remaking the world and ourselves--and we have really made the move
toward doing without God. The secular society and the modern state
show that the Old Testament's language about becoming a god was not
too strong.
    C) So, if human accomplishments have tended to confirm the
truth of part of the Old Testament doctrine of man, why should we
not take the rest of it seriously?
        1) It says that man can, indeed, act like a god, but
cannot do it successfully, that the results of such hybris

have always been disastrous and are bound to be, because
his greatness is not his own attribute but a gift derived
from a higher being; and that when he acts in denial of
his dependence on that source he loses his greatness, and
reverts to bestiality. The existence of that higher
being history cannot prove, but I believe it has confirmed
the truth of what the Bible says about the results of
hybris.
2) It says also that the fact of death proves that man is
no god, and that the effort to cheat death is a manifestation of hybris. Now if hybris is the great destroyer of
humanity perhaps acceptance of the reality of death is a
necessary part of being fully human.

D) The Old Testament sees the state as the fullest development
of human powers and hence as the entity most subject to hybris.
History, and our own fears of the power of the modern state tend to
confirm this as well. We ask practical questions about this, for
we want to know what we can do to prevent such fears from coming
true, but theology does not always provide answers to satisfy the
pragmatic mind. Men in ancient Israel addressed "the Word of God"
to the rulers of foreign nations, and as far as we can tell the Word
had no effect on those kings, although we should admit that once
again the essential truth of that Word has been confirmed by history
But we still ask about effectiveness, as well as truth, and their
effect in the day they were uttered seems to have been little enough
Later such words did perhaps preserve Calvin and Cromwell from hybri
so that God's Word has had some demonstrable effects on the great
powers through the behavior of men of faith.

The most effective thing about this Word, however, in the past
and potentially in our own day, is the doctrine of man which it
teaches. The way human societies deal with the issues raised by
tyranny and the difficult ethical decisions which face us will
depend on the conception of the nature of man which predominates in
those societies. If the Biblical concept of man is true, then the
future of humanity depends upon our constant and convincing enunciat
of those truths at all levels of society.

EXCURSUS

THE PROBLEM OF MYTH

The extravagance of human accomplishments in the world's
economy leads one who takes them seriously to strain with language
in the effort to find adequate words for them, as the reader may
have noted in some of the passages quoted in the Prologue. Old
Testament authors who dealt with the matter had the same problem,
and it has already been pointed out that they make use of some
unusual (for the Bible) materials exactly at the points where the
exaltation of man to near divinity becomes the issue. These are
materials for which parallels can be found in ancient Near Eastern
myths. But the term "myth" is so vague and so much discussed and
disputed that anyone who uses it in more than a casual way must
explain what he means by it even though it may be true, as in this
book, that the conclusions drawn from the material are not dependent
on one's theory of myth.

There have been many helpful studies of the problem of myth in
the Old Testament in the past few years but at one fundamental
point no appreciable progress seems to have been made. That is the
question of how the term "myth" ought to be defined. The promise
that Childs' monograph of some years ago might provide a basis for
a consensus has not been fulfilled,[1] for the great variety of
earlier definitions has been continued in the literature which has
appeared since. This confusion in Old Testament study is only a
reflection of a general confusion about the use of "myth", which
one dictionary calls "one of the obscurest notions of comparative
religion",[2] and which is a problem as well for anthropologists,
folklorists, psychologists, and philosophers. Despite the fact
that one is brought near to despair when he attempts to find an
adequate definition for a word which is used in literally dozens of
ways, no one has suggested that we ought to give it up as an empty
word. It has a power over us; we seem to have an instinctive feeling that "myth" does correspond to something real which it is
important to talk about, and so the discussion of definition goes
on. The problem is that we cannot agree as to which of several
aspects of human experience the term ought to be made to refer. It
is now functioning as a signal which points to several, not necessarily closely related aspects of reality, and it is doubtful that
a single definition should try to include them all. Furthermore,
many discussions of the term seem to begin a priori and make little

if any contact with the subject matter of other discussions which presume to be about the same word. Often, of course, conflicting definitions are listed and discussed, but eventually one comes around to that concept which the author believes to be the appropriate meaning for the word, while the other definitions and the concerns they represent are simply dismissed.

As one example out of many, we may note Childs' brief rejection of the philosophical definition offered by Hartlich and Sachs in favor of a phenomenological approach.[3] It is certainly true that Childs' approach to the problem of myth in the Old Testament has been a valuable one, but it begs several important questions. By saying, "Myth means this and not that," he has set himself over against a very large number of scholars who still use myth to mean "that", and has by implication dismissed the questions raised by "that". So despite the value of what Childs or Hartlich and Sachs have done, to restrict ourselves to two examples, the fact that each insists on using the same word to refer to quite different realities and to claim his use as the legitimate one means that the confusion continues.

In this state of affairs the last thing that is needed is a new definition of myth, and the next-to-last thing is a defense of one of the popular approaches as the one which should be used in dealing with the Old Testament. To do the latter is to dismiss important questions which have been raised by other definitions or to claim a precision for one's thought which will not bear examination. In this chapter we shall attempt to categorize the different subjects which scholars talk about when they use the word "myth" and to comment on what they seem to want to say about their subject by applying the term to it. Having done so, if one could then propose a new set of words which would receive acceptance as substitutes for the offending one, then some real progress might be made, but myth is a word with such power over us that any diminution of its domain seems unlikely at present. At best, one might hope for a moratorium on the use of the word in certain of the less helpful contexts where it has been employed. This is especially true for Old Testament study. It will be argued here that what most Old Testament scholars really want to discuss when they deal with "the problem of myth in the Old Testament" could be pursued with greater clarity and less confusion if the term "myth" were not made the focus of discussion. In order to justify this position I must show that the concerns of most (not all) of the Old Testament scholars who discuss myth are not the philosophical (including phenomenological) problems denoted by the word, but are simply concerns about the uniqueness of the Old Testament.

My attempt to categorize the uses of myth cannot hope to deal fairly with every one of them, for the variety is too great. Althou

the approach is aimed at the Old Testament, it begins in general
terms, so that a narrowing of the field occurs as we progress.
The approach takes the form of three cycles, beginning with a
categorization of the subjects which scholars really want to talk
about when they say they are going to discuss "myth" with an
identification of the occurrences of these interests among Old
Testament scholars, continuing with a discussion of the value
judgments which have been made by the latter as they use the term,
and concluding with some comments about the results of the appli-
cation of these various definitions to Old Testament study.
Finally, a suggestion will be made about how useful research
might continue even though the problem of definition remains unsolved.

The Subject Matter of "Myth"

The categories which follow are of necessity highly schematized.
Although the work of certain scholars will fall very neatly within
one category this will not be true of others, either because they
have consciously attempted to construct a broad definition, because
their work does not always agree with their explicit definition,
or because they do not deal explicitly with the question of definition. At any rate the effort here is not to devise a classification
system into which every scholar's work would neatly fit--that is
impossible--but to identify as clearly as possible the major concerns
of those who say they are going to discuss myth. Obviously in some
cases several of these concerns may be combined in a given work and,
with good reason, be called the problem of myth.

A) Myth as a Literary Genre: If on form-critical principles
one could develop a description of a Gattung to be called "myth"
it would provide for us an objective and neat definition of the term
by which all other uses could be judged. Efforts have been made to
do this and they are to be found especially in the works of those
scholars who emphasize the narrative character of myth.[4] As a
traditional narrative myth must then be distinguished from saga,
legend, and fairy tale, but despite the helpful descriptions of
these various types which have been offered, a purely literary
approach has not provided a consensus from which discussion could
proceed, for two reasons. First, a good many influential scholars
will not be restricted to defining myth as a narrative. They are
interested in "mythical thought", the evidence for which may be
found in symbols, rituals, and customs as well as in the mythical
story.[5] Hence, the narrative form is for them only a rather narrow
manifestation of a much larger phenomenon rather than the basis

upon which to build one's definition. The other reason for a
lack of agreement on a form-critical definition is the recognition
that there is no purely formal criterion by which one can distinguish myth from other narratives. Efforts to define myth are
really based on content or on theories of origin, and in too many
cases these criteria do not enable one to draw sharp boundaries
between myth and the other narrative types; legend, saga, and
fairy tale.[6]

B) <u>Myth as an Intellectual Mistake</u>: The popular use of the
word to mean "something false" or "something which others believe
and I don't" might be included under this heading. It is a use
which has a long history. The Greeks used it in this way as did
the New Testament and Christian apologists.[7] It was almost the
only way the word was used in subsequent history until the rise of
Romanticism, and despite the modern efforts to appreciate myth as
something of value the word is still used in a deprecatory sense
more often than any other way. We shall look briefly at four
rationalistic depreciations of myth, with comment on their use by
Old Testament scholars where possible.

1) Myth versus History. These two categories are frequently used in opposition to one another as ways of differentiating between what can be established with some degree of certainty on the
basis of historical evidence, and what can not. When used in this
way a myth is an account of something which did not really happen.
As Tylor wrote, myth is "sham history, the fictitious narrative
of events that never happened".[8]
Another approach which defines myth in contrast to history
may be included here, although it does not necessarily categorize
the mythical as automatically untrue. It is the definition of myth
as cyclic in its concept of time as contrasted with the linear view
of time found in history.[9]
Frequently Old Testament scholars who are nominally operating
with a more sophisticated definition of myth continue to use the
contrast between myth and history as one of their real criteria for
determining the nature of an Old Testament text. One example only
will be cited: speaking of the crossing of the Red Sea, Holm says,
"Historically a real event can be present here, but the account also
contains mythical material--Yahweh's direct intervention--which can
only be adhered to by an act of faith and never by knowledge concerning historical facts."[10]

2) Myth versus Science. The term is used in this sense to
denote something which <u>could</u> not have happened according to our
present understanding of the laws of nature. We shall include here

both those who concentrate on the difference between our cosmology and those of other cultures and those who use the following type of definition: "Myth originates wherever thought and imagination are employed uncritically or deliberately used to promote social delusion."[11]

The problem of the archaic cosmology to be found in the Old Testament is a perennial one and it will frequently be called "mythological". Among several definitions with which Burrows works is, "It involves the personal, even anthropomorphic element, treating as the acts of a personal being or beings what a scientific world-view sees as the operation of impersonal forces and laws. But for the modern man who accepts the scientific point of view a mythological conception in this sense is at the same time false, or at best only a poetic, figurative expression of truth. Much of ancient Hebrew and early Christian thought is obviously mythological in this sense."[12]

3) Myth as a Category Mistake. This is the approach which leads to the demythologizing enterprise. It is related both to 1) and 2) above and to category C) below. As several scholars have pointed out,[13] Bultmann's famous definition calling for demythologizing,[14] which at first reading seems straightforward, is not a clear statement of his deepest concerns. Shubert Ogden, who believes the definition is essentially adequate for expressing the concerns of Protestant theologians, has, I believe, improved on it considerably. He says myth is language which represents a field of human experience, that of the "original internal awareness of our selves and the world as included in the circumambient reality within which all things come to be, are what they are, and pass away,"[15] and that it represents this awareness in terms based on our external perception of reality. These terms are inappropriate ways of representing the reality which lies behind them, so myth involves a "category mistake", and demythologization is necessary in order to express in appropriate language the truth expressed inappropriately in myth. This approach agrees with 1) and 2) above in contrasting myth with science and history but disagrees with them in accepting it as a conveyer, however inept, of truth.[16]

Demythologizing has not been taken up with enthusiasm by Old Testament scholars but occasionally one will denote by "myth" those elements which he believes need to be restated in order to make them understandable or acceptable to modern man[17] (who is himself a myth, incidentally[18]).

4) Myth as a Disease of Language. One of the earliest efforts to interpret myth scientifically was the philological approach of Max Müller, now abandoned. He believed that the development of

language accounted entirely for the origin of mythology. Words
having personal connotations were applied in a metaphorical sense
to the non-human world in a very early period, and eventually men
forgot that these words were not to be interpreted literally and
took them to be the names and qualities of real persons. Myths
then had to be invented to explain the use of such terms with
respect to objects in nature.[19]

C) <u>Myth as Language Representing a Peculiar Type of Reality</u>:
A great many different approaches to myth are included under this
category. They differ from those under B) in that they are likely
to emphasize the value or necessity of myth. Rather than using the
term to mark off the false from the true, they use it to mark off a
peculiar type of reality or a special way of apprehending reality
which may or may not then be judged to be true. The sub-categories
which we shall discuss here are not mutually exclusive by any means
so they should be considered to be differing <u>emphases</u>.

1) Myth as a Mode of Perception. In the writings of Ernst
Cassirer the term myth is used to denote a distinctive way of per-
ceiving the world by the human mind. "If myth did not <u>perceive</u> the
world in a different way it could not judge or interpret it in its
specific manner."[20] No interest is shown in the subject matter of
myth nor in any external reality to which it might refer.[21] The
reality of myth is in itself; it is an autonomous creation of the
human spirit which, alongside art, language, and science produces
and posits a world of its own.[22] Hence, although there is a myth-
making mentality characteristic of archaic peoples, and it is this
which interested Cassirer most, myths are also to be found among
modern men, so that in his last work he discussed the myths of Nazi
Germany.[23]

Since Cassirer emphasized the intimate connection between myth
and language it may be permissible to mention under this heading
those modern literary critics who believe that words have a reality
in and of themselves, even though they use the term myth in a variety
of ways.[24]

Cassirer's work has influenced Old Testament scholars as well
as others but seldom will one find an explicit effort to apply a
Cassirer-like definition to Old Testament study. One example will
be found in Gaster's <u>Myth</u>, <u>Legend</u>, <u>and</u> <u>Custom</u> <u>in</u> <u>the</u> <u>Old</u> <u>Testament</u>:
"Myth, or <u>mythopoeia</u>, is an independent and autonomous faculty of
the mind which may operate at any time and in any age, alongside of
intellection and speculation. . . . It is, as Cassirer pointed out,
the stuff of the affective, as distinct from the intellectual, side
of the mind, and equally determines meaning and significance."[25]

2) Emphasis on Psychology. In the writings of Jung and his followers myths, dreams, visions, and stories are taken to be manifestations of archetypes of the collective unconscious. "The primitive mentality does not invent myths, it experiences them. Myths are original revelations of the pre-conscious psyche, involuntary statements about unconscious psychic happenings, and anything but allegories of physical processes."[26] They are symbols, then, of a given kind of reality, of truths about the human psyche. In referring to those human fantasies which cannot be reduced to experiences in an individual's past, Jung said they "resemble the types of structures to be met within myth and fairy-tale so much that we must regard them as related."[27]

Some of the followers of Jung are studying the Old Testament with considerable interest. The author of Satan in the Old Testament says of her work: "This presupposes, however, that such mythologems be understood as spontaneous expressions of psychic reality. . . . My subject will not be God and the devil, not their essence as such--that would be metaphysical speculation--but the psychological contents and the experiences of the superhuman in a religiously creative time . . ."[28]

3) Emphasis on Another World: The Supernatural or the Sacred. This emphasis is often included as one of several aspects of myth in definitions which attempt to be comprehensive,[29] but some authors will be found to stress it above all else. It would say that anything which speaks of a world apart from ours, of a reality utterly different from that which is normally accessible to the senses (the reality which we commonly call "the sacred") is to be called "myth". John Cobb has put it in a relatively extreme form: "If Christian faith apprehends a reality radically different from all other reality, even to the extent that the term 'reality' cannot be used univocally, then the language of faith must be sui generis. We may assign the term 'myth' to such sui generis language."[30]

Seldom will an Old Testament scholar make this the single key to the understanding of myth but it often is combined with other elements. To cite one example, Davies argues against restricting myth to polytheism by asserting, "Myth is a way of thinking and of imagining about the divine, regardless of the number of gods," and by finding material for Israelite myths within the concept of Yahweh's personality.[31]

4) Emphasis on Metaphysics. This approach is closely related to the preceding one and may not be distinguished from it by many authors. The emphasis here tends to be on the necessity of using symbolic language to express certain kinds of truth which cannot be put in rational terms. Some will use the term metaphysics,[32]

others emphasize the irrational,[33] while others speak of "knowledge of the unknowable" or unverifiable;[34] but all seem to be expressing a similar interest in dividing human experience into that which is rationally expressible and empirically verifiable on the one hand and that which is not, on the other.

Definitions of this type occur frequently in the works of Old Testament scholars. A good example is this one: "Myth is always an attempt to express, and thereby to make comprehensible, some truth about the world and man's existence in it, a truth inaccessible and unknown in itself, but capable of being expressed in and by symbols."[35]

5) Emphasis on Ideals and Universals. Here again myth is used as a symbol but the metaphysical nature of its referent may not be emphasized so strongly. A fair example of this approach is Alan Watts' definition: "Myth is to be defined as a complex of stories--some no doubt fact, and some fantasy--which, for various reasons, human beings regard as demonstrations of the inner meaning of the universe and of human life."[36] Others emphasize that myths seem to be the appropriate medium for expressing what are believed to be universal truths about mankind.[37]

Occasionally a statement of this type about myth will be found in works on the Old Testament. After discussing the transformation of myth in Israel, G. E. Wright comments, "The problem, however, is this: Granted that Israel's sense of reality transformed all mythical references when used in the new context, something of the original meaning must have been retained in the mythical references or else they would not be used. Perhaps it would be safe to say that God's war of conquest likened to his slaughter of the dragon at creation served to heighten the importance of the event. It becomes something of universal significance, far transcending its own time and place. . . .While the myth is drawn into Israel's historical tradition, it retains its mythical flavor to the extent that the significance of the history is enhanced and understood as of universal import."[38]

D) Myth as an Instrument Functioning to Maintain the Life of the Human Community: A large number of scholars are interested in myth not as an approach to questions of truth, scientific or historical, nor as a possible revelation of a supra-rational reality, but are interested in the function it performs in the human community. Hence they are more likely to discuss the value (i.e., the usefulness) of myth than its truth.[39] The group can be divided into two: one which uses the term in a broad sense, finding myths which function in all cultures, and the other which defines only certain cultures as mythological and then tends to use that word to denote the entire orientation of such cultures as opposed to others.

1) The Broad Use. The interest which leads scholars to use the term in this way is well expressed by this definition: "Every culture will create and value its own myths, not because it may not be able to distinguish between truth and falsity, but because their function is to maintain and preserve a culture against disruption and destruction. They serve to keep men going against defeat, frustration, disappointment; and they preserve institutions and institutional processes."[40]

Since Old Testament scholars are much less concerned with the universal myth-making tendency than they are with the discrepancies between the myths of antiquity and modern thought, one would not expect to find them speaking of the functions of myth in all societies save as an occasional prelude to an apology for Biblical myth.

2) The "Mythological Culture" Use. Within this category we shall try to include a good many scholars who disagree with one another at many points. Yet they all agree in rejecting the ways of understanding myth given above in A, B, and C. They do share a "phenomenological" methodology,[41] emphasize the ways in which myth functions in society, and are concerned to achieve a sympathetic understanding of the purpose and value of myth. Their major concern is primitive or archaic societies; that is, they do not normally use quite so broad a definition of myth as those described in D) 1). Although they can discover vestiges of traditional myths which still are preserved in attenuated forms in modern societies,[42] their chief contribution has been to help us to appreciate cultures in which myth is normative, whose outlook on the world and human life is far removed from ours. They discuss what is a myth and what is not, within those cultures,[43] but it is usually the entire culture and not merely one portion of it which they wish to describe.

Several of the emphases of the "mythological culture" approach which have been described in the preceding paragraph are contained in this partial definition: "But note that the majority of myths, simply because they record what took place 'in illo tempore', themselves constitute an exemplar history for the human society in which they have been preserved, and for the world that society lives in."[44] A portion of another definition may be cited as an illustration of the functional emphasis: " . . . a form of reasoning which transcends reasoning in that it wants to bring about the truth it proclaims."[45] How does it bring about the truth it proclaims? There is general agreement that this occurs through the intimate relationship between myth and ritual. The question of the exact nature of the relationship between the two is hotly disputed, and it is not necessary for us to attempt to follow that entire discussion here.[46] One quotation from a representative of the "Myth and Ritual" school which would be accepted, with modifications, by a good many scholars, will have to suffice: "Now the ritual in this ancient pattern of religion did not consist only of actions, but the actions were accompanied by spoken words, chants, and incantations, whose magical efficacy was an essential part of the ritual. . . . In the ritual the myth was the spoken part which related the story of what was being done in the acted part, but the story was not told to amuse an audience, it was a word of power; the repetition of the magic words had power to bring about or re-create the situation which they described."[47]

As it functions in a mythological culture, then, myth may be defined as a sacred narrative of beginnings the chief purpose of which is "to stabilize the established order both in nature and in society, to confirm belief, to vouch for the efficacy of the cultus, and to maintain traditional behaviour and status by means of super-natural sanctions and precedents."[48]

Several Old Testament scholars have affirmed that the only proper use for the term "myth" in Biblical studies is the type just described. They believe that myth properly denotes the world-views to be found among ancient cultures so that the problem of myth in the Old Testament is to be approached by comparing the Israelite world view with those of Israel's neighbors. Their interest is to emphasize the contrast between the view of time and space, God, man and nature, held by Israel and by people of other ancient civilizations.[49]

Questions of Intent and Judgments about Truth

The variety of definitions which has been briefly outlined reflects a series of rather different concerns which have motivated scholars. The question of truth is central, but it is raised and answered in many ways. A comment by Altizer, although perhaps not applicable to every use of the word, raises the issue which lies behind most discussions of myth in the Old Testament: "It should be emphasized that the very word 'myth' indicates a loss of the meaning--or reality--to which myth points. For a conscious awareness of the mythical as a distinct language arises only when man has established a gulf between himself and the sacred. The mythical appears as the 'mythical' only when the reality to which it refers can no longer immediately be grasped."[50] Even when a scholar asserts that myth is essential and universal it may very well still be true that he bothers to use the term only because some problem has been felt about the truth of certain kinds of language or certain claims about reality.[51]

We shall look again at each of these uses of myth by Old Testament scholars, now asking about the question of truth. Those under B) need not be discussed further since by definition myth has something false about it. The interest of those who use C) 2) is psychological, and they claim to discover a certain kind of truth about man's inner being preserved in myths. C) 1) and C) 4) involve a recognition of the inadequacy of a purely rationalistic view of truth and will suggest that there may be more than one kind of truth, so that myth may have a legitimate function.

Many of the scholars whose opinions have been gathered under C) 3) have probably been motivated to use myth as they do because of a recognition of the problem created for us by our loss of apprehension of the realm of the sacred. As long as the existence of two realms, the sacred and the profane, was experienced and accepted unquestioningly there was no awareness of a problem of myth in the sense in which it is used by these scholars. The Old Testament <u>may</u> be anti-mythological in its outlook (whatever that means) but it must be observed that it never questions the reality of the sacred, nor does it identify anything as "myth" and argue against it.[52] This is a modern problem and it is a legitimate problem of faith for us. As to the question of truth, four options seem to be available:

a) The existence of the realm of the sacred is denied, so myth is obviously false.[53]

b) We confess that we have lost contact with the sacred, although we have no basis for denying it exists. Myth is then meaningless for us although it may be true in itself.[54]

c) Myth is just an improper way of conveying truth about the sacred and that truth is accessible to us through demythologizing.[55]

d) Myth is the only language available to speak about the sacred, and its reality is still accessible to us through it.[56]

Those who use the term as defined in C) 5) and D) 1) may talk about the sacred, but they tend to use myth in a broader way to refer to any narrative, dramatic or pictorial way of expressing one's understanding of his existence. This also refers to something real which is a legitimate part of the study of man's intellectual and social history. It might be asserted that all men have and need myths of some kind to live by, and the absolute truth of such myths may or may not be questioned, but it must be observed that normally one labels as a myth only an outlook on life which one does not accept.[57]

The concern of those who use the D) 2) approach to myth is not <u>initially</u> this life and the faith of modern man, as is true of all

the others. Although contemporary faiths often do come into the
picture eventually, these scholars begin with an effort to explain
and help us to understand cultures which are very different from
ours. Since these cultures contain world-views which are foreign
to us and since these views are called mythological, then no matter
how sympathetic the treatment may be the implicit judgment contained
in the word "myth" is likely to be "untrue".[58]

Results of the Application of Concerns
about Myth to Old Testament Study

Once more we shall look at the several uses of myth in Old
Testament study which were outlined above, having considered in
general terms the problems to which each of them is addressed, in
order to learn what scholars have concluded about the nature of the
Old Testament witness and the faith of Israel as they have approached
it with their own individual concerns.

A) Some scholars believe that there are certain truths about
human existence which are naturally conveyed in narrative and
dramatic form, i.e., by myths as they define them. Under this heading we may be justified in grouping the psychological approach (C2),
the "ideals or universals" approach (C5), and the broad functional
approach (D1), since all would agree in finding myth in the Old
Testament. Indeed, from this point of view if there were no myth
in the Old Testament we would have to conclude that it says nothing
of importance about the human experience. This must be called a
legitimate and useful area of study of the intellectual and social
dimensions of humanity; what is questionable about it per se is its
use of myth as a meaningful term. One might suggest that "narrative"
or "story", or even Gaster's title, Thespis would be less confusing
ways of denoting this type of value-charged language.

B) The problem of the existence of realities which are not
rationally perceptible or expressible has exercised scholars in
several disciplines and we have seen that one of the terms used in
discussion of certain aspects of the problem is myth. Categories
B and C 3 and 4 of the approaches to the Old Testament listed above
have this in common. B 1, 2 and 4 simply deny its existence; the
others are most concerned with the difficulty of finding ways of
expressing truths about non-rational realities. But all these
approaches do find myth in the Old Testament, for it is founded on
that other reality. It makes statements which are not in accord
with "objective" historical and scientific standards, it affirms
things to be true which are not empirically verifiable, and it speaks

of the actions of a divine being in the world. Given one of these
approaches, some scholars then frankly admit the Old Testament
contains myth, but others attempt to qualify their definition at
this point. For example, they may want to separate nature myth
from language about the realm of the sacred in general, then say
the Old Testament has the latter but not the former.[59] Or they
may separate cosmological ideas from the efficacious story itself
and say that Israel has the former but not the latter.[60] And so
forth. At this point much confusion is to be found. If the
analysis of the basic intent of these scholars is correct, they
really have been motivated by secular man's problem of the loss of
contact with the realm of the sacred. It is this which has led them
to speak of myth but many of them have not been content to deal with
the Old Testament on the same level with other cultures as they do
so. Hence, they introduce another criterion for defining myth, that
of comparison with the thought of other ancient cultures. At this
point both the concern and the definition found in the works of
some of these scholars overlaps the concerns and definitions found
in our next group.

C) As indicated above, the phenomenologists or functionalists
(D2) want to display the contrast between Israelite and other ancient
cultures. They reject the concerns which have been described in the
two preceding paragraphs as introducing concepts which are foreign
to the Old Testament, which is true enough; however, we must point
out that they are _not_ concerns which are foreign to _us_ as we deal
with the Old Testament and try to understand it. They are legitimate
questions which confront us, and a reasonably good case can be made
for using the term myth with respect to each of them. The phenomenologists can, of course, make just as good a case for their right to
the word, if not better, but by their claim to possess the proper way
of approaching the Old Testament they tend either to bypass completely
the other questions, or to introduce a criterion of truth which has
not been very critically examined.
    The reasoning is about as follows: 1) The tacit assumption is
that the understandings of reality found in cultures different from
our own are untrue. 2) The Old Testament can be shown to have an
understanding of reality different from that labeled "mythological".
3) Therefore, the superiority of the Old Testament is upheld.

Now at last we have come to the heart of the matter. The real
point at issue when most Old Testament scholars discuss myth is the
truth of the Bible. They have been distressed either by the manifest
difference between the Bible's understanding of reality and that
which is believed by modern, secularized man, or by the obvious similarities between the religion of Israel and that of her pagan neighbors,

or both. They have attempted to cope with the second embarrassment
by emphasizing the differences between Old Testament thought and
that of "mythological cultures".[61] They have reacted to the first
in a variety of ways. Building on the difference between the Old
Testament and "myth", we and the Old Testament come out together
on one side as non-mythological, so the difference between us is
minimized. Or one of the other approaches we have mentioned may
be taken. Cosmology may be minimized, demythologizing may be
attempted, the necessity of symbolic language may be maximized, etc.
And all of these enterprises are conducted under the title, "The
Problem of Myth." The problem is not myth but the Truth of the Old
Testament.

If it could be possible to call a moratorium on the use of
the word "myth" by Old Testament scholars for a few years we might
be able to understand one another (and even our own work) better.
We may continue to discuss archaic cosmologies, differing concepts
of space and time, sacredness and secularity, varying understandings
of the nature of man and his relation to God and the world, symbolic
language, etc., and use the term myth incidentally as we do so (we
cannot escape it), but I see no reason why it needs to be the key
word for any of these discussions. When it serves as the key word
for all of them (and more), as it does now, we flounder, as a reading of almost any of the recent articles on myth in the Old Testament
in the light of the analysis given here will reveal.

If our immediate concern is the difference between our own
secularized apprehension of reality and that to be found in the Bible
the problem can be discussed without the pejorative word "mythology".
"Symbolic" is perhaps more appropriate than "mythological" for
Jungian, Tillichian or other concerns about certain kinds of reality.
And when a comparison is to be made between the religion of the Old
Testament and other ancient religions I believe the Old Testament
itself can provide some guidance as to appropriate terminology.

Myth is not an Old Testament word nor is it used in a significant way in the New Testament, where it is equivalent to "fable".
I see no evidence that Israelites were aware of the existence of
myths in the sense of any of the definitions discussed, except that
probably they could identify a given piece of material as a cult text
and another as a text which was not considered sacred. There is
certainly no conscious anti-mythological bias in the Old Testament,
but there is an anti-Canaanite bias, a henotheistic bias (at least),
a bias against idolatry. There is little evidence that pre-exilic
Israelites cared to deny the truth of the great seasonal myths and
the myths of the famous sanctuaries. Had they done so we would have
no "fragmentary mythology" left in the Old Testament. It seems likely
that most of them looked upon nature much as the Canaanites did, much
as all men (including Christians[62]) have done until the rise of

secularism. But conservative Israelites before the exile did not
agree to worship the Canaanite gods or to frequent their sanctuaries.
The issue, as they appear to have understood it, was not world-view,
concept of reality, or myth, but which god is to be worshiped?[63]
And the jealousy of the God of Israel tended to rule out not only
participation in the cults of other gods but anything else which
the believer was consciously aware of as the property of those gods.
So it is that there are no substantial pieces of Canaanite mythology
brought over into the Old Testament; they were known to be cult
texts for other gods. But polemic against the truth claimed for
those texts nowhere appears explicitly, in striking contrast to the
polemics against the other gods and their cults. Indeed parts of
those texts are used, when convenient, as if they were true, much
to our embarrassment.

Since this is true, the term myth would not seem to be the
most useful one to use in discussing the differences between the
Yahwistic faith of pre-exilic Israel and the faiths of Canaan. As
understood by the average believer (including some psalmists and
prophets) these faiths were probably much more like the phenomenologists' descriptions of mythology than like our own. This is not
at all to deny that the seeds of the desacralization of nature are
to be found in the Yahwistic faith nor that there is a significant
emphasis on history as over against the natural cycle. It does call
for a more cautious approach to the comparative studies which need
to be made than has often been taken.

We must take seriously the true parallels which we find. The
language of hymns, of wisdom, and of sacrificial regulations may be
very much the same in different cultures, e.g., and the implications
of this are important.

We must take seriously those aspects of other cultures which
are missing from the Old Testament. Incantations, e.g., are the
most common form of religious literature in Babylonia but there are
none to be found in the Old Testament.[64]

We must take seriously the quantitative differences which can
be demonstrated but without the error of interpreting them as quali-
tative in nature. The prime example here is history-writing, which
has been made the key to the distinctiveness of the Old Testament
by some scholars in a way which may have overstated the case.
Albrektson has recently demonstrated that on a small scale the same
kind of concerns for history can be found outside the Old Testament,
warning us that care must be used in talking about history as the
special Biblical means of revelation, but he agrees that quantita-
tively the comparatively large amount of history in the Old Testament
is important and must be accounted for.[65]

Finally we must take seriously those Biblical materials which
represent a point of view which is common elsewhere but rare in the

Old Testament. For the most part these are the passages which have
been labeled mythological (as I have already done earlier in this
book) because they are to be compared not so much with the laws or
hymns or cultic regulations or wisdom literature of other cultures,
as with texts such as Enuma Elish, which everyone calls myths.
These passages do stand in some contrast with most of the Old Testament and have remarkable affinities with extra-Biblical literature,
and so perhaps one could still call them mythological if no less
compromising a term can be found. But they are important not because they might be given such a label--we have seen how meaningless
that is. Rather, here what is peculiarly Israelite impinges
directly upon materials which are the common property of ancient
Near Eastern peoples so that they provide an especially valuable
basis for comparison.

Our criterion for picking out these Old Testament passages for
special treatment is not our instinctive separating out of everything
supernatural or sacred, as one does when he puts everything involving
divine activity, other worlds, etc., into the category of myth. It
is not legitimate to do this unless we can show that the ancients
(Israelites and others) recognized such categories, and that I doubt.
Rather, our criterion is the observation that certain passages are
peculiar in the Old Testament in that they contain themes and images
which occur only a few times in its hundreds of pages. This is an
objective criterion since it is based on counting. Some of these
unusual passages may be of little importance for us; they may be
merely peculiar (e.g., Moses' circumcision, Ezekiel's statement
that God gave Israel laws that were not good). But our interest in
other passages will be heightened by the fact that certain themes
and images which are rare in the Old Testament are common elsewhere.
Then one is justified in looking for reasons why the material is
present in the Old Testament but not in the mainstream of its
testimony.

As we deal with the theme of hybris we find that several of
the most striking passages which are concerned with it use motifs
which never occur in the Old Testament outside of hybris passages,
and they are motifs which are common in other ancient Near Eastern
literature. It is because of this connection between hybris and
material which is common elsewhere but rare in the Old Testament
that such texts become of special interest to us.

Some scholars have studied these texts as a contribution to the
problem of myth, as they have understood it. Others have attempted
to explain the relationship of these passages to other literature in
terms of borrowing; asking where the Israelites got this material.
It has already been made clear that the philosophical problem of
myth is not central for us, but neither will hypothetical sources
concern us much either. It will be shown that the themes to be
discussed in this book are extremely common; they can be found almost

everywhere. So it will not be as surprising to find them in the
Old Testament as if something uniquely Egyptian, let us say (such
as the eye of Horus), appeared there. If it could be shown that
precisely the same form of a theme appeared both in the Old Testament and elsewhere then the question of borrowing would also be
important. That may indeed occur at times (e.g., the flood story),
but in the passages which will concern us no such clear relationships can be shown. And this is what we should expect, from the
results of studies of comparative folklore. Similar themes recur
again and again in folklore all over the world, but they are used
in different contexts, in free combination with other themes, and
they clearly do not always mean the same thing. Hence it appears
that what is significant is not so much something inherent in the
theme itself, nor the fact that the same theme appears in different
places, but how the theme is used in a given culture.

In chapters III-V we sort out those common "mythological"
themes from the great hybris passages of the Old Testament, look
for all possible parallels to each, and try to understand what each
theme meant in a given context. As we do this it will become
evident that there are certain distinctive teachings which may be
called the Old Testament view of man, as contrasted with views held
by other peoples. No attempt will be made to trace the history of
the sources used by the Old Testament writers, since our evidence
is insufficient for any secure conclusions about that. It will
simply be assumed that these themes were so well known in the
ancient East that they were available to anyone, perhaps in several
forms. Our working hypothesis will then be that the Old Testament
authors used these themes quite deliberately in order to say what
they believed, and that they used them because apparently such
language was the best or only way to convey precisely this belief
about man.

NOTES

NOTES TO THE PROLOGUE

1. B. Russell, Power, A New Social Analysis (New York, W. W. Norton, 1938), p. 11.

2. Genesis 3:5.

3. J.-P. Sartre, Being and Nothingness: An Essay on Phenomenological Ontology (New York, Philosophical Library, 1956), p. 566.

4. L. Feuerbach, Principles of the Philosophy of the Future, trans. M. H. Vogel (Indianapolis, Bobbs-Merrill, 1966), p. 58.

5. S. Freud, Civilization and Its Discontents (New York, W. W. Norton, 1962), p. 39.

6. Swinburne, Poems, selected and intro. by B. Dobrée (Baltimore, Penguin Books, 1961), p. 92.

7. In a work such as this the use of the word "man" over and over again in the generic sense is almost inescapable. To substitute "man and woman" or even "mankind" or "humankind" becomes inordinately clumsy when the term must be used so often, and unfortunately English does not possess a good equivalent to the Hebrew 'ādām or the Greek anthrōpos, which denote the human race, in contrast to 'ish and anēr, which mean "male". The reader is asked to think of the former, rather than the latter meaning whenever he or she sees "man" in the text.

8. For recent discussions of humanism from various Christian perspectives, note W. F. Albright, History, Archaeology and Christian Humanism (New York, McGraw-Hill, 1964); O. Guinness, The Dust of Death (Downers Grove, Ill., InterVarsity Press, 1973), Chap. I; R. L. Shinn, Man: The New Humanism (Philadelphia, Westminster Press, 1968).

9. M. Eliade, The Sacred and the Profane (New York, Harper, 1961), p. 203.

Notes to Pages 2-5

10. Oevres Complètes de P.-J. Proudhon, nouvelle ed. (Paris, 1959), Vol. 15, Écrits sur la Religion, Introduction par Th. Ruyssen, p. 45; A. Noland, "History and Humanity: The Proudhonian Vision," in The Uses of History, ed. H. V. White (Detroit, Wayne State University Press, 1968), pp. 66-72.

11. The New Humanist, 6, No. 3 (May-June, 1933), 2f. Cf. "The Humanist Manifesto: Twenty Years After," The Humanist, 13 (1953), 58-71.

12. Sartre's definition of God is, "the ideal of a consciousness which would be the foundation of its own being-in-itself by the pure consciousness which it would have of itself." Being and Nothingness, p. 566. Freud's comments which form the context of the quoted statement are, "Long ago he formed an ideal conception of omnipotence and omniscience which he embodied in his gods. . . . Today he has come very close to the attainment of this ideal, he has almost become a god himself. . . . Not completely; in some respects not at all, in others only half way." Civilization and Its Discontents, pp. 38f.

13. E. Fromm, You Shall Be As Gods: A Radical Interpretation of the Old Testament and Its Tradition (New York, Holt, Rinehart and Winston, 1966), pp. 22f.

14. Ibid., pp. 13, 81, 225f.

15. A. Camus, The Rebel: An Essay on Man in Revolt (New York, Knopf, 1957), p. 306.

16. Pascal's Pensées, with an English translation, brief notes and introduction by H. F. Stewart (New York, Pantheon Books, 1950), pp. 90-91.

17. Isthmian Odes, V, 14-16. Trans. J. E. Sandys, The Odes of Pindar (London, W. Heinemann, 1937), p. 473.

18. A. MacLeish, "When We Are Gods," Saturday Review 50 (Oct. 14, 1967), 22. Used by permission.

19. Ibid.

20. M. Muggeridge, "Men Like Gods," The Christian Century, 86 (Feb. 5, 1969), 176-178.

21. Quoted by Muggeridge, ibid., 176.

22. (New York, 1969).

23. Cf. a recent discussion from another point of view by
J. F. Priest, "Humanism, Skepticism, and Pessimism in Israel,"
JAAR 36 (1968), 311-326, emphasizing the Wisdom literature. A
work on a similar theme drawn on broader lines is K. Cragg's
The Privilege of Man: A Theme in Judaism, Islam and Christianity
(London, Athlone Press, 1968).

24. Parts of these chapters are based on work originally
done under the guidance of Professor J. Coert Rylaarsdam at the
Divinity School of the University of Chicago for my doctoral
dissertation, "The Significance of the Oracles against the Nations
in the Message of Ezekiel" (unpublished, 1964).

25. See especially R. Payne, Hubris; a Study of Pride, rev.
ed. (New York, Harper, 1960).

26. Quoted by R. Gordis in The Book of God and Man: A Study
of Job (Chicago, University of Chicago Press, 1965), p. 131. B.
Gemser says of the Old Testament that its view of man is not
singular but plural: humilitas and dignitas, vanitas and majestas,
pravitas and nobilitas, "Humilitas or Dignitas," in Adhuc Loquiter:
Collected Essays of Dr. B. Gemser, ed. A. van Selms and A. S. van
der Woude (Leiden, E. J. Brill, 1968), p. 75.

27. R. Jungk, Tomorrow Is Already Here (New York, Simon and
Schuster, 1954), quoted by W. G. Pollard in "God and His Creation,"
in This Little Planet, ed. M. Hamilton (New York, Scribner, 1970),
p. 68.

NOTES TO CHAPTER I

1. Greece is included because of our relatively full knowledge
of this culture (and because hybris is their own word), while the
Hittites are not included because little can be said as yet about
this aspect of their thinking. One must have devoted himself to the
study of these ancient peoples for a long time before he is able to
make a judgment about the general conception of man which they held.
The author's reading of as many texts as possible in translation
scarcely qualifies him to do this, so he is very strongly dependent,

in the first part of this chapter, on the opinions of men such as Wilson, Jacobsen and Kramer, whose years of work with the primary materials make their opinions worth respecting.

2. The many implications of Biblical humanism for modern theology have been surveyed by R. L. Shinn in _Man: The New Humanism_, "New Directions in Theology Today," 6 (Philadelphia, Westminster Press, 1968).

3. H. & H. A. Frankfort et. al., _The Intellectual Adventure of Ancient Man_ (Chicago, The University of Chicago Press, 1946), p. 96.

4. _Ibid._, p. 98.

5. H. Frankfort, _Ancient Egyptian Religion_ (New York, Columbia University Press, 1948), pp. 69f.

6. _Ibid._, p. 70.

7. J. Černý, _Ancient Egyptian Religion_ (London, Hutchinson's University Library, 1952), p. 67.

8. Cf. Frankfort, _Ancient Egyptian Religion_, p. 81.

9. _Intellectual Adventure_, pp. 106-117; Černý, pp. 68f.

10. _Intellectual Adventure_, pp. 113f.

11. Černý, _op. cit._, pp. 75f. In the light of this evidence Frankfort's statement that "the actions of individuals lacked divine guidance altogether," (_Ancient Egyptian Religion_, p. 81) probably needs to be restricted to the early periods.

12. The Instruction of Amenemope 19:14-17; translation from _Intellectual Adventure_, p. 115.

13. _Intellectual Adventure_, p. 117.

14. Note, however, some differences between the interpretations of sin given by Wilson, _Intellectual Adventure_, p. 116, and Frankfort, _Ancient Egyptian Religion_, pp. 73f., 77.

15. _ANET_, pp. 405, 407, 441, 444.

16. There is a description in the Pyramid Texts of the ferocity with which the dead Pharaoh makes a place for himself in the other world, but he is, after all, a god to begin with, so this cannot be called a case of human hybris. J. A. Wilson, The Burden of Egypt: The Culture of Ancient Egypt (Chicago, University of Chicago Press, 1951), pp. 85, 146f.; R. O. Faulkner, "The 'Cannibal Hymn' from the Pyramid Texts," JEA, 10 (1924), 97-103.

17. ANET, pp. 8, 366, 417.

18. A. Heidel, The Babylonian Genesis (2nd ed.; Chicago, University of Chicago Press, 1951), pp. 120f.; W. G. Lambert & A. R. Millard, Atra-Hasis: The Babylonian Story of the Flood (Oxford, Clarendon Press, 1969), p. 15.

19. S. N. Kramer, The Sumerians: Their History, Culture, and Character (Chicago, University of Chicago Press, 1963), p. 258.

20. T. Jacobsen, in Intellectual Adventure, pp. 202, 205.

21. Kramer, op. cit., p. 123.

22. Ibid., pp. 264ff.

23. Enuma Elish, The Myth of Zu, Atrahasis, and many other shorter works; cf. ANET, pp. 37-47, 52-57, 60-72, 103-109, 111-113.

24. ANET, pp. 434-440.

25. "The Etiological Myth of the 'Seven Sages'" Orientalia, N.S. 30 (1961), pp. 1-11.

26. ANET, p. 85.

27. ANET, pp. 83f.

28. ANET, p. 101.

29. ANET, pp. 93-95. Lambert's work on Atrahasis must now be the guide to any study of the flood traditions; supra, note 18.

30. Lambert, op. cit., p. 18.

31. Cf. the flood stories, the Erra myth, the Lamentation over the Destruction of Ur.

32. As in the end of the Gilgamesh Epic, where the magnificent walls of Eridu are his consolation for the loss of eternal life.

33. Cf. A. van Selms, *Marriage and Family Life in Ugaritic Literature* (London, Luzac, 1954); J. Gray, "Social Aspects of Canaanite Religion," *VTS* 15 (1966), 170-192.

34. A. S. Kapelrud, *The Violent Goddess: Anat in the Ras Shamra Texts* (Oslo, Universitetsforlaget, 1969), pp. 70-75.

35. *Nemean* vi. 1; translation from F. M. Cornford, *Greek Religious Thought from Homer to the Age of Alexander* (London, J. M. Dent, 1923), p. 116.

36. Other exceptions would be Plato's belief in the unity of all life (outside the main current of Greek thought, Cornford, *op. cit.*, p. xxiv) and the promise of the mystery religions to make the believer one with the deity.

37. M. P. Nilsson, *Greek Piety*, trans. H. J. Rose (Oxford, Clarendon Press, 1948), p. 20.

38. M. H. Jameson, in *Mythologies of the Ancient World*, ed. S. N. Kramer (Chicago, Quadrangle Books, 1961), pp. 248f.; G. Murray, *Five Stages of Greek Religion*, 3rd ed. (Boston, Beacon Press, 1952), pp. 45f.

39. Nilsson, *op. cit.*, p. 9f.

40. *Description of Greece* viii. *Arcadia* ii.4-5. Trans. W. H. S Jones, Loeb Classical Library (Cambridge, Mass., Harvard University Press, 1939), III, 353. A. W. H. Adkins, *From the Many to the One: A Study of Personality and Views of Human Nature in the Context of Ancient Greek Society, Values and Beliefs* (Ithaca, N.Y., Cornell University Press, 1970), p. 36, comments on Aristotle's reference to the deification of heroes as a common belief (Nicomachean Ethics, 1145a22).

41. W. K. C. Guthrie, *In the Beginning. Some Greek Views on the Origins of Life and the Early State of Man* (Ithaca, N.Y., Cornell University Press, 1957), chap. 4.

42. Hesiod *Works* 109-120.

43. *Ibid.*, 121ff.

44. Guthrie, op. cit., pp. 95; 69, 74-77.

45. Ibid., 96ff.

46. Since every creature except man was given the natural endowments to enable its species to survive. Ibid., pp. 86f.

47. Ibid., p. 82.

48. C. Kerényi, Prometheus: Archetypal Image of Human Existence, trans. R. Manheim (New York, Pantheon Books, 1963), pp. xxif., 53.

49. E.g., Alcman Partheneion i.8; Herodotus History vii.10; Sophocles Ajax 118; cf. E. R. Dodds, The Greeks and the Irrational (Berkeley, University of California Press, 1951), pp. 30f.; A. W. H. Adkins, op. cit., p. 86.

50. Dodds, op. cit., pp. 30f.; on the moralizing tendencies see C. H. Moore, The Religious Thought of the Greeks from Homer to the Triumph of Christianity (Cambridge, Harvard University Press, 1916), pp. 78-81, 87.

51. W. Jaeger, Paideia: The Ideals of Greek Culture, trans. G. Highet (New York, Oxford University Press, 1945), Vol. I, p. 103, n. 18.

52. Ibid., p. 168.

53. F. R. Walton, "Hybris," RGG[3], III, 497f.; G. Bertram, "Hybris," TDNT, VIII, 295-307; Nilsson, op. cit., pp. 52-59; Moore, op. cit., pp. 32f., 78-81, 86ff.; a book-length study by C. del Grande, Hybris, Colpa e castigo nell'espressione poetica e letteraria degli Scrittori della Grecia antica (Napoli, R. Ricciardi, 1947).

54. Op. cit., p. 53.

55. Ibid., p. 54.

56. Ibid., p. 57.

57. Ibid., p. 58.

58. Dodds, op. cit., p. 31.

59. Walton, RGG[3], III, 497f.

Notes to Pages 14-19

60. Cornford, op. cit., p. xix.

61. Nilsson, op. cit., pp. 58f.

62. Herodotus History vii.10; translation from Cornford, op. cit., p. 88.

63. J. A. Wilson, Intellectual Adventure, pp. 107f.

64. The mystery religions' offer of immortality while still on earth and the gnostic concept of the divine spark in man provide interesting exceptions to this statement, but they are too remote from the Old Testament temporally to be compared with it profitably. The deification of kings practiced in the Hellenistic-Roman period was almost exclusively political rather than religious in orientation but it is probably referred to in the book of Daniel (11:36ff.). On deification of kings cf. W. W. Tarn & G. T. Griffith, Hellenistic Civilisation, 3rd ed. (London, E. Arnold, 1952), pp. 52-55.

65. E.g., Heidel, op. cit., pp. 65, 67; Lambert, op. cit., pp. 57-65.

66. To the extent, at least, that man participated in the creation of the animals by giving them their names, Gen. 2:19f.

67. By that I mean to do more than to observe that there is a dependence on foreign materials and to try to identify them, as of course has been done for a long time.

NOTES TO CHAPTER II

1. E. König, Theologie des Alten Testaments (Stuttgart, Belser U.G., 1923); P. Heinisch & W. Heidt, Theology of the Old Testament (Collegeville, Minn., Liturgical Press, 1950); O. J. Baab, The Theology of the Old Testament (New York, Abingdon-Cokesbury, 1949); J. Barton Payne, The Theology of the Older Testament (Grand Rapids, Zondervan, 1962).

2. For a good, recent treatment of the subject, W. F. May, A Catalogue of Sins (New York, Holt, Rinehart and Winston, 1967), chap. 11.

3. (New York, 1953), pp. 186-203.

4. _Ibid._, p. 179; cf. pp. 188-194.

5. The few Old Testament theologies which do discuss the subject are, it will be noted, strongly influenced by the loci of dogmatics.

6. "Démesure et Chute dans l'Ancien Testament," in _Hommage a Wilhelm Vischer_ (Montpellier, Causse, Graille, Castelman, 1960), pp. 63-82.

7. R. Payne's equation of the two terms in his title, _Hubris; A Study of Pride_, thus has some historical justification. His book traces the theme of pride (meaning _hybris_) largely in literature and art from ancient Greece to modern times.

8. _Op. cit._, p. 188.

9. H. W. Robinson, _Inspiration and Revelation in the Old Testament_ (Oxford, Clarendon Press, 1946), pp. 14-15; e.g., "his face fell," Gen. 4:5.

10. See chapter five and the last part of this chapter.

11. Verb: Isa. 3:16; Jer. 13:15, 48:29; Ezek. 16:50, 28:2,5,17; Ps. 131:1; Prov. 18:12; 2 Chron. 17:6, 26:16, 32:25. Infinitive: Zeph. 3:11. Gābē(a)h: Ps. 101:5; Prov. 16:5; Eccl. 7:8. Gābō(a)h: 1 Sam. 2:3; Isa. 5:15. Gōbah: Ps. 10:4; Prov. 16:18; 2 Chron. 32:26. Gabhūt: Isa. 2:11,17. These references are all taken from Humbert's article.

12. Verb: Deut. 8:14, 17:20; Hos. 13:6; Ezek. 31:10; Dan. 11: 12,36. Rām: Exod. 14:8; Num. 15:30, 33:3; 2 Sam. 22:28; Isa. 2:12; Ps. 18:28; Prov. 6:17. Rūm: Isa. 2:11,17, 10:12; Jer. 48:29; Prov. 21:4; Rōmā: Mic. 2:3. Verb (hifil): Ps. 75:5,6.

13. Ga'awā: Isa. 9:8, 13:11, 16:6, 25:11; Jer. 48:29; Ps. 10:2, 31:19, 73:6; Prov. 29:23; Zeph. 3:11. Gē'ē: Isa. 2:12, 16:6; Jer. 48:29; Ps. 94:2, 140:6; Prov. 8:13, 15:25, 16:19; Job 40:11,12. Gē'ut: Ps. 17:10. Gā'ōn: Lev. 26:19; Am. 6:8; Hos. 5:5, 7:10; Isa. 13:11, 14:11, 16:6; Jer. 13:9, 48:29; Ezek. 16:56, 32:12; Zech. 9:6, 10:11; Ps. 123:4; Prov. 8:13, 16:18.

14. TDNT, VIII, 299. See also his article, "'Hochmut' und verwandte Begriffe im griechischen und hebräischen Alten Testament,"

WO 3 (1964), 32-43, in which he concludes that the LXX gives a relatively greater emphasis to the concept of hybris than the Hebrew Bible does.

15. D. Neiman, in a paper read to the Society of Biblical Literature in November of 1969, suggested that hnp might be close in meaning to the Greek hybris.

16. Op. cit., p. 67.

17. Pride is said to be Uzziah's downfall in 2 Chron. 26:16; "and when he was strong his heart was haughty." The downfall of Alexander is also introduced by "and when he was strong," Dan. 8:8. Presumably David could have been accused of hybris in the census incident (2 Sam. 24 = 1 Chron. 21), but he was not (Humbert, op. cit., p. 68).

18. Humbert, op. cit., p. 77. Note the rhetorical questions, "Who has . . . ?" in Job 9:4b, 41:3.

19. To be discussed in chapter four.

20. Op. cit., p. 70.

21. S. Thompson, Motif-Index of Folk-Literature (Bloomington, Indiana University Press, 1958), C54, C771.1, C771.2, F772.1. G. Fohrer, in Introduction to the Old Testament (Nashville, Abingdon Press, 1968), pp. 160-165, has proposed a hypothetical N-source in the Pentateuch which he believes came from the cattle raisers of southern Judah whose hostility toward civilization would explain the exmphasis of the three stories just mentioned. Its view of civilization is that when man begins to make progress he either goes astray or oversteps his limits and then God must intervene to restrain him.

22. Cf. J. Skinner, Genesis (ICC, 1910), pp. 223f.

23. L. Ginzberg, The Legends of the Jews (Philadelphia, The Jewish Publication Society of America, 1947), I, 179-181; V, 201-206.

24. J. G. Frazer, Folklore in the Old Testament, abridged ed. (New York, The Macmillan Company, 1927), chap. 5.

25. O. E. Ravn, "Der Turm der Babel," ZDMG 91 (1937), 352-372; N. H. Sarna, Understanding Genesis (New York, Jewish Theological Seminary of America, 1966), pp. 66-77.

26. E. G. H. Kraeling, "The Tower of Babel," _JAOS_ 40 (1920), 276-281.

27. M. Eliade, "The Yearning for Paradise in Primitive Tradition," in _Myth and Mythmaking_, ed. H. A. Murray (New York, G. Braziller, 1960), pp. 61-75.

28. H. Gunkel, _Genesis_ (6th ed., Göttingen, Vandenhoeck & Ruprecht, 1964), p. 96.

29. Gen. 11:1-9 is assigned to the Yahwistic document which traces the deepening predicament of man in his sinfulness from the sin in the Garden throughout the primal history; cf. G. von Rad, _Genesis_, trans. J. H. Marks (Philadelphia, 1961), pp. 148ff.

30. Sarna, _op. cit._, pp. 67, 72f.

31. One question which will be raised about this is whether the reference to Gen. 1:28, which is part of the Priestly, not the Yahwistic, document, is justifiable as providing the background of the story.

32. Von Rad, _op. cit._, pp. 145, 147.

33. _Ibid._, p. 145.

34. W. Zimmerli, _1. Mose 1-11, Die Urgeschichte_, 3rd ed. (Zürich, Zwingli-Verlag, 1967), pp. 400f.

35. Sarna, _op. cit._, pp. 74f.

36. Ravn, _op. cit._, pp. 358ff. Cf. Jer. 51:53.

37. Von Rad, _op. cit._, p. 146f.

38. D. D. Luckenbill, _Ancient Records of Assyria and Babylonia_ (Chicago, University of Chicago Press, 1926-27), II, 60.

39. _Ibid._, pp. 55f.

40. _Ibid._, p. 115f.

41. R. Labat, _Le caractére religieux de la royauté assyro-babylonienne_ (Paris, Librairie d'Amérique et d'Orient, 1939), pp. 253ff.

42. E. J. Banks, "Eight Oracular Responses to Esarhaddon," _AJSL_ 14 (1898), 267-277; G. Contenau, _La Divination chez les Assyriens et les Babyloniens_ (Paris, Payot, 1940), p. 128; F. Martin, _Textes religieux assyro-babyloniens_ (Paris, Letouzey et Ané, 1903), pp. 109-111.

43. M. Jastrow, _The Religion of Babylonia and Assyria_ (Boston, Ginn & Company, 1898), chap. 19; Labat, _op. cit._, pp. 255-257; F. Martin, _op. cit._, pp. 109-111, 301-307.

44. _The Book of Isaiah_, rev. ed. (New York, Harper and Brothers, n.d.) I, 171-182.

45. V. Herntrich, _Der Prophet Jesaja_, Kapitel 1-12 (_ATD_ 17, 1950), p. 197, accepts 16, uncertain whether 17-19 is a reworked Isaianic fragment or by a later author; A. Bentzen, _Introduction to the Old Testament_, 5th ed. (Copenhagen, G. E. C. Gad, 1959), II, 108, says it is difficult to abandon the tradition of Isaianic authorship of 5-18; O. Eissfeldt, _The Old Testament: An Introduction_ (New York, Harper and Row, 1965), p. 312, ascribes 16-23 to the early Isaiah, 5-15 to late in his ministry.

46. E.g., several accept all, or all except 12; doubts are often expressed about 10 and 11; some question 15. The most recent commentary, H. Wildberger, _Jesaja_ (_BKAT_ 10, 1970), pp. 390-393, accepts 5-9, 13b-15a.

47. Eissfeldt, _op. cit._, p. 329; J. Gray, _I and II Kings_ (Philadelphia, Westminster Press, 1963), p. 625.

48. Cf. this from an inscription of Sennacherib: "In the midst of the high mountains I rode on horseback, where the terrain was difficult, and had my chariot drawn up with ropes; where it became too steep, I clambered up on foot like the wild-ox." Luckenbill, _op. cit._, II, 117. That such texts were known to inhabitants of the Levant is proved by the discovery of a broken Sargon stele at Ashdod; M. Dothan, _Ashdod II-III_ (_'Atiqot_ 9-10; Jerusalem, 1971), pp. 193-197. Although inscribed in Akkadian, these texts surely must have been proclaimed aloud in the vernacular by royal officials so that all might know the greatness of their conqueror. This kind of language is not common in the Old Testament, but is almost confined to the book of Isaiah.

49. C. Westermann, _Basic Forms of Prophetic Speech_ (Philadelphia, Westminster Press, 1967), p. 143, cites this passage as a good example of the type in its expanded form.

50. H. W. Wolff, "Die Begründungen der prophetischen Heils-
und Unheilssprüche," ZAW 52 (1934), 18-22.

51. D. E. Gowan, "The Significance of the Oracles Against
the Nations in the Message of Ezekiel" (unpublished Ph.D. dissertation, University of Chicago, 1964), pp. 24-64.

52. G. von Rad, Der Heilige Krieg im alten Israel, 3rd ed.
(Göttingen, Vandenhoeck & Ruprecht, 1958), pp. 15-29. Cf. Judg.
4-5; 1 Sam. 11, 14-15.

53. Ibid., pp. 6-13. Cf. some qualifications of von Rad's
theory in R. Smend, Yahweh War and Tribal Confederation, trans.
M. G. Rogers (Nashville, Abingdon Press, 1970), chap. 2.

54. Especially 1 Kings 22, also 2 Kings 3:18-19, 6:8-10, 21-
22, 7:1, 13:15-19; Jer. 27. Additional evidence for special
functions of prophets in warfare in R. Bach, Die Aufforderungen
zur Flucht und zum Kampf im alttestamentlichen Prophetenspruch
(WMANT 9; Neukirchen, Kreis Moers, Neukirchener Verlag, 1962).

55. E.g., Isa. 13, 34; Ezek. 30.

56. The early date of this passage has been questioned by,
among others, G. Fohrer, "Remarks on Modern Interpretation of the
Prophets," JBL 80 (1961), 310; Introduction to the Old Testament,
p. 409; but the unity of vss. 1-34 has been upheld with impressive
arguments by A. Jepsen, Nabi (München, Beck, 1934), pp. 90f.; M.
Noth, Überlieferungsgeschichtliche Studien, 2nd ed. (Tübingen,
M. Niemeyer, 1957), I, 80, n. 1; N. H. Snaith (IB, 1954), III,
166; G. von Rad, Der Heilige Krieg, p. 54; and W. Zimmerli,
Erkenntnis Gottes nach dem Buche Ezechiel, ATANT 27 (Zürich,
Zwingli-Verlag, 1954), p. 18.

57. E. Würthwein, "Jesaja 7, 1-9. Ein Beitrag zu dem Thema:
Prophetie und Politik," in Theologie als Glaubenswagnis, Festschrift
für Karl Heim (Hamburg, Furche-Verlag, 1954), pp. 47-63; H. W.
Wolff, Frieden ohne Ende; Jesaja 7, 1-17 und 9, 1-6 ausgelegt (BS,
35; Neukirchen, Kreis Moers, 1962), pp. 18, 24ff.; G. von Rad, Der
Heilige Krieg, pp. 56-62.

58. J. A. Soggin, "Der prophetische Gedanke über den heiligen
Krieg, als Gericht gegen Israel," VT, 10 (1960), 79-83.

59. On pride see B. D. Napier, "Isaiah and the Isaian," VTS
15 (1966), 240-251; J. M. Ward, Amos and Isaiah (Nashville, Abingdon

Press, 1969), pp. 168-171; S. Erlandsson, The Burden of Babylon:
A Study of Isaiah 13:2-14:23, Coniectanea Biblica, OT Series 4
(Lund, Gleerup, 1970), pp. 139-142.

60. E.g., Sargon: "Before me Ursâ, the Armenian, who does
not respect (lit., guard) the word of Assur and Marduk, who does
not fear the curse of the lord of lords,--a mountaineer, of
murderous seed, who was without judgment, whose speech was evil,
whose lips kept bawling indecencies, who had no respect for the
honored name of Shamash, supreme judge of the gods, and who was
forever, without let-up, overstepping his bounds; after (all) his
earlier crimes (lit., sins), he committed the grievous (lit.,
great) offense of destroying this land and overwhelming its
people." Luckenbill, op. cit., II, 79.

61. Isaiah I-XXVII (ICC, 1912), p. 199. Questioned now by
Wildberger, BKAT 10, p. 392.

62. In addition to Westermann's emphasis on the originality
of the reason-judgment form in Basic Forms of Prophetic Speech,
note the discussion of the use of questions (such as occur in vs.
15) in the reason, pp. 142ff.

63. An excellent discussion of Isaiah's political counsel
appears in N. K. Gottwald, All the Kingdoms of the Earth (New York,
Harper and Row, 1964), pp. 147-208.

64. H. Junker, "Sancta Civitas, Jerusalem Nova," in Ekklesia,
Festschrift für Bischof Dr. Matthias Wehr (Trier, Paulinus-Verlag,
1962), pp. 17-33; R. Davidson, "The Interpretation of Isaiah II
6ff.," VT 16 (1966), 1-7.

65. R. B. Y. Scott, "Isaiah" (IB, 1956), V, 182f.; H. Wildberger, Jesaja (BKAT 10, Neukirchen Kreis Moers, Neukirchener
Verlag, 1966), pp. 95f.

66. G. B. Gray, ICC, pp. 48f.; V. Herntrich, ATD 17, pp. 34f.

67. Well-done in Wildberger's commentary, op. cit.

68. J. M. P. Smith, "The Day of Yahweh," AJT 5 (1901), 512;
G. von Rad, "The Origin of the Concept of the Day of Yahweh," JSS
4 (1959), 97-108. Erlandsson, op. cit., pp. 146-153, thinks the
term is too broad to be associated unilaterally with holy war and
emphasizes especially its connections with pride.

69. Wildberger, op. cit., p. 108.

70. H. G. Wells, "The Man Who Could Work Miracles."

71. Paraphrasing Herntrich, op. cit., p. 38.

72. Other references to nations and kings: Isa. 13:11, 16:6; Jer. 48:26,42; Zeph. 2:8,10; Dan. 8:25, 11:36-39. Note also the condemnations of Nineveh and Babylon for the attitude expressed by "I am and there is none else." Zeph. 2:15, Isa. 47:10.

NOTES TO CHAPTER III

1. E.g., W. H. Cobb, "The Ode in Isaiah xiv," JBL 15 (1896), 18-35; H. L. Ginsberg, "Reflexes of Sargon in Isaiah After 715 B.C.E.," JAOS 88 (1968), 49-53; Erlandsson, op. cit., pp. 111-114, 160-166. Arguments against: Babylon (vs. 4a) an anachronism, vocabulary includes late elements, nationalistic tone. Arguments for: similarity to 10:5ff., emphasis on downfall of the proud, literary quality.

2. L. S. Chafer, Systematic Theology (Dallas, Dallas Seminary Press, 1947) II, 33-50. This is not a standard position for conservative theology; cf. E. J. Young, The Book of Isaiah (Grand Rapids, Eerdmans, 1965) I, 441.

3. Against Marcion V, 11 and 17; justified traditionally by combining Isa. 14:12 with Luke 10:18. Cf. K. L. Schmidt, "Lucifer als gefallene Engelmacht," TZ 7 (1951), 161-179. Early occurrences in Vita Adae et Evae 15:3, Slavonic Enoch (A text) 29:4-5.

4. "The exposition of this passage, which some have given, as if it referred to Satan, has arisen from ignorance; for the context plainly shows that these statements must be understood in reference to the king of the Babylonians. But when passages of Scripture are taken up at random, and no attention is paid to the context, we need not wonder that mistakes of this kind frequently arise. Yet it was an instance of very gross ignorance, to imagine that Lucifer was the king of devils, and that the Prophet gave him this name. But as these inventions have no probability whatever, let us pass by them as useless fables." Commentary on the Book of the Prophet Isaiah (Grand Rapids, Eerdmans, 1948), p. 442.

Notes to Pages 46-48

5. B. S. Childs, <u>Myth and Reality in the Old Testament</u>, <u>SBT</u>, 27 (London, 1960), p. 70.

6. Some of the suggestions for rearrangement (often including emendations of individual words which will not be noted here): 17c, 18c; 18a, 18b (Cheyne, Marti, Procksch); 17c, . . . ; 18a, . . . ; 18b, 18c; 19a, 19b; 20b - 21d; 19c, 19d; 19e, . . . ; 20a, 19f (Dumont-Sommer, "Note exégétique sur Isaïe 14,16-21," <u>RHR</u> 134 [1947/48], 72-80); 18a, 19e; 18b, 18c; 19a, 19b; 19c-d, 19f (L. Alonso Schökel, <u>Estudios de Poética Hebrea</u> [Barcelona, J. Flors, 1963], p. 413); 19a, 19d; 19e, 19f; . . . , 19b; . . . 19c (Duhm).

7. Cf. O. Eissfeldt, <u>Der Maschal im Alten Testament</u>, BZAW 24 (Giessen, A. Töpelmann, 1913); A. R. Johnson, "Māshāl," <u>VTS</u> 3 (1955) 162-169; A. H. Herbert, "The 'Parable' (māsāl) in the Old Testament," <u>Scottish Journal of Theology</u> 7 (1954), 180-196.

8. H. Jahnow, <u>Das Hebräische Leichenlied</u>, BZAW 36 (Giessen, A. Töpelmann, 1923), pp. 242-250; P. Lohmann, <u>Die anonymen Prophetien gegen Babel aus der Zeit des Exils</u> (Berlin, 1910).

9. K. Budde, "Das Hebräische Klagelied," <u>ZAW</u> 2 (1882), 1-52. Most of the following comparison of Isa. 14:4ff. with the dirge is based on Jahnow's work.

10. Notes on the translation: Vs. 4b: Usually madhēbā is emended to marhēbā "storming", since the root dhb has been unknown. However, it occurs twice in the Hodayoth from Qumran (III, 25 and XII, 18) and once in the Damascus Document (XIII, 9), so the existence of the root ought not to be denied, and it is here assumed that the LXX epispoudastēs is a reasonably accurate translation of the Hebrew. Cf. H. M. Orlinsky, <u>JQR</u> 43 (1952-53), 335f., <u>VT</u> 7 (1957), 202f.; H. L. Ginsberg, <u>JAOS</u> 88 (1968), p. 53, n. 38; Erlandsson, <u>op. cit.</u>, pp. 29-32. Vs. 6: Accepting the common emendation mirdath for murdāph. Vs. 12: hōlēš is probably not from the same root as the adjective meaning "weak" (Exod. 32:18; Joel 4:10); cf. A. Guillaume, <u>JTS</u> NS 14 (1963), 91f. The parallelism has led to the acceptance of I. Eitan's conjecture that the LXX "depart, disappear" and the cognate Arabic root "snatch away, carry off" point to the correct meaning here. He suspects the Arabic vernacular hls "reap with a sickle" to be a loan word from ancient Hebrew without the usual interchange of sin and shin, and although this is conjectural the rendering "reaper" provides an excellent parallel to "felled" in the first half of the line; <u>A Contribution to Biblical Lexicography</u> (New York, Columbia University Press, 1924), pp. 42ff. Vs. 14: The usual translation "heights" may very well

be correct, but several modern scholars prefer "back". Ginsberg,
op. cit., p. 51; M. Dahood, Biblica 44 (1963), 302. Vs. 17:
Accepting the common emendation to a feminine pronoun, to agree
with "world"; although "he ruined his cities" may not be as
completely out of the question as some have suggested. Pointing
pth as a piel, with many commentators. Vs. 21: This rendering
of the last line is suggested very diffidently, following Ginsberg
and earlier Jewish commentators who point out that ml' is qal and
that as a contrast to vs. 17 this is a natural reading. The usual
"and fill the face of the world with cities" has led many to drop
the last word or emend it to "ruins" or "tyrants".

11. By Gruppe in 1883, according to W. Baumgartner, "Israel-
itisch-Griechische Sagenbeziehungen," in Zum Alten Testament und
seiner Umwelt (Leiden, Brill, 1959), p. 157.

12. E.g., H. Gressmann, Der Messias (Göttingen, Vandenhoeck,
1929), p. 165f.

13. Schöpfung und Chaos (Göttingen, Vandenhoeck, 1895), p.
134.

14. Vs. 12: a deity named Shaḥar appears in Ras Shamra text
52. Vs. 13: bᵉhar mōʿēd is similar to Ug. pḫr mʿd, used three
times in text 137 of the assembly of the gods on Mount Lala; yarkᵉthē
ṣāphōn is identical in meaning to bṣrtt ṣpn, the site of
Baal's throne in 49:I,29,34. Ṣpn has been identified with the
present Mt. Casios in Syria. Vs. 14: the translation of bmh as
"back" is supported by the designation of Baal as one who "mounts
the clouds", (rkb ʿrpt, text 68:9); the divine name Elyon is not
found at Ugarit but has appeared in Syria on the Sfire-Sudjin stele
I, in a long list of pairs of gods who are witnesses to the treaty,
in the form ʿl wʿlwn (line 11).

15. G. Quell, "Jesaja 14, 1-23," in Festschrift Friedrich Baum-
gärtel, ed. J. Herrmann & L. Rost (Erlangen, Universitätsbund
Erlangen, 1959), pp. 156f.; W. F. Albright, Yahweh and the Gods of
Canaan (London, Athlone Press, 1968), pp. 201f.

16. P. Grelot, "Isäie XIV, 12-15 et son arriere-plan mytholo-
gique," RHR 149 (1956), 18-48. An attempt by U. Oldenburg to reinforce Grelot's theory, "Above the Stars of El: El in Ancient South
Arabic Religion," ZAW 82 (1970), 187-208, has added more information
about Athtar in South Arabia but must still admit there is no trace
of the myth presumed to lie behind Isa. 14; pp. 203f., 207f.

Notes to Pages 51-52

17. The root <u>hll</u> is evidently related to Akkadian <u>ellu</u> "bright" and Arabic <u>hll</u> "begin to shine", and the probable correctness of the Masoretic vocalization has been upheld by Grelot, <u>VT</u> 6 (1956), 303f., following von Soden. The word <u>shaḥar</u> commonly means "dawn" in the Old Testament, however it has been suggested that Amos 4:13; Job 3:9, 38:12 contain reminiscences of its use as a divine name.

18. In Hesiod's <u>Theogony</u> 986f. Phaethon is the son of Eos and Kephalos. All that is said of him is that he was ravished by Aphrodite who made him the nocturnal acolyte in her temple. The parents of the Phaethon who drove the sun's chariot were Helios and Klymene; cf. Grelot, <u>RHR</u> 149 (1956), 25-32.

19. Told in its fullest form in Ovid <u>Metamorphosae</u> ii. 19ff. Nicely summarized with parallels by J. G. Frazer in <u>Apollodorus</u> (Loeb Classical Library, 1946), II, 388-394. Another effort to connect Isa. 14 with Greek myth has been made by J. W. McKay, "Helel and the Dawn-goddess," <u>VT</u> 20 (1970), 451-464; but see P. C. Craigie, "Helel, Athtar and Phaethon (Jes. 14:12-15)" <u>ZAW</u> 85 (1973), 223-225.

20. D. Nielsen, <u>Ras Schamra Mythologie und biblische Theologie</u> (Leipzig, Deutsche morgenländische gesellschaft, in Kommission bei F. A. Brockhaus, 1936), p. 58.

21. A. Caquot, "Le dieu 'Athtar et les texts de Ras Shamra," <u>Syria</u> 35 (1958), 48-51.

22. Grelot, <u>RHR</u> 149 (1956), 32ff.; J. Gray, <u>The Legacy of Canaan</u>, 2nd ed.; <u>VTS</u> 5 (Leiden, Brill, 1965), p. 170, believe he is; Caquot, <u>op. cit.</u>, 55-59 believes he is basically a fertility deity and his astral characteristics are secondary.

23. Nielsen, <u>op. cit.</u>, pp. 53ff.

24. Gunkel, <u>Schöpfung und Chaos</u>, p. 133; Childs, <u>op. cit.</u>, p. 69.

25. So Gray, <u>Legacy</u>, p. 288, n. 1, and M. C. Astour, <u>Hellenosemitica</u> (Leiden, Brill, 1965), p. 270, n. 1, have commented on Grelot's interpretation of the text as a case of <u>hybris</u>. Slightly different interpretations of the same passage by Albright, <u>op. cit.</u>, p. 201; Caquot, <u>op. cit.</u>, pp. 58f.

26. S. Thompson, <u>Motif-Index of Folk-Literature</u>, A781, A781.1, F383.4.2.

27. *Ibid.*, A106, A162.

28. See R. Luyster, "The Study of Myth: Two Approaches," *JBR* 34 (1966), 235-243, for a convenient, brief summary of the problem.

29. The new interest in tracing connections between Greece and the Semitic world is exemplified by C. Gordon, *Before the Bible: The Common Background of Greek and Hebrew Civilisations* (New York, Harper, 1962); M. Astour, *Hellenosemitica*.

30. This touches on another debate, that of Lévi-Strauss with Jung, summarized by R. Cooley, "Jung, Levi-Strauss and the Interpretation of Myth," *Criterion* (University of Chicago) 8 (1968-69), 12-16.

31. In a recent book dealing entirely with the question of derivation, P. Walcot, *Hesiod and the Near East* (Cardiff, Wales U. P., 1966), occasional statements are made concerning the change in meaning of symbols, pp. 25f., 136, n. 39.

32. Cf. the references in Cooley, *op. cit.*, 12f.

33. E.g., in tree symbolism, see Chap. V.

34. H. Frankfort, *The Problem of Similarity in Ancient Near Eastern Religions* (Oxford, Clarendon Press, 1951).

35. After developing this method of dealing with mythological materials I was pleased to read the following comments by H. Ringgren in "Remarks on the Method of Comparative Mythology," *Near Eastern Studies in Honor of William Foxwell Albright* (Baltimore, Johns Hopkins Press, 1971), pp. 410f.: "It is obvious that certain mythical elements can be present in various mythologies without the myths themselves being identical as totalities. One element—which obviously must be supposed to express a certain limited idea—can be combined with one set of elements in one religion and with other sets of elements in other religions. . . . It seems important for an analysis to break down the myths into small units and to ascertain where these units occur. It is also necessary to pay attention to the way these units are combined with one another, that is, to study the patterns and structures they form together with other units."

36. W. von Soden, "Eine altassyrische Beschwörung gegen die Dämonin Lamastum," *Orientalia*, NS 25 (1956), 141-148. My translation from von Soden's German rendering. An earlier partial translation of the text appeared in J. Lewy, "Les Textes paleo-assyriens et l'Ancien Testament," *RHR* 110 (1934), 41.

37. *Iliad* xix. 83ff.

38. Hephaestus fell from the heavenly realm twice (*Iliad* i. 590ff.), but for different reasons. At birth he was dropped from Olympus by Hera because he was weak and sickly, but later he returned. Once he took his mother's part in a quarrel with Zeus, and the latter seized him by the leg and threw him down, but again he returned and mediated the quarrel between mother and father.

39. *ANET*, p. 120.

40. E. Reiner, *Orientalia*, NS 30 (1961), 4.

41. *ANET*, pp. 114-118; J. V. K. Wilson, "Some Contributions to the Legend of Etana," *Iraq* 31 (1969), 8-17.

42. *Ibid.*, 15-17.

43. Frazer, *Apollodorus*, II, p. 139.

44. A similar story is that of Helle, who with her brother Phrixus flew away from danger on the back of the ram with the golden fleece, but she fell into the sea, which was named after her—Hellespont (*Apollodorus*, I, pp. 75ff.).

45. A series of remarkable American Indian parallels is related by Frazer in *Apollodorus*, II, pp. 388-394.

46. Euripides, *fragments*, 285, 286, 306-308. Discussion of various forms of the story in Astour, *op. cit.*, pp. 266f.

47. Although as Pindar put it the last statement might almost apply: " . . . who would fain have gone to the homes of heaven and the goodly company of Zeus." *Isthmian Odes* vii. 45ff., trans. J. Sandys (Loeb Classical Library, 1937).

48. Trips back and forth from the netherworld by certain deities do include ascents to heaven, but these are not significant parallels at this point and will be discussed under the theme "Descent into Sheol".

49. M. Eliade, *Myths, Dreams and Mysteries*, pp. 99-107, distinquishes the two groups of material involving on the one hand horizontal flight, as escape; and on the other vertical flight, as ascent to heaven.

50. Helle, on a ram with golden fleece; Idas, on a winged chariot; Abaris, on a golden arrow; discussed by Astour, _op. cit._, pp. 272-275, 282f.

51. A similar expression appears in Amarna letter 264 (Knudtzon's numbering), translated by H. Winckler, "Whether we mount up to heaven or descend to earth, our head is still in your hand," _The Tell-El-Amarna Letters_ (New York, Lemcke & Buechner, 1896), p. 317, his number 189.

52. _ANET_, pp. 101-103; T. Jacobsen, "The Investiture and Anointing of Adapa in Heaven," _AJSL_ 46 (1929-30), 201-203; F. M. T. deL. Böhl, "Die Mythe vom weisen Adapa," _WO_ 2 (1959), 416-431; G. Roux, "Adapa, Le Vent et l'Eau," _RA_ 55 (1961), 13-33.

53. Roux, _op. cit._, 13-26.

54. _ANET_, p. 102a.

55. Storming of heaven does occur elsewhere, as illustrated by Frazer's American Indian examples (_Apollodorus_, II, 318-326), but on quite a different level from the cases we have been considering.

56. The ascent and descent of the heavenly redeemer in Gnostic myths is too far removed from the concerns expressed by the materials discussed here to be worth including.

57. T. Jacobsen, "Primitive Democracy in Mesopotamia," _JNES_ 2 (1943), 159-172; Ras Shamra text 137 (_ANET_, p. 130).

58. This passage has been used to support the theory that the prophets did believe that they had been admitted to the divine council and received their messages there, but it is not strong support, for all Jeremiah does is deny that certain men have listened in the council. J. F. Ross, "The Prophet as Yahweh's Messenger," in _Israel's Prophetic Heritage_, ed. B. Anderson & W. Harrelson (New York, Harper, 1962), pp. 98-107.

59. Such worthies as Utnapishtim and Atrahasis only learn the decisions of the divine assembly when a personal god leaks the news to them, _ANET_, pp. 93a; Lambert & Millard, _Atra-hasis_, p. 89.

60. Nielsen, _op. cit._, p. 47. Albright, _op. cit._, p. 202, translates "circumpolar stars", comparing the expression to the Egyptian conception that the stars which never set represent eternity.

Notes to Pages 59-62

The Targum, which does a broad de-mythologizing job on this passage, substitutes "people of God", J. F. Stenning, The Targum of Isaiah (Oxford, Clarendon Press, 1949).

61. G. Fohrer, Das Buch Jesaja (Stuttgart, 1960), I, 172.

62. "Back": Albright, op. cit., p. 202; Dahood, Biblica 44 (1963), 302; Ginsberg, op. cit., 51; most others translate "height". Targum: "I will ascend above all the people; I will be higher than all of them."

63. A. S. Kapelrud, Baal in the Ras Shamra Texts (Copenhagen, Gad, 1952), pp. 98f.

64. Nonnos Dionysiaca vi. 155-175, x. 293-297.

65. H. G. Güterbock, "Hittite Mythology," in Mythologies of the Ancient World, ed. S. N. Kramer, pp. 161-164.

66. Cf. the varying judgments of M. H. Pope, El in the Ugaritic Texts (VTS 2, 1955), pp. 27ff.; Kapelrud, Baal, pp. 98-109; Gray, Legacy, op. cit., pp. 154-169.

67. ANET, pp. 111-113, 515f.; ANES, pp. 514-517.

68. T. Fish, "The Zu Bird," BJRL 31 (1948), 162-171.

69. ANET, pp. 112b-113a.

70. Grelot, op. cit., pp. 32-42; cf. Albright, op. cit., p. 201.

71. Caquot, op. cit., 46f., 53f.; Gray, Legacy, p. 288, n. 1; Astour, op. cit., p. 270, n. 1.

72. Kapelrud, Baal, 99-103, believes that Yam is put up against Baal in an effort to regain El's throne, but that Mot and Athtar belong to a different pattern.

73. H. G. Güterbock, "The Hittite Version of the Hurrian Kumarbi Myths: Oriental Forerunners of Hesiod," AJA 52 (1948), 123-134; Walcot, op. cit.; Astour, op. cit., pp. 217ff.

74. ANET, p. 120.

75. AJA 52 (1948), 123-134.

76. ANET, pp. 121-125.

77. Lines 820-880; cf. N. O. Brown, Hesiod's Theogony (New York, Liberal Arts Press, 1953), p. 12, with Walcot, op. cit., pp. xiif.

78. Pope, op. cit., pp. 29ff.; Kapelrud, Baal, p. 103.

79. Gray, Legacy, pp. 154f.

80. Grelot, op. cit., p. 43; Nielsen, op. cit., pp. 106f., cf. note 72 above.

81. Cf. note 55 above.

82. Iliad xxiv. 605-612; Odyssey viii. 223-228; Apollodorus I.iii, 3-4; I.iv,2; Nonnus Dionysiaca i.486ff.; Statius Thebaid x.827-939.

83. C. Kerényi, Prometheus: Archetypal Image of Human Existence, offers a Jungian interpretation which makes of Prometheus an expression of the condition of man; cf. pp. 44f., 77f., 99.

84. Gilgamesh, X.iii,3-5; ANET, p. 90.

85. Inanna: ANET, pp. 52-57; Ishtar: ANET, pp. 106-109; Kore: the Homeric Hymn to Demeter contains the basic myth.

86. ANES, pp. 507-512.

87. ANET, p. 52, n. 6; cf. S. N. Kramer, "Dumuzi's Annual Resurrection: An Important Correction to 'Inanna's Descent'," BASOR 183 (1966), 31.

88. ANET, pp. 87, 97ff.

89. Cf. ANET, pp. 109f.; A. Heidel, The Gilgamesh Epic and Old Testament Parallels (Chicago, University of Chicago Press, 1949), pp. 119-223, has translated and commented on most of the relevant materials.

NOTES TO CHAPTER IV

1. See above, p. 45.

2. "In these words, and those which immediately follow, the boasting is so absurd that it is impossible to believe that they proceeded from the lips of a mortal man; but as the Prophet did not intend to quote the very words which Nebuchadnezzar employed, let us be satisfied with examining the subject itself." J. Calvin, <u>Commentary on the Book of the Prophet Isaiah</u> (Grand Rapids, Eerdmans, 1948), p. 443.

3. See the Prologue.

4. See above, p. 33.

5. D. E. Gowan, "The Use of <u>ya'an</u> in Biblical Hebrew," <u>VT</u> 21 (1971), 168-185.

6. Cf. the book of Malachi for the use of the diatribe form.

7. For two very different efforts to improve the poem, one based on rearrangement and the other on deletion, cf. Jahnow, <u>Das Hebräische Leichenlied</u>, pp. 222f. and W. Zimmerli, <u>Ezechiel</u> (<u>BKAT</u> 13, 1969), pp. 676-680.

8. Jahnow, <u>op. cit.</u>, p. 228.

9. C. Mackay, "The King of Tyre," ChQR, 117 (1934), 239-58; and J. Dus, "Melek Ṣor--Melqart?" <u>Archiv Orientalni</u> 26 (1958), 179-85, think the first poem refers to the king, the second to the god Melqart.

10. E.g., Zimmerli, <u>BKAT</u>, p. 662.

11. The only occurrences of ḥokmā in Ezekiel are in chap. 28; twice in vss. 11-19 and three times in vss. 1-10. The words yōpī and r^ekullā occur twice each in vss. 11-19 and once each in vss. 1-10, while the former occurs three times in chap. 27 and an alternate form of the latter ten times. The expression gābah lēb occurs in 28:2,5, and 17, while the only occurrences of yip'ătekā are in 28:7 and 17. Other relationships with chap. 27 are kālīl (27:3,4, 11; 28:12 and 'eben y^ekārā (27:22; 28:13).

12. Although Ezekiel's ministry was to the exiles, according
to the testimony of his book, much of chapters 4-24 concerns
Jerusalem directly. This was seen as a serious problem by a
generation of scholars, from G. Hölscher, Hesekiel, der Dichter
und das Buch, BZAW 39 (Giessen, A. Töpelmann, 1924) to H. G. May,
"Ezekiel" (IB 6, 1956), and an original Judean setting for these
oracles was proposed by many. The work of C. G. Howie, The Date
and Composition of Ezekiel (JBL Monograph Series, 4; 1950) and
G. Fohrer, Die Hauptprobleme des Buches Ezechiel, BZAW 72 (Giessen,
A. Töpelmann, 1952) has provided a firm basis for the traditional
date and setting of the prophet's ministry, and it may be seen
that his words to and concerning Jerusalem had a direct and
crucial relevance for the exiles. As the book of Jeremiah shows
(e.g., chap. 7) faith in Yahweh tended to take the form of faith
in his temple, his city and his land. Ezekiel realized that if
there was to be any hope for the survival of a Yahwistic faith
after the impending fall of Jerusalem there must be a release
from this attachment to the holy city, and much of his work was
dedicated to that aim. Cf. W. Eichrodt, Ezekiel (Philadelphia,
Westminster Press, 1970), pp. 7-11.

13. Cf. chap. 26 on impregnability and 27 on wealth. Since
Hölscher the opinions which have been expressed about the authorship of Ezekiel have varied widely, from rejection of all but a
few verses to acceptance of most of the book. Nearly all have
ascribed at least part of vss. 11-19 to Ezekiel; as justification
for my treatment of both oracles as being for the most part the
work of Ezekiel see the reasons given in the text and the commentaries of Fohrer, Eichrodt, Zimmerli and Wevers.

14. Difficulties for this theory are created by the presence
of the date in 26:1, the appearance of two oracles against Ammon,
and the presence in chap. 28 of an oracle against a seventh nation
(Sidon) which is not in the "because . . . therefore" form. But
the very close similarities of form and content of the seven listed
above still lead us to consider them together, even though there
may be doubts about whether they originated as a separate series.

15. Chap. 35 contains what appear to be two doublets of the
Edom oracle in 25:12-14 so would be included with the materials
just described. Partial parallels to this point of view occur in
36:2-4, 6-7, 13-14.

16. G. von Rad, "The Origin of the Concept of the Day of
Yahweh," JSS 4 (1959), 97-108.

Notes to Pages 73-75

17. Compare the theme of creation, which has played such an important role in Christian theology but which is given no more and perhaps less attention in extended Old Testament passages than is the hybris of nations.

18. Notes on the translation: Vs. 12b: ḥōtēm toknīt has been much disputed and its meaning remains uncertain. The most common interpretation, which emends to ḥōtam taknīt, has been accepted, cf. G. R. Driver, Biblica 35 (1954), 158f. Vs. 13: The translation assumes the root of mᵉsukāteka to be sūk. Whether it is intended to describe a bejeweled garment or something else remains uncertain; cf. H. J. Van Dijk, Ezekiel's Prophecy on Tyre, "Biblica et Orientalia," 20 (Rome, Pontifical Biblical Institute, 1968), pp. 116-118. The appropriate translation of most of the precious stones mentioned in the Bible remains very uncertain; see J. S. Harris, "The Stones of the High Priest's Breastplate," ALUOS 5 (1963-65), 40-62; W. H. Schoff, The Ship "Tyre" (New York, Longmans, Green, 1920), pp. 117-134. Purely for the sake of consistency the LXX has been followed here, since anglicized forms of these Greek words are currently used as names for gem stones. But this is not to imply that the modern terms are exact equivalents of the Hebrew words. The identifications of gem stones in antiquity varied greatly, as a comparison of ancient versions of, and references to, Exod. 28 and Ezek. 28 will show. I have given up as hopeless the effort to understand tuppēkā and nᵉqābēkā and have simply transliterated them. Vs. 14: Although several scholars accept the MT, which identifies the king with the cherub, the translation agrees with those who believe 'at must be emended to 'ēt, for reasons given in the text. The verbs of this verse cannot be translated without some emendation, but if the first word is read as the preposition "with" then the verse can be made sense of if the conjunction is dropped from nᵉtattīkā. Vs. 16: MT can scarcely be translated. Emendations proposed by BH3 have been accepted.

19. M. Pope, El in the Ugaritic Texts, pp. 12, 98, compares vs. 2 to El's dwelling "at the confluence of the two streams in the midst of the source of the two deeps." For Daniel, read here as Danel since it is probably a reference to the figure known from the Ugaritic texts, see M. Noth, "Noah, Daniel und Hiob in Ezechiel xiv," VT 1 (1951), 251-60.

20. O. Procksch, Geschichtsbetrachtung und geschichtliche Ueberlieferung bei den vorexilischen Propheten (Leipzig, Hinrichs, 1902), pp. 161-64; J. L. McKenzie, "Mythological Allusions in Ezek. 28:12-18," JBL 75 (1956), 322-27; H. G. May, "The King in the Garden of Eden: A Study of Ezekiel 28:12-19," in Israel's Prophetic Heritage, ed. B. W. Anderson & W. Harrelson, pp. 168f.

21. I. G. Matthews, _Ezekiel_, "An American Commentary on the Old Testament," (Philadelphia, The American Baptist Publication Society, 1939), p. 105; K. Yaron, "The Dirge over the King of Tyre," _ASTI_ 3 (1964), 51-54.

22. J. Skinner, _The Book of Ezekiel_, "The Expositors' Bible," (New York, Armstrong & Son, 1895), p. 257; G. Fohrer, _Ezechiel_ (_HAT_ 13, 1955), p. 162.

23. H. Gunkel, _Genesis_ (_HKAT_ 1, 2nd ed., 1902), p. 32.

24. _HAT_, p. 162.

25. P. Humbert, "Emploi et portée du verbe bārā (créer) dans l'Ancien Testament," in _Opuscules d'un Hébraïsant_ (Neuchatel, Secrétariat de L'Université, 1958), pp. 146-65. Most interpreters believe the subject to be the first man; those who do not, take it to be Melqart: Mackay, _op. cit._, Dus, _op. cit._; or otherwise identify it with the cherub: G. Widengren, _The Ascension of the Apostle and the Heavenly Book_, "Uppsala Universitets Arsskrift," 7 (Uppsala, Ludenquistska bokhandeln, 1950), pp. 94-97, T. H. Gaster, _Myth, Legend and Custom in the Old Testament_ (New York, Harper & Row, 1969), pp. 621-24.

26. A. Bentzen, _King and Messiah_ (London, Lutterworth, 1955), chap. 5, identified king and First Man with _Urmensch_, and was severely criticized for this by S. Mowinckel, "Urmensch und 'Königsideologie'," _StTh_ 2 (1948), 71-89. In "King Ideology--'Urmensch'--'Troonsbestijgingsfeest'," _StTh_ 3 (1950), 148-53, Bentzen agreed that his terminology ought to be corrected and "Urmensch" replaced by "First Created Man". I. Engnell, "Die Urmenschvorstellung und das Alte Testament," _Svensk Exegetisk Arsbok_ 22-23 (1957-58), 265-89, also concluded that the two concepts must be kept separate.

27. Mowinckel, _op. cit._, p. 71f.

28. _Ibid._

29. Engnell, _op. cit._, pp. 268, 289.

30. C. J. Gadd remarked about the "unevenness" in the ancient accounts of the creation of man in _Ideas of Divine Rule in the Ancient East_ (London, Oxford University Press, 1948), p. 3.

31. H. Frankfort, _Ancient Egyptian Religion_, pp. 50f., 131f.

Notes to Pages 76-79

32. R. T. Rundle Clark, <u>Myth and Symbol in Ancient Egypt</u>
(New York, Grove Press, 1960), p. 91. A useful survey of the
kinds of statements that are made about man in Egyptian texts
is made by E. Otto, "Der Mensch als Geschöpf und Bild Gottes in
Ägypten," in <u>Probleme biblischer Theologie</u>. Gerhard von Rad zum
70. Geburtstag. Ed. H. W. Wolff (München, C. Kaiser, 1971), pp.
335-348.

33. <u>ANET</u>, p. 43.

34. S. N. Kramer, <u>Sumerian Mythology</u>, rev. ed. (New York,
1961), pp. 70-71.

35. <u>Ibid.</u>, pp. 72f.

36. <u>ANET</u>, p. 68.

37. <u>Ibid.</u>, p. 99.

38. <u>Ibid.</u>, p. 100.

39. Heidel, <u>Babylonian Genesis</u>, p. 70. A collection of
Babylonian creation stories is to be found on pp. 61-81 of this
work.

40. <u>Ibid.</u>, p. 68.

41. Eusebii Pamphili <u>Evangelicae Praeparationis</u>, trans. E. H.
Gifford, i (Oxford, Clarendon Press, 1903), p. 10.

42. 1 Krt 37, 43, 136, 151, 278.

43. Pope, <u>op. cit.</u>, pp. 49-54.

44. <u>ANET</u>, p. 38, ll. 13-25.

45. <u>Ibid.</u>, p. 40, l. 172; S. N. Kramer, "Dilmun: Quest for
Paradise," <u>Antiquity</u> 37 (1963), 111-115.

46. G. Widengren, <u>The King and the Tree of Life in Ancient
Near Eastern Religion</u>, "Uppsala Universitets Arsskrift," 4 (Uppsala,
Lundequist, 1951), pp. 9-11.

47. G. A. Barton, <u>The Royal Inscriptions of Sumer and Akkad</u>
(New Haven, Yale University Press, 1929), p. 313.

48. ANET, p. 110.

49. Widengren, The King and the Tree of Life, p. 17.

50. ANET, p. 119.

51. Ibid., p. 267.

52. Ibid., p. 84.

53. F. M. T. deL. Böhl, "Das Zeitalter der Sargoniden nach Briefen aus dem königlichen Archiv zu Nineve," in Opera Minora, pp. 417f. Nebuchadnezzar II, e.g., is called "der Ackerbauer Babylons" in S. Langdon, Die Neubabylonische Königsinschriften (Leipzig, Hinrichs, 1912), p. 105, no. 13, 1. 19.

54. A. L. Oppenheim, "Mesopotamian Mythology II," Orientalia 17 (1948), 47.

55. Ibid., p. 48.

56. Gilgamesh Epic V. 1. 6; ANET, p. 82.

57. A. Brock-Utne, Der gottesgarten. eine vergleichende religionsgeschichtliche Studie, "Avhandlinger utgitt av det Norske Videnskaps-Akademi i Oslo," II. "Historisk-Filosofisk Klasse," 2 (Oslo, I Kommisjon hos Jacob Dybwad, 1935), p. 129; D. Neiman, "Eden, the Garden of God," Acta Antiqua 17 (1969), 109-124.

58. B. Alfrink has discussed in full the Babylonian concept of the world mountain in "Der Versammlungsberg im äussersten Norden," Biblica 14 (1933), 41-67. Cf. R. J. Clifford, The Cosmic Mountain in Canaan and the Old Testament, Harvard Semitic Monographs, 4 (Cambridge, Harvard University Press, 1972).

59. Luckenbill, op. cit., I, section 217. Cf. Alfrink, op. cit., p. 50. Eharsagkurkurra means "world mountain".

60. O. Eissfeldt, Baal Zaphon. Zeus Kasios und der Durchzug der Israeliten durchs Meer (Halle, M. Niemeyer, 1932).

61. Op. cit., pp. 99-102.

62. F. C. Fensham, "Thunder-Stones in Ugaritic," JNES 18 (1959), 273-74.

Notes to Pages 82-85

63. Op. cit., pp. 38f.

64. The jewels would not be as brilliant as we are used to, since faceting was not practiced in antiquity, but the term still might well describe translucent or transparent stones.

65. I.e., in Ezek. 28 and in references to the high priest's breastplate, Exod. 28 and 39. Yaron, op. cit., p. 36, incorrectly claimed that seven of the nine stones are mentioned nowhere else.

66. Terms from Ezek. 28 which occur in Exod. 28: hōtām, three times; hokmā and kālīl, once each; "full of the spirit of wisdom" in Exod. 28:3 recalls "full of wisdom" in Ezek. 28:12; the connection of the gems with gold-work in Exod. 28 perhaps explains the reference to gold after the list of stones in Ezek. 28, and the description of stones inscribed as seals may explain the occurrence of "seal" in Ezek.

67. The MT is suspect not only because it makes the cherub the subject of the poem but also because of a disagreement in gender; the pronoun is feminine, cherub masculine.

68. T. H. Gaster, "Angel," IDB, I, 131-32.

69. The recent studies of the passage by May and Yaron agree on this point.

70. A faint reflection of some connection between the First Man and the garden may occur in Sanchuniathon's statement, "Aeon discovered the food obtained from trees," Eusebii Pamphili, i, 10.

71. Heidel, The Babylonian Genesis, pp. 124f.; James, Myth and Ritual in the Ancient Near East, p. 202.

72. ANET, p. 101, text A, 1. 2.

73. Ibid., 11. 8-18.

74. Ibid., n. 1a.

75. E. Ebeling, Tod und leben nach den vorstellungen der Babylonier (Berlin, Walter de Gruyter, 1931), I, 27, n. a.

76. W. Bousset, Hauptprobleme der Gnosis (Göttingen, Vandenhoeck 1907), p. 220.

177

77. S. N. Kramer, "The Death of Gilgamesh," <u>BASOR</u> 94 (1944), 6, n. 11.

78. <u>ANET</u>, pp. 51f., section B.

79. <u>Op</u>. <u>cit</u>., p. 127, ll. 4-16; cf. No. 30, p. 131, ll. 40f.

80. F. M. T. deL. Böhl, <u>Der babylonische furstenspiegel</u>, "Mitteilungen der altorientalischen Gesellschaft," 11, No. 3 (Leipzig, O. Harrassowitz, 1937), p. 36.

81. Chap. 5.

82. <u>Ibid</u>., p. 41.

83. <u>Ibid</u>., pp. 42f. Cf. Gunkel, <u>Genesis</u> (<u>HKAT</u> 1, 2nd ed.; 1902), p. 28.

84. <u>King and Messiah</u>, p. 41.

85. <u>Ibid</u>., p. 43.

86. <u>Ibid</u>., pp. 45-47.

87. "Die Urmenschvorstellung," pp. 271f. Cf. also I. Engnell, "'Knowledge' and 'Life' in the Creation Story," <u>VTS</u> 3 (1955), 112-113.

88. J. Pedersen, <u>Israel: Its Life and Culture</u> (London, 1940), I, 46-60, III, 81-86. Also, H. W. Robinson, "The Hebrew Conception of Corporate Personality," <u>BZAW</u> 66 (1936), 46-62; A. R. Johnson, <u>The One and the Many in the Israelite Conception of God</u> (Cardiff, University of Wales Press, 1961). Cf. S. Mowinckel, <u>He That Cometh</u>, trans. G. W. Anderson (Nashville, Abingdon, 1954), pp. 69-74.

89. <u>ANET</u>, pp. 265f.

90. <u>Ibid</u>., p. 101, ll. 3,4,8.

91. <u>Ibid</u>., p. 75, I.v.22.

92. Brock-Utne, <u>op</u>. <u>cit</u>., pp. 113, 118f.

93. R. Gordis, "The Knowledge of Good and Evil in the Old Testament and the Qumran Scrolls," <u>JBL</u> 76 (1957), 125ff.

178

Notes to Pages 88-90

94. <u>ANET</u>, p. 101, l.4.

95. <u>Ibid</u>., p. 50, l.35.

96. Heidel, <u>Babylonian Genesis</u>, pp. 124f. Cf. the discussion of various explanations for Adapa's failure by Roux, <u>RA</u> 55 (1961), 27-31.

97. H. T. Obbink's suggestion that eternal life could be had only through continual eating of its fruit, and that Adam and Eve had eaten thereof up until the Fall, seems very probably to be correct ("The Tree of Life in Eden," in <u>Old Testament Essays</u>, by the Society for Old Testament Study [London, Charles Griffin and Company, 1927], pp. 25-28). Cf. Gordis, <u>JBL</u> 76 (1957), 134; and Engnell, <u>VTS</u> 3 (1955), 116. P. Humbert, <u>Etudes sur le récit du paradis et de la chute dans la Genèse</u>, "Memoires de l'Université de Neuchâtel," 14 (Neuchâtel, Secrétariat de l'Université, 1940), devoted a chapter to the theories which had been proposed concerning the mortality or immortality of the first man. He concluded by saying that man is essentially mortal, but that obedience had offered to man a chance to obtain from God the gift of immortality, which he forfeited through his choice of disobedience (p. 151). In the most recent commentary on Genesis, C. Westermann has refused to speculate, saying we know only the <u>Grundmotiv</u> and the negative conclusion, <u>BKAT</u> 1 (1970), pp. 291f.

98. A. A. Bevan, "The King of Tyre in Ezekiel xxviii," <u>JTS</u> 4 (1902-1903), 500-505; Yaron, <u>op</u>. <u>cit</u>., 40-45.

99. I. Engnell, <u>Studies in divine kingship in the ancient Near East</u>, 2nd ed. (Oxford, Blackwell, 1943), and others.

100. The poem has an integrity of its own, reflecting Ezekiel's peculiar interests, style and vocabulary. Since his interests and vocabulary obviously are closely related to the priestly materials in the Old Testament it is not surprising that his form of the paradise myth might reflect details of the priesthood and the sanctuary. It is very likely that these resembled their Phoenician prototypes, and of course there might be a relationship to Phoenician myths here too, but at present that cannot be demonstrated, and as we have shown in the preceding chapter the integrity of the present passage is of more significance than hypothetical sources. Recently T. H. Gaster has suggested that the closest parallel to the poem is not Gen. 3 but the myth of Prometheus (<u>Myth, Legend, and Custom in the Old Testament</u>, pp. 622f.). The parallels he finds are: the culprit is a divine being (which depends on MT, "You are a cherub"

[vs. 14], rejected by most scholars), he was blameless and wise, unlike Adam but like Prometheus (an interpretation of Gen. 2-3 different from the one accepted here, which finds hints of the wisdom of the First Man in Genesis), and he dies in fire which comes from his own body, reminiscent of the fiery character of Prometheus (but we take vs. 18 to be a realistic reference to the burning of a city and not part of the myth).

101. For a similar interpretation, see Eichrodt, op. cit., pp. 354, 367f.

NOTES TO CHAPTER V

1. It may be appropriate at this point to offer another comment on "myth" as it applies to the materials studied here. In Isa. 14 the dominant characteristics of the themes so labeled were polytheism and occurrences in otherworldly realms, in Ezek. 28 it was the theme of beginnings, while here the theme is cosmological. But in each case the decision to call them "myth" was not made initially because of these characteristics but on the basis described at the end of the Excursus: the materials are common in literature from outside of Israel but are non-typical for the Old Testament.

2. F. K. Kienitz, Die politische Geschichte Ägyptens vom 7. bis zum 4. Jahrhunderts vor der Zeitwende (Berlin, Akademie-Verlag, 1953), p. 27. For comments on the Tyre and Egypt oracles in Ezekiel in relation to the historical context see K. S. Freedy and D. B. Redford, "The Dates in Ezekiel in Relation to Biblical, Babylonian and Egyptian Sources," JAOS 90 (1970), 462-485.

3. Notes on the text: Vs. 3: omit 'aššūr, for which there is as yet no adequate explanation; omit wᵉḥōreš mēṣal "shadowing place," since it breaks the context, is unnecessary metrically, and is missing from some LXX witnesses. Vs. 4: Tᵉhōm "the deep", is transliterated rather than translated in order to call attention to a word with overtones of cosmic myth; BH³'s emendations are accepted for grammatical reasons. Vs. 10: The change in Hebrew from second to third person may be original but for the sake of clarity the tree is referred to in third person in the translation. Vs. 14: "Trees of water" is painfully literal, the usual paraphrase is "trees that drink water". "In height" could be translated "in

their pride". Vs. 15: Omit kissētī, which seems meaningless in
the context and is missing from the LXX; 'ulpē is difficult and
the correct form and translation are not completely certain.
Vs. 17: Follow Driver (Biblica, 19, p. 179) in reading wᵉzōrᵉ'ū,
"were dispersed"; emend yāsᵉbū to yōsᵉbē.

4. Cf. R. A. Bowman, "Ezra," (IB, 1954), III, loc. cit.

5. The dream reports of Gudea of Lagash are well known. Cf.
A. L. Oppenheim, The Interpretation of Dreams in the Ancient Near
East, "Transactions of the American Philosophical Society," 46
(Philadelphia, American Philosophical Society, 1956), pp. 245f.,
250, 251, 254f.

6. Cf. 1 Esdras 3-4, Ahikar, and later literature.

7. The change of person is ably discussed by J. A. Montgomery
in Daniel (ICC, 1927), pp. 222f.

8. Cf. W. Dommershausen, Nabonid im Buche Daniel (Mainz,
Matthias-Grünewald, 1964).

9. Cf. the commentaries. For the view that the book is much
earlier than the second century see E. J. Young, The Prophecy of
Daniel (Grand Rapids, Eerdmans, 1949).

10. Montgomery, ICC, pp. 89f.; O. Eissfeldt, The Old Testament:
An Introduction, pp. 522-525.

11. Nabonidus' reputation was poor just before and after the
fall of Babylon, as the "Verse Account of Nabonidus" shows (ANET,
pp. 312-315). Cf. Dommershausen, op. cit., pp. 55-58.

12. Notes on the text (verse numbering according to the MT):
Vs. 6: read hezwē as an imperative. Vs. 32: the repetition of
"those who dwell on earth" after "with the army of the heavens"
seems inappropriate and is probably a dittography.

13. Convenient sources are M. Eliade, Patterns in Comparative
Religion, chap. 8; E. O. James, The Tree of Life, "Studies in the
History of Religions," 11 (Leiden, E. J. Brill, 1966); E. A. S.
Butterworth, The Tree at the Navel of the Earth (Berlin, de Gruyter,
1970).

14. Eliade, The Sacred and the Profane, pp. 32-42.

15. U. Holmberg (Harva), Der Baum des Lebens, "Annales Academiae Scientiarum Fennicae," Series B, Vol. XVI (Helsinki, 1922-23), pp. 51-69.

16. Zimmerli, BKAT 13, p. 752. If "plant of life" is not to be identified with "tree of life" then the latter is found only in the Bible, according to H. Genge, "Zum 'Lebensbaum' in den Keilschriftkulturen" Acta Orientalia 33 (1971), 321-334.

17. R. Campbell Thompson, The Devils and Evil Spirits of Babylonia, "Luzac's Semitic Text and Translation Series," 14 (London, Luzac, 1903), pp. lvii-lxiii, 201-207; W. F. Albright, "The Mouth of the Rivers," AJSL 35 (1918-19), 164ff.; S. H. Langdon, "The Legend of the Kishkanu," JRAS (1928), 846-48; H. Danthine, Le palmier-dattier et les arbres sacrés dans l'icon-ographie de l'Asie Occidentale ancienne, "Bibliotheque archeo-logique et historique," 25 (Paris, P. Geuthner, 1937), p. 150; N. Perrot, Les représentations de l'arbre sacré sur les monuments de Mésopotamie et d'Élam (Paris, P. Geuthner, 1937), pp. 6-11. Genge concludes kishkanu is to be identified with neither tree of life nor world tree, op. cit., pp. 332f.

18. E. O. G. Turville-Petre, Myth and Religion of the North: The Religion of Ancient Scandanavia (New York, Holt, Rinehart and Winston, 1964), p. 279.

19. Ibid., pp. 244-246.

20. Ibid., p. 279.

21. Ibid. The Ragnarök is the tremendous battle between the frost giants and the gods in which almost universal destruction ensues, followed by a new and better age.

22. I. Paulson, "Die Religionen der nordasiatischen (sibirischen) Völker," in Die Religionen Nordeurasiens und der amerikanischen Arktis, "Die Religionen der Menschheit," 3 (Stuttgart, W. Kohlhammer, 1962), p. 31.

23. Ibid. Cf. Holmberg's extensive descriptions of Siberian material, op. cit., pp. 51-61.

24. H. Gressmann, Altorientalische Texte (Berlin, de Gruyter, 1929), p. 218. My translation from the German. Possible evidence for an expression similar to that in the last line has been found in a Ugaritic text by M. Margulis, "A Weltbaum in Ugaritic Litera-ture?" JBL 90 (1971), 481f.

25. E. Reiner, Šurpu: A Collection of Sumerian and Akkadian Incantations, "Archiv für Orientforschung," Beiheft 11 (Graz, Im Selbstverlage des Herausgebers, 1958), p. 45, ll. 1-8.

26. Ibid., p. 46, ll. 42-48.

27. Ibid., ll. 49-55.

28. Danthine, op. cit., pp. 148f. Cf. the plates in Perrot.

29. H. Frankfort, Cylinder Seals (London, Macmillan, 1939), pp. 275f.; Perrot, plates 13-14.

30. Holmberg, op. cit., pp. 14f., 65.

31. Danthine, op. cit., figs. 576, 577; cf. figs. 571, 574, 581; Frankfort, Cylinder Seals, plate xlii, cf. a and e with i and k.

32. Clark, op. cit., p. 58.

33. S. A. B. Mercer, The Pyramid Texts (New York, Longman's, 1952), I, lines 916b, 1433b; pp. 166, 228.

34. H. Kees, Der Götterglaube im alten Aegypten, 2nd ed. (Berlin, Akademie-Verlag, 1956), p. 84.

35. The point has never been seriously disputed although Cooke says nothing of the parallels in his Ezekiel commentary (ICC) and A. Brock-Utne, Der Gottesgarten, questioned the presumed parallels to either the world tree or the tree of life, p. 125.

36. S. N. Kramer, Gilgamesh and the Huluppu-Tree, "Assyriological Studies," No. 10 (Chicago, 1938), p. 7.

37. S. N. Kramer, Sumerian Mythology, p. 34.

38. ANET, pp. 48f., 80, 82, 83. T. H. Gaster, Myth, Legend, and Custom in the Old Testament, has concluded, however, that these are the closest parallels to be found, pp. 626f.

39. S. H. Hooke, The Origins of Early Semitic Ritual (London, Oxford University Press, 1938), p. 14; H. Frankfort, "Gods and Myths on Sargonid Seals," Iraq, I (1934), pp. 24f., plates IVf., Va.

40. W. H. Ward, The Seal Cylinders of Western Asia (Washington, The Carnegie Institute of Washington, 1910), pp. 149-151.

41. S. Smith, "Notes on the 'Assyrian Tree'," BSOS 4 (1926), 72.

42. Two attempts at translating the text will reveal this: "Now Pulu the kalu priest when he prepared . . . in the house of Nabu, in the festal house of . . . and in the festal house of Tashmetum of the city of A . . . the shubshat, vessels(?) he removed, others he seized and the span(?) he cut off; as for the golden vessels of the temples(?) which Sargon had made, the goldsmith placed gold thereon. The old work he removed, he renewed it and the mighty ruler Nabu, who stands upon it." L. Waterman, Royal Correspondence of the Assyrian Empire (Ann Arbor, University of Michigan Press, 1930), II, letter 951. "Now Bulu, the kalu-priest, prepared the ornamental trees(?) in the temple of Nabu. Out of the festal house of Bel(?) and into the festal house of Tashmetum of the city . . . he removed the supsate, "yoked" others, cut off the "yoke"; and the banquet dishes of gold, which Sarru-ukin had made, the goldsmith set down for that purpose . . . " C. Frank, Studien zur babylonischen Religion (Strassburg, Schlesier & Schweikhardt, 1911), p. 100. My translation from Frank's German.

43. For recent contributions to the discussion see L. Vanden Berghe, "Réflexions critiques sur la nature de Dumuzi-Tammuz," La Nouvelle Clio, 6 (1954), 298-321; the papers by A. Moortgat, A. Falkenstein, A. Parrot, H. Otten, and F. R. Kraus in Compte Rendu de la troisième Rencontre assyriologique internationale (Leiden, Brill, 1954), pp. 18-74; S. N. Kramer's remarks in Mythologies of the Ancient World, pp. 10-11, 109-115; BASOR 183 (1966), 31; O. R. Gurney, "Tammuz Reconsidered: Some Recent Developments," JSS 7 (1962) 147-160; T. Jacobsen, "Toward the Image of Tammuz," History of Religions 1 (1962) 189-213.

44. Clark, op. cit., p. 105; S. A. B. Mercer, The Religion of Ancient Egypt (London, Luzac, 1949), p. 103.

45. Plutarch Moralia, trans. F. C. Babbitt, "Loeb Classical Library" (Cambridge, Mass., Harvard University Press, 1936), Book V, De Iside et Osiride, sec. 15. K. Sethe noted the following in the Pyramid texts: "Your mother Nut takes you, she seizes your arms so that you will not become gᶠu, so that you will not become 'shu." (Text 2107) He recognized that 'shu is the name of a tree, the cedar. This is a prayer to save the deceased from the fate of Osiris. "Zur ältesten Geschichte des ägyptischen Seeverkehrs mit

Notes to Pages 108-114

Byblos und dem Libanongebiet," <u>Zeitschrift für ägyptische Sprache
und Altertumskunde</u>, 45 (1908), 7-14.

46. Plutarch, <u>op</u>. <u>cit</u>., Section 16.

47. Clark, <u>op</u>. <u>cit</u>., p. 235.

48. Diodorus Siculus I. 14. 2. 3.

49. Kees, <u>op</u>. <u>cit</u>., p. 97.

50. <u>ANET</u>, pp. 126-128.

51. F. V. M. Cumont, <u>The Oriental Religions in Roman Paganism</u>
(Chicago, The Open Court Publishing Company, 1911), p. 46.

52. Eliade, <u>Patterns</u>, p. 273; James, <u>The Tree of Life</u>, pp.
147f.

53. Eliade, p. 274; James, pp. 148-150.

54. G. Widengren, <u>The King and the Tree of Life</u>, proposes this
theory, pp. 50-61; contrary opinions by Fohrer, <u>HAT</u> 13, p. 176;
Zimmerli, <u>BKAT</u> 13, p. 752; Mowinckel, <u>He That Cometh</u>, pp. 453f.
Herodotus speaks of dreams of Persian kings which used vegetation
imagery for royalty in i.108, vii.19.

55. S. Langdon, ed., <u>Building Inscriptions of the Neo-
Babylonian Empire</u>: Part 1, Nabopolassar and Nebuchadnezzar (Paris,
E. Leroux, 1905), p. 171.

56. These additional chapters also deal with Tyre and Egypt.
Parts of them might have been discussed in detail, since they make
use of the common theme of dragon-slaying in ways analogous to the
texts which have been studied (Ezek. 29:3-5, followed by two reason-
announcement oracles; and 32:2-8), for they accuse the Pharaoh of
hybris. "Because you said, 'The Nile is mine, and I made it,' . . .
(29:9b). "You consider yourself a lion among the nations, . . ."
(32:2) But nothing new is added by these texts, and the message we
found in the others appears in a truncated form since the dragon
is an enemy from the beginning and the emphasis on legitimacy under
God and the tragedy of the corruption of human splendor is missing.

57. E.g., W. O. E. Oesterley, <u>Immortality and the Unseen World</u>
(London, S.P.C.K., 1921); E. F. Sutcliffe, <u>The Old Testament and
the Future Life</u> (London, Burns, Dates & Washbourne, 1946); A. Heidel

The Gilgamesh Epic and Old Testament Parallels, chap. iii; R.
Martin-Achard, From Death to Life (Edinburgh, Oliver and Boyd,
1960); N. J. Tromp, Primitive Conceptions of Death and the
Nether World in the Old Testament (Rome, Pontifical Biblical
Institute, 1969).

58. Cf. the background to Isa. 14 described in Chapter III.

59. Pedersen, Israel, II, 461-62; J. J. McGovern, "The
Waters of Death," CBQ, 21 (1959), 350-58.

60. BKAT 13, p. 783.

61. H. G. May, "Some Cosmic Connotations of MAYIM RABBIM,
'Many Waters'," JBL, 74 (1955), 19.

62. A comparison with Eridu, which in Babylonian texts is a
garden site, and is the subterranean home of Enki (Ea), suggests
itself, but does not seem to be a real analogy to this text
(Albright, AJSL, 35 [1918-19], 164f.).

63. Eichrodt, op. cit., pp. 374-377, also believes a topography
of Sheol is represented in 26:19-21, although he thinks the metaphor
in 31:17f. is confused, pp. 428f.

64. A. Lods, "Note sur deux croyances hebräiques relatives à
la mort et à ce qui la suit: le sort des incirconcis dans l'au-
delà et la victoire sur Leviathan," Comptes rendus de l'Academie
des Inscriptions et Belles Lettres (June 4, 1943), pp. 271-83.

65. O. Eissfeldt, "Schwerterschlagene bei Hesekiel," in
Society for Old Testament Study, Studies in Old Testament Prophecy,
ed. H. H. Rowley (London, Lutterworth Press, 1950), pp. 73-81.

66. E. Ebeling has published some Sumerian Texts which may
indicate a belief in a different fate for the good and the evil
(Tod und Leben, pp. 22f.; "Eine Beschreibung der Unterwelt in
sumerischer Sprache," Orientalia, 18 [1949], 285-87). S. N.
Kramer has found evidence of the judgment of the dead in an elegy
recently published, but the basis for the judgment is not ascer-
tainable, The Sumerians, pp. 210, 214.

67. Thompson, Devils and Evil Spirits, p. 39.

68. Cf. Eichrodt, op. cit., pp. 436-438, 441.

NOTES TO THE EPILOGUE

1. See, e.g., Science and Public Affairs, a journal initiated in 1945 as Bulletin of the Atomic Scientists, and, among many books, L. Augenstein, Come, Let Us Play God.

2. Cf. the definition of tyranny offered by M. Latey in Patterns of Tyranny (New York, Atheneum, 1969), p. 18: "A tyrant is a ruler who exercises arbitrary power beyond the scope permitted by the laws, customs and standards of his time and society and who does so with a view to maintaining or increasing that power."

3. Latey, op. cit., p. 277.

4. Reinhold Niebuhr, The Children of Light and the Children of Darkness (New York, Scribner, 1960), p. xiii.

5. "Traditional Attitudes towards Death" in Man's Concern with Death by A. Toynbee and others (London, Hodder and Stoughton, 1968, pp. 62f.

6. Ibid., p. 65.

7. Ibid., p. 66.

8. In addition to the Toynbee volume just cited, see R. Fulton (ed.), Death and Identity (New York, John Wiley and Sons, 1965) and L. O. Mills (ed.), Perspectives on Death (Nashville, Abingdon Press, 1969).

9. The plan to freeze the body at death in the faith that one day science will make it possible to thaw out, bring to life, heal and rejuvenate so that those who die now may have the opportunity to share in the utopia which science will soon create for us.

10. J. S. Dunne, The City of the Gods. A Study in Myth and Mortality (New York, Macmillan, 1965), pp. 2, 4.

11. R. C. W. Ettinger, "Cryonics and the Purpose of Life," The Christian Century 84 (1967), pp. 1250-53.

12. Quoted by W. R. Bowie in IB, I, 505.

13. Cf. our references to Niebuhr's _Nature and Destiny of Man_ in Chap. II and V. Taylor's definition of "atonement": "how man is delivered from his pride and his overweening confidence in himself," _The Cross of Christ_ (London, Macmillan, 1956), p. 87.

14. There are even more texts we might have discussed: Isa. 47:10, Dan. 8:8, 10f., 25; 11:36ff., Ps. 82.

15. _Leviathan_, chap. 17; quoted by Dunne, _op. cit._, p. 195.

16. (London, 1954), VII, 7ff.

17. Latey, _op. cit._, p. 122.

18. _Ibid._, p. 190.

19. _Ibid._, p. 191.

20. _Ibid._, p. 135.

21. _Ibid._, p. 306.

22. _Ibid._, pp. 202-204.

23. _Ibid._, pp. 205-209; W. L. Shirer, _The Rise and Fall of the Third Reich_ (Greenwich, Conn., Fawcett, 1962), pp. 324-333; A. C. Cochrane, _The Church's Confession Under Hitler_ (Philadelphia, Westminster Press, 1962).

24. Latey, _op. cit._, pp. 209-213: C. de Grunwald, _The Churches and the Soviet Union_ (New York, Macmillan, 1962).

25. Latey, _op. cit._, pp. 199f.

26. _Ibid._, p. 294.

188

NOTES TO THE EXCURSUS

1. B. S. Childs, _Myth and Reality in the Old Testament_, _SBT_ 27 (Naperville, Ill., A. R. Allenson, 1960).

2. K. Rahner & H. Vorgrimler, _Theological Dictionary_, ed. C. Ernst, trans. R. Strachen (New York, Herder & Herder, 1965), p. 303. Another insult worth quoting: "one of the most widely traveled semantic hobos of our times," R. H. Ayers, "'Myth' in Theological Discourse: A Profusion of Confusion," _AngThR_ 48 (1966), 200. Cf. M. Barnard, _The Mythmakers_ (Athens, Ohio, Ohio University Press, 1966), p. 181: "At every point in our definition a door stands open to let 'myths' wander in and out. None of the doors will lock."

3. _Op. cit._, pp. 13-14; with reference to C. Hartlich & W. Sachs, _Der Ursprung des Mythosbegriffes in der Modernen Bibelwissenschaft_ (Tübingen, J. C. B. Mohr, 1952). G. S. Kirk, in _Myth: Its Meaning and Function in Ancient and Other Cultures_ (Cambridge, University Press, 1970), pp. 252ff., refuses to accept any unitary theory of myth and suggests a three-fold typology of mythical functions: 1. narrative and entertaining, 2. operative, iterative and validatory, 3. speculative and explanatory. His work is of considerable value for its criticisms of several of the more popular theories.

4. E.g., J. Sløk, "Mythos" _RGG_3, IV, 1263; E. O. James, _Myth and Ritual in the Ancient Near East_ (New York, 1958), 280-290; S. Langer, _Philosophy in a New Key_ (New York, 1942), pp. 142f.

5. E.g., T. H. Gaster, "Myth and Story," _Numen_ I (1954), 184-212.

6. A. Bentzen, _Introduction of the Old Testament_, I, 241f.; G. Fohrer, _Introduction to the Old Testament_, p. 86; S. Thompson, "Myths and Folktales," in _Myth: A Symposium_, ed. T. A. Sebeok (Bloomington, Ind., 1958), pp. 104-107.

7. G. Stählin, "mythos," _TDNT_, IV, 766-779, 792f.

8. E. B. Tylor, _Anthropology_ (New York, 1898), p. 387.

9. F. M. T. deL. Böhl, "Mythos und Geschichte in der alt-babylonischen Dichtung," in _Opera Minora_ (Groningen, 1953), p. 221.

10. S. Holm, "Mythos und Symbol," ThLZ 93 (1968), p. 565.
A more extreme example in F. Festorazzi, "Il 'mito' e l'Antico
Testamento," RBibIt 9 (1961), pp. 144-171.

11. D. Bidney, "Myth, Symbolism, and Truth," in Myth:
A Symposium, p. 13. Cf. E. B. Tylor, Primitive Culture (New
York, H. Holt and Company, 1889), I, 284ff.

12. M. Burrows, An Outline of Biblical Theology (Philadelphia, Westminster Press, 1946), p. 115.

13. M. Barth, "Introduction to Demythologizing," JR 37
(1957), 148; J. Macquarrie, The Scope of Demythologizing
(London, SCM Press, 1960), pp. 198-216.

14. "Mythology is the use of imagery to express the other
worldly in terms of this world and the divine in terms of human
life, the other side in terms of this side." R. Bultmann, "New
Testament and Mythology," in Kerygma and Myth, ed. H. W. Bartsch,
trans. R. H. Fuller (London, S.P.C.K., 1961), p. 10, n. 2.

15. S. Ogden, "Myth and Truth," McCormick Quarterly 18
(Jan. 1965), p. 62.

16. It will be observed that most of the discussions of
Bultmann attempt to work with a variety of definitions of myth
in addition to Bultmann's own. Cf. Macquarrie, op. cit.; G. V.
Jones, Christology and Myth in the New Testament (London, G.
Allen & Unwin, 1956), Part IV; G. Miegge, Gospel and Myth in the
Thought of Rudolf Bultmann, trans. S. Neill (Richmond, John Knox
Press, 1960), chap. 3; etc.

17. E. L. Allen, "On Demythologizing the Old Testament,"
JBR 22 (1954), 236-241.

18. H. H. Brunner, "Der Mythos vom modernen Menschen,"
Reformatio 16 (1967), 100-106.

19. "In some few cases only . . . could mythology rightly be
considered as a disease, as a premature hardening, so to say, of
the organic tissues of language, namely, when a word had lost its
original meaning, and was afterwards interpreted, or rather mis-
interpreted, in accordance with the ideals of a later age." F.
Max Müller, Natural Religion (London, Longman's, Green and Co.,
1907), p. 22.

20. E. Cassirer, <u>An Essay on Man</u> (New Haven, Yale University Press, 1944), p. 76.

21. E. Cassirer, <u>The Myth of the State</u> (Garden City, N.Y., Doubleday, 1955), pp. 41-43.

22. E. Cassirer, <u>Language and Myth</u>, trans. S. K. Langer (New York, Harper & Brother, 1946), p. 8.

23. <u>The Myth of the State</u>, chap. 18.

24. E.g., P. Wheelwright, "The Semantic Approach to Myth," in <u>Myth: A Symposium</u>, pp. 95-103.

25. (New York, 1969), pp. xxxiv, xxxvi. But note definitions with slightly different emphases in Gaster's other works; <u>Thespis</u> (2nd ed.; Garden City, N.Y., 1961), pp. 24f.; <u>Numen</u> 1 (1954), 185-187.

26. C. G. Jung & C. Kerényi, <u>Essays on a Science of Mythology</u> (New York, Pantheon Books, 1949), p. 101.

27. <u>Ibid.</u>, p. 103.

28. R. V. Kluger (Evanston, Ill., Northwestern University Press, 1967), p. 3.

29. Three examples of rather comprehensive definitions: J. Knox, <u>Myth and Truth</u> (Charlottesville, Va., University Press of Virginia, 1964), p. 35, cites four characteristics of myth: 1) It is an imaginative narrative dealing with cosmically significant acts of God (or some superhuman being); 2) Its source is in the common life of a human community; 3) The community prizes it because it explains something distinctive and important in human existence; 4) It is an inseparable and indispensable part of the community's life. A. Dulles, "Symbol, Myth and the Biblical Revelation," <u>Theological Studies</u> 27 (1966), 8-10, narrows the field somewhat with seven characteristics: 1) It is a communal possession; 2) It is a "figurative representation of a reality which eludes precise description or definition"; 3) It "deals with a numinous order of reality beyond the appearances of the phenomenal world"; 4) It contains a numinous presence portrayed in personal terms; 5) It takes place on a cosmic scale with a permanent causal influence on earthly happenings; 6) It is a drama which occurs in its own order of time (vs. legends); 7) It is immediately connected with the present concerns of men. He adds that since the forces

of nature are multiple myth can scarcely be anything other than polytheistic. W. H. Schmidt, "Mythos im Alten Testament," EvTh 27 (1967), 237-240, cites four aspects of "myth as word": 1) It describes the gods as acting persons; 2) Its events occur in their own time, beyond the time of history, but on earth or in a heaven revealed to men; 3) It is the foundation of reality; 4) It stands in close connection to the cult; is not only description but the thing itself.

30. "Christianity and Myth," JBR 33 (1965), 315. Cf. the article on Tillich's concept of myth by A. D. Foster, "Myth and Philosophy: Theology's Bipolar Essence," JBR 34 (1966), 316-328.

31. G. Henton Davies, "An Approach to the Problem of Old Testament Mythology," PEQ 88 (1956), 88f.

32. Rahner, op. cit., p. 303: "If we assume that every concept bearing upon a metaphysical or religious reality, remote from direct experience, must work with a sensible image . . . which is not the original phenomenal form of that reality . . . then every meta-physical or religious utterance is a mythical one or can be inter-preted in mythical terms."

33. K. Jaspers in Jaspers & Bultmann, Myth and Christianity (New York, The Noonday Press, 1958), p. 16: "The myth is a carrier of meanings which can be expressed only in the language of myth. The mythical figures are symbols which, by their very nature, are untranslatable into other language."

34. E. Buess, Die Geschichte des Mythischen Erkennens (München, C. Kaiser, 1953), p. 27: "knowledge of the unknowable"; cf. Hartlich & Sachs, op. cit., pp. 159-161.

35. R. A. F. Mackenzie, Faith and History in the Old Testament (New York, Macmillan, 1963), p. 71; cf. John McKenzie, "Myth and the Old Testament," CBQ 21 (1959), 268-274; M. Burrows, op. cit., p. 116.

36. Myth and Ritual in Christianity (New York, Vanguard Press, 1954), p. 7; cf. R. H. Ayers, op. cit., p. 201: "A value-charged story expressing to some degree the life orientation of a group and/or individual."

37. B. H. Throckmorton, Jr., The New Testament and Mythology (Philadelphia, Westminster Press, 1959), pp. 94f.

38. <u>The Old Testament and Theology</u> (New York, Harper, 1969), p. 133; cf. H. M. Buck, Jr., "From History to Myth: A Comparative Study," <u>JBR</u> 29 (1961), 219-226.

39. R. Pettazoni, "The Truth of Myth," in <u>Essays on the History of Religions</u>, trans. H. J. Rose ("Studies in the History of Religion, Supplements to <u>Numen</u>," I, 1954), pp. 11-23.

40. R. Gotesky, "The Nature of Myth and Society," <u>AmAnthropologist</u> 54 (1952), p. 530; quote from G. Sebba, "Symbol and Myth in Modern Rationalistic Societies," in <u>Truth, Myth, and Symbol</u>, ed. T. J. J. Altizer, <u>et. al.</u> (Englewood Cliffs, N.J., Prentice-Hall, 1962), pp. 141-168, whose entire article is an excellent example of this approach to myth.

41. Childs, <u>op. cit.</u>, p. 16.

42. E.g., M. Eliade, <u>Myth and Reality</u>, trans. W. R. Trask (New York, Harper & Row, 1963), Chap. IX; and <u>Myths, Dreams and Mysteries: the Encounter between Contemporary Faiths and Archaic Realities</u>, trans. P. Mairet (London, Harvill Press, 1960).

43. E.g., B. Malinowski, "Myth in Primitive Psychology," in <u>Magic, Science and Religion and Other Essays</u> (Garden City, N.Y., Doubleday and Company, 1955), pp. 101-108.

44. M. Eliade, <u>Patterns in Comparative Religion</u>, trans. R. Sheed (New York, Sheed & Ward, 1958), p. 430.

45. H. Frankfort, <u>Intellectual Adventure</u>, p. 8.

46. See esp. <u>Myth, Ritual, and Kingship</u>, ed. S. H. Hooke (Oxford, Clarendon Press, 1958). Questions are raised about the hypothetical relationship by C. Kluckhohn, "Myths and Rituals: A General Theory," <u>HThR</u> 35 (1942), 45-79; W. G. Lambert, "Myth and Ritual as Conceived by the Babylonians," <u>JSS</u> 13 (1968), 104-112.

47. S. H. Hooke, <u>In the Beginning</u> ("The Clarendon Bible," 6; Oxford, Clarendon Press, 1947), p. 18.

48. E. O. James, <u>op. cit.</u>, p. 283.

49. Especially Childs, <u>op. cit.</u>, J. Barr, "The Meaning of 'Mythology' in Relation to the Old Testament," <u>VT</u> 9 (1959), 1-10.

50. T. J. J. Altizer, "The Religious Meaning of Myth and Symbol," in Truth, Myth and Symbol, p. 91.

51. Cf. Pettazoni, op. cit., on the loss of truth from myths, and Gaster's discussion of the same question in Numen 1 (1954), 207ff. But P. Ricoeur thinks an awareness of the existence of myth need not mean the loss of its effective truth, The Symbolism of Evil (New York, Harper & Row, 1967), pp. 5, 161-164.

52. Nor does the LXX. The word occurs only in Sir. 20:19 in its old sense of "word", and in a compound, mythologos, in Bar. 3:23; Stählin, op. cit., pp. 780f.

53. E.g., the "myth-school" of 19th century Germany.

54. Altizer, op. cit., Cobb, op. cit.

55. Bultmann, op. cit., Ogden, op. cit.

56. Jaspers, op. cit., Knox, op. cit., Mackenzie, op. cit.

57. E. Dardel says that the effectiveness of myth is largely dependent upon ignorance of its actual motivation. "The Mythic," Diogenes, No. 7 (Summer 1954), pp. 33-51; reference from Bidney, op. cit., pp. 11f.

58. Eliade hesitates to judge myth as untrue; see, e.g., Cosmos and History; the Myth of the Eternal Return (New York, Harper, 1959), pp. 154-159; The Sacred and the Profane (New York, Harcourt, Brace, 1959), pp. 201-213.

59. A. Ohler, Mythologische Elemente im Alten Testament (Düsseldorf, Patmos-Verlag, 1969), p. 11, intends not to deal with myth as the effort to speak of God in external terms, but only with pagan ways of speaking of gods not in history but in natural cycles and as part of the forces of nature.

60. O. W. Schmidt, op. cit., pp. 237-242, sees two approaches to myth, as a narrative (through Religionswissen-schaft) and as a manner of understanding the world (as in Bultmann's definition). Israel shares the mythological world-view but has no myth itself.

61. E.g., H. D. Beeby, "The Old Testament and the Redemption of Culture," South East Asia Journal of Theology 8, No. 4 (1966/67), 17-28; B. W. Anderson, "Myth and the Biblical Tradition," ThToday

Notes to Pages 142-143

27 (1970), 44-62; J. Barr, op. cit.; Childs, op. cit.; Dulles, op. cit.; Old Testament theologies in general. Another possibility, that truth is to be found not only in what is distinctive in the Old Testament but also in much that it has in common with other religions, is seldom discussed. Is the common assumption that revelation is confined to the unique material in the Bible a continuing result of the shock of the discovery of ancient cultures in the nineteenth century? It was not an assumption of the apologists in the early church, at any rate. Suppose one day we discover that the only distinctive thing in the Old Testament is the teaching about the one whom we ought to worship? Would that destroy the Biblical faith? Perhaps not, since that may have been the Old Testament's major concern all along.

62. Cf. Eliade's references to customs in eastern Europe throughout his works, and J. Frazer, The Golden Bough, passim. Some of the quibbling over how much mythological thought there is in the Old Testament might be lessened if more emphasis were put on the fact that both scholarship and popular piety are reflected there.

63. Note the comments of this type by two reviewers of Childs' book; U. Simon, ChQR 161 (1960), 503, and J. P. M. Sweet, JTS NS 12 (1961), 69f. The latter has suggested that by substituting "Yahweh" for "a deity" in Childs' definition of myth one could make of it an acceptable definition of Old Testament thought.

64. W. W. Hallo, "Akkadian Apocalypses," IEJ 16 (1966), 231.

65. B. Albrektson, History and the Gods, "Coniectanea Biblica," OT Series 1 (Lund, Gleerup, 1967).